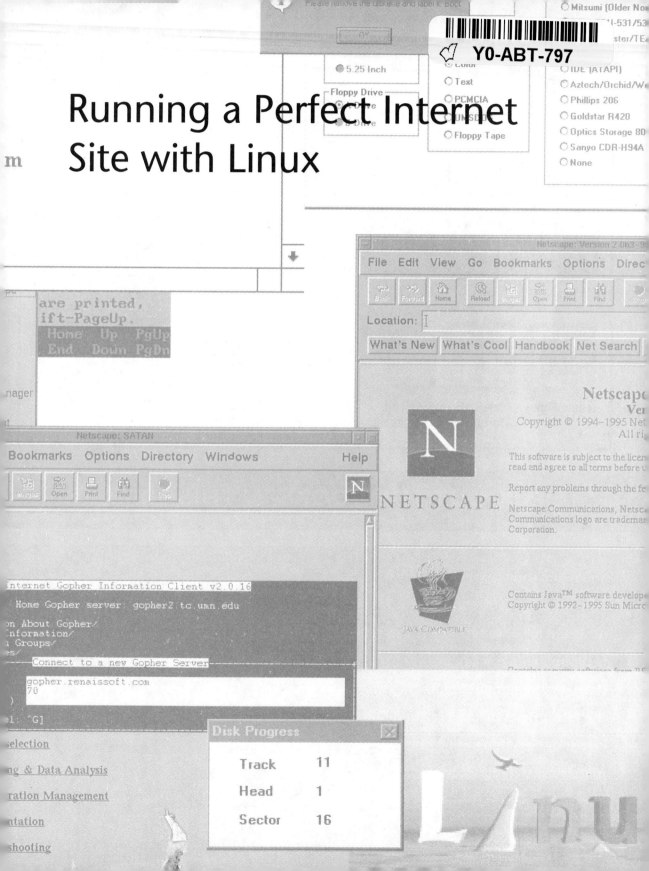

Running a Perfect Internet Site with Linux

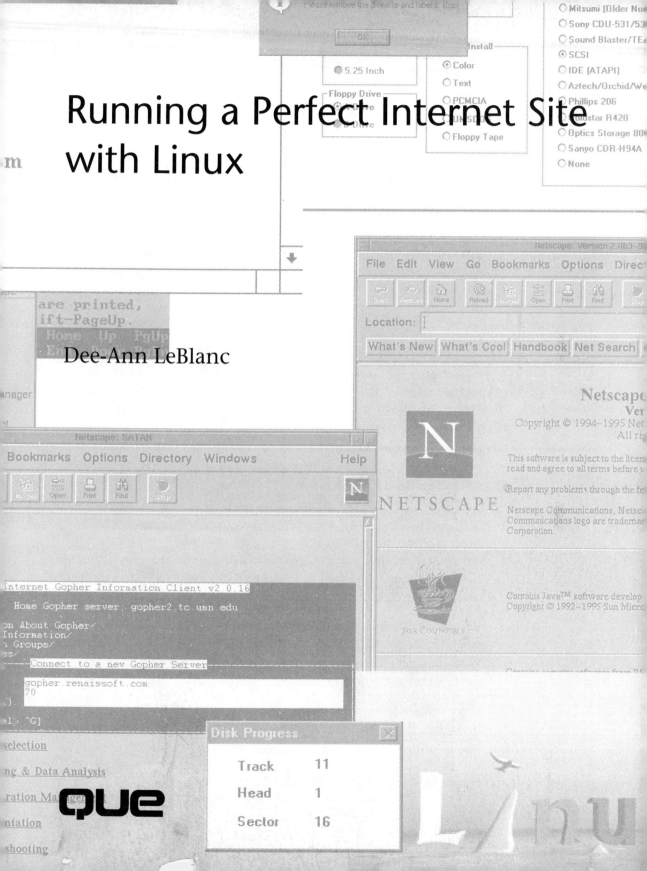

Running a Perfect Internet Site with Linux

Dee-Ann LeBlanc

Que

Running a Perfect Internet Site with Linux

Copyright© 1996 by Que® Corporation.

Library of Congress Catalog No.: 95-72569

ISBN: 0-7897-0514-1

98 97 96   6 5 4 3 2 1

Interpretation of the printing code: the rightmost double-digit number is the year of the book's printing; the rightmost single-digit number, the number of the book's printing. For example, a printing code of 96-1 shows that the first printing of the book occurred in 1996.

All terms mentioned in this book that are known to be trademarks or service marks have been appropriately capitalized. Que cannot attest to the accuracy of this information. Use of a term in this book should not be regarded as affecting the validity of any trademark or service mark.

Screen reproductions in this book were created using Collage Plus from Inner Media, Inc., Hollis, NH.

Composed in *Stone Serif* and *MCPdigital* by Que Corporation

Credits

President
Roland Elgey

Publisher
Stacy Hiquet

Editorial Services Director
Elizabeth Keaffaber

Managing Editor
Sandy Doell

Director of Marketing
Lynn E. Zingraf

Senior Series Editor
Chris Nelson

Title Manager
Jim Minatel

Acquisitions Manager
Cheryl D. Willoughby

Acquisitions Editor
Doshia Stewart

Product Director
Benjamin Milstead

Production Editor
Danielle Bird

Copy Editor
Thomas Cirtin

Assistant Product Marketing Manager
Kim Margolius

Technical Editor
James O'Donnell

Figure Specialist
Nadeem Muhammed

Acquisitions Coordinator
Ruth Slates

Operations Coordinator
Patricia J. Brooks

Editorial Assistant
Andrea Duvall

Book Designer
Ruth Harvey

Cover Designer
Dan Armstrong

Production Team
Steve Adams
Brian Buschkill
Jason Carr
Anne Dickerson
Chad Dressler
Bryan Flores
DiMonique Ford
Trey Frank
Jason Hand
Glenn Larson
Stephanie Layton
Michelle Lee
Julie Quinn
Bobbi Satterfield
Jody York

Indexer
Tim Griffin

About the Author

Dee-Ann LeBlanc co-owns Renaissoft Enterprises, a computer services firm that specializes in Internet consulting and training, and custom software development. She co-authored Que's *Using Eudora* and *The Internet CD Tutor*. Dee-Ann has a background in technical writing and engineering. She wears several hats for Renaissoft Enterprises as a computer consultant, technical writer, and manager.

Acknowledgments

I would like to thank all of the people who sent me prompt and helpful responses on my questions about their services and applications. Also, I'd like to acknowledge the many folks who put a lot of effort into making sure a wide range of documentation is available for Linux, such as the Linux Documentation Project.

Trademarks

Que Corporation has made every effort to supply trademark information about company names, products, and services mentioned in this book. Trademarks indicated below were derived from various sources. Que Corporation cannot attest to the accuracy of this information.

We'd Like To Hear from You!

As part of our continuing effort to produce books of the highest possible quality, Que would like to hear your comments. To stay competitive, we *really* want you, as a computer book reader and user, to let us know what you like or dislike most about this book or other Que products.

You can mail comments, ideas, or suggestions for improving future editions to the address below, or send us a fax at (317) 581-4663. For the online inclined, Macmillan Computer Publishing has a forum on CompuServe (type **GO QUEBOOKS** at any prompt) through which our staff and authors are available for questions and comments. The address of our Internet site is **http://www.mcp.com/que** (World Wide Web).

In addition to exploring our forum, please feel free to contact me personally to discuss your opinions of this book: I'm **102121,1324** on CompuServe, and I'm **bmilstead.que.mcp.com** on the Internet.

Thanks in advance—your comments will help us to continue publishing the best books available on computer topics in today's market.

Benjamin Milstead
Product Director
Que Corporation
201 W. 103rd Street
Indianapolis, Indiana   46290
USA

Contents at a Glance

Preparations

Installing Linux

Setting Up Your Site

Maintenance

Upgrading and Adding

Appendixes

Contents

III Setting Up Your Internet Site   111

6 Installing E-mail Server Software   113

7 Installing Web Server Software   129

8 Installing Gopher Server Software   163

Introduction

As this book is being written, a new Internet site is "born" every 15 minutes somewhere in the world. Why?

Because the number of people on the Internet is skyrocketing, more and more people are able to make a living by providing Internet connections. Businesses find the Net useful for disseminating information about themselves; communicating with clients, potential clients, and co-workers; as well as networking with people who may be helpful to the company in the future. Even governments are staking claims in cyberspace. They make information about their country and people available online, and they use the Net to help their citizens track down information they otherwise might have to stand in line in a government office to obtain.

One of the first problems you run into when setting up a site is deciding which operating system to use. Many people choose Linux. After all, it's a free version of UNIX, and constantly being updated; there is an amazing amount of support available for it on the Internet in forums used by other Linux users; and it's a stable operating system.

Linux is also, in a strange way, a more "social" operating system than most. Its primary designer reads and responds to the Linux newsgroups; anyone who develops the proper skills—and good ideas—can help Linux continue to evolve; and it's fully available online along with its documentation.

The true beauty of Linux for our purposes is that it's feasible to set up an Internet site with it whether you're a hobbyist, business user, or service provider! You can also make the operating system as bare bones or feature-rich as you like.

What This Book Is

Running a Perfect Internet Site with Linux is a comprehensive guide to setting up, running, and maintaining an Internet site with Linux. All you have to do is follow the book, step by step, for the setup process. Later, when you need a refresher on site maintenance, you can pick it up from your bookshelf and use it as a handy reference.

The following is a brief overview of each chapter:

- Chapter 1, "Why Create Your Own Site With Linux?," discusses why you would want to create your own site, and why you would want to use Linux. Also discusses Linux history, and applying for the domain name of your site (something that *must* be done ahead of time).

- Chapter 2, "What Kind of Hardware and Connection You'll Need," discusses how to choose the hardware and connection you need for what you want to do with your site.

- Chapter 3, "Getting Ready To Install Linux from the CD-ROM," discusses what kinds of preparations you need to make to be able to install Linux.

- Chapter 4, "Installing Linux from the CD-ROM," walks you through one possible Linux installation, explaining the choices made along the way.

- Chapter 5, "Setting Up Your Site for General Use," walks you through how to set up accounts, passwords, use virtual consoles, and shut down your system.

- Chapter 6, "Installing E-Mail Server Software," discusses setting up sendmail (your e-mail server), and POP mail if you need it. Also covers testing your e-mail server.

- Chapter 7, "Installing Web Server Software," discusses setting up and testing your Web server.

- Chapter 8, "Installing Gopher Server Software," discusses setting up and testing your gopher server.

- Chapter 9, "Installing UseNet Server Software," discusses setting up and testing your news server, as well as whether you need to run one.

- Chapter 10, "Installing FTP Server Software," discusses setting up and testing your Telnet and FTP servers.

- Chapter 11, "Installing Finger Server Software," discusses setting up and testing your Finger server.

- Chapter 12, "Security," discusses security measures you can take to protect your site from mischief coming over the Internet.

- Chapter 13, "Maintaining Linux," discusses managing users, disk space, and resources on your site.

- Chapter 14, "Maintaining Your System," discusses managing things for each of your servers.

- Chapter 15, "Upgrading Your System," discusses various hardware upgrade options, ideas, and considerations.

- Chapter 16, "Upgrading Your Software," discusses various software upgrade options, ideas, and considerations.

What This Book Is Not

This book is not an introduction to the Internet or to UNIX. You should have experience with the Internet and UNIX to use this book.

Further, this book is not a reference for writing programs for your site. I will, however, point you to online references as necessary.

The CD-ROM: Everything You'll Need to Get Things Going

You get all of the instructions you'll need in this book, and you also get a CD-ROM with all of the software as well! I've also tracked down all of the documentation I could find, so you won't have to go digging around online too often to find what you need.

As you may know, Linux software is frequently updated. The CD with this book is current at this time, but there may be a time in several months when you want a newer version of Linux and you don't want to download it. To help save you some time and money getting an updated version of Linux, we have arranged for a special discount offer with InfoMagic, a major provider of CD-ROM Linux software. With this one-time offer, you get the complete InfoMagic Linux CD-ROM set that includes Slackware and other Linux distributions as well as additional software archives. Please see the coupon included at the back of the book for the details of this special offer.

Conventions Used in This Book

This book uses various conventions that make it easier for you to get the most out of it. After all, I'm sure you want to get your site up and running as quickly and smoothly as possible!

Typeface	Meaning
italics	Variables inside commands; new terms
bold	Internet addresses; words or letters you have to type
`computer type`	Commands you type in; on-screen messages

Tip

Tips suggest easier or alternative ways to get things done.

Note

Notes contain information that I thought would be helpful or interesting.

Caution

Cautions contain important warnings. Please read any that you encounter as you work through this book to prevent unwanted results, including system damage and loss of data.

Now, let's get down to business!

Part I

Preparations

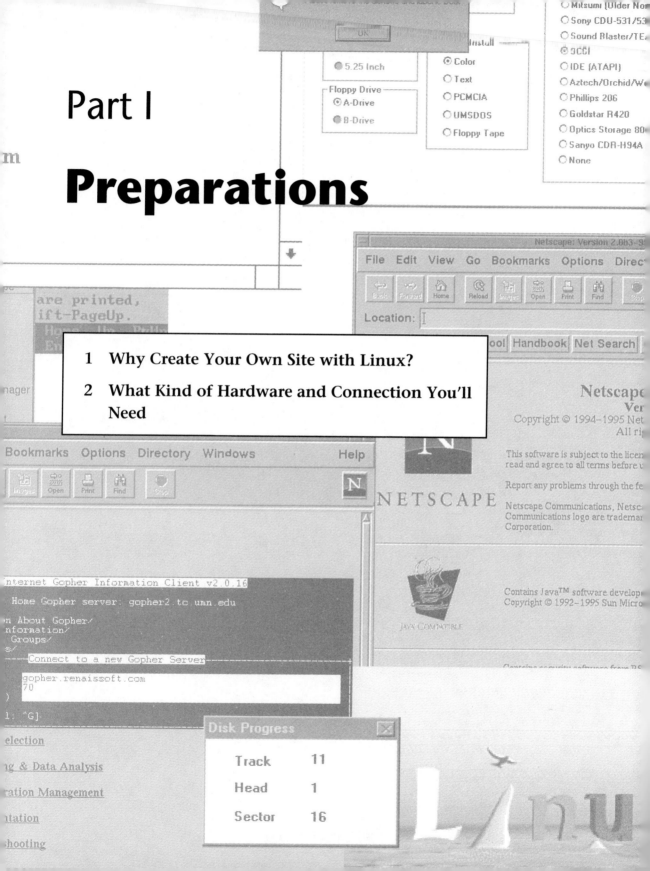

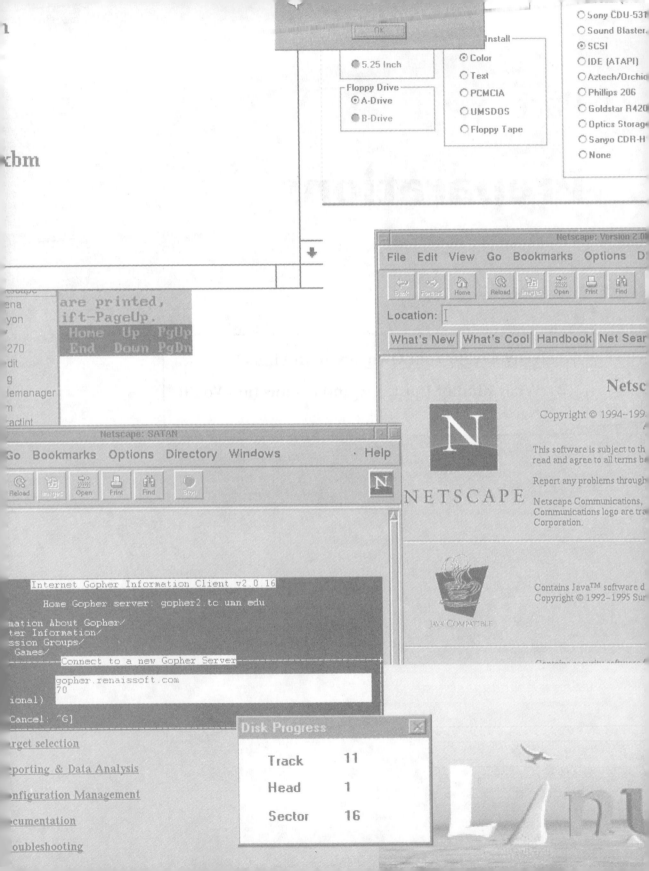

## Chapter 1

Why Create Your Own Site with Linux?

Because you bought this book, I obviously don't need to sell you on the idea of having your own Internet site nor on the idea of using Linux. After all, Linux is a full-fledged version of UNIX. Servers and clients for all the major Internet services (electronic mail, the World Wide Web, and so on) are available for this operating system. This makes Linux an excellent choice for running an Internet server.

Linux makes an especially good Internet server because you don't have to get any programs to teach it how to speak TCP/IP (the protocol the computers on the Internet use to communicate with one another). Most operating systems require extra software to be able to handle it.

In this chapter, you learn the following about Linux:

- What Linux is
- How to follow Linux versions
- How to register a name for your site

What Is Linux?

Linux is a free clone of the UNIX operating system for machines with 386, 486, and 586 (Pentium) processors (see fig. 1.1). It's full-featured and flexible, and is constantly being updated and improved.

Fig. 1.1
The Linux shark is
the unofficial
Linux logo.

Who Wrote and Who Maintains Linux?

The Linux operating system began in 1991 in Finland when Linus Torvalds wrote *Minix* (mini-UNIX) for a school project. As he enhanced the system during that year on his own, it grew from the mini-UNIX "Minix" to "Linux."

Torvalds wrote the initial Linux (which was little more than a kernel way back then) and still oversees its progression. A team of people worldwide now contribute to its growth and maintenance.

> **Tip**
>
> Are you wondering exactly how Linux is pronounced? On the World Wide Web, you can actually find a sound file of Torvalds himself pronouncing it! Just go to **http:// sunsite.unc.edu/mdw/mdw.html** and choose the link to Linus's pronunciation.

Linux Features

With Linux, you won't feel as though you're using a backwater version of UNIX because of a lack of key features. You get the same features you expect with any other version of UNIX, including the following:

- *True multitasking*   Very few operating systems offer full multitasking. Many OS's claim to do multitasking but their claim is only half correct.

These OS's let you do more than one thing at a time, but those processes are not fully running at the same time. If you try to background one process to let it finish, it either stops or crawls along until you return to it.

With an operating system like Linux, while the priority is given to the task you are working on at that very second, the tasks in your background continue until completed or until they need input.

■ *Virtual memory*   Sometimes you need to be able to access more RAM than you physically have in your system. *Virtual memory* is space on your hard drive that acts as extra RAM for when you need it.

■ *Shared libraries*   Many operating systems require that your programs be completely self-contained, which makes them a lot larger than they often need to be. OS's like Linux can generate binaries (programs) that access libraries of code that already exist on your system. This way, the size of your binaries is kept down. Smaller binaries save RAM and hard drive space.

■ *Demand loading*   Many operating systems keep everything in physical RAM until they run out of space, and then start using their virtual memory (if they have it). This means that if you leave a process open but don't use it for a while, it's probably sitting there eating up its RAM space and pushing the new things you're doing into swap!

This works a bit differently with OS's that can handle demand loading. When processes are still active, but not in use for quite some time, a Linux system will move them over to its swap space to free up more of its physical RAM for tasks that are being attended to.

■ *Proper memory management*   An important thing in any operating system is memory management. If your OS doesn't manage memory properly, you can end up with unpredictable crashes of your programs that can vary from just having to restart to having to completely reboot your machine. Needless to say, this is not what most people consider a productive working environment. Linux does have proper memory management, which is a relief when you're fond of running a lot of programs at once!

■ *TCP/IP networking*   Most operating systems for personal computers don't have TCP/IP networking built-in. Instead, if you want to connect to the Internet, you must get a program to handle the connection and conversion of the computer's own internal communication protocols to the Internet's TCP/IP protocols.

Linux uses TCP/IP for its own networking. Therefore, you don't need a conversion program. This makes for faster access to the Internet, and less chance for error since your processes don't have to go through as many program layers.

Linux also aims for the UNIX POSIX (Portable Operating System Interface) Federal Information Processing Standard set forth by the National Institute of Standards and Technology. This fact means that applications for other flavors of UNIX port to Linux without too much difficulty.

Linux and Microsoft DOS and Windows Programs

Linux itself cannot run MS-DOS or Windows applications. However, a DOS emulator (dosemu) can run most DOS applications and is constantly improving. You can run Windows applications on top of the DOS emulator, but you can't run Windows in enhanced 386 mode. So, while it will soon be possible to run Windows on Linux on top of the DOS emulator, the process will be slower than you may prefer. To run Windows for serious use with multiple applications on top of Linux will require the Windows emulator that is still under development.

Copyright Status

The "ownership" of Linux can get a little complex. Linus Torvalds owns the copyright on the Linux kernel. However, Linux itself (including the kernel) is all under the GNU Public License (GPL), often referred to as the *copyleft* because of how different it is from most copyright agreements. The full GPL is in Appendix B, "The GNU General Public License."

The GPL requires that those who use items that it covers to create programs make the source of those programs available to those who ask, and it insists that a copy of the GPL document be included with the product. This agreement allows the programmers to offer their software to the general public while retaining copyright over it so that it remains their work. It also ensures that code is available for others to enhance and modify (giving proper credit to the previous programmers, of course). The goal is to increase the total amount of free software available.

How To Follow Linux Version Numbers

Linux has two different sets of version numbers called *version trees*. It's important to understand the difference between the two trees so that when you see updates on the Internet, you know which patch files to get. One tree, the *experimental tree,* is a line of versions that is experimental; the code is still in the testing stages. The other tree, the *production tree,* has the code that is considered to be stable.

How To Tell the Difference Between Experimental and Stable

To determine the type of Linux version, look at the version numbers. Each number is made up of three digits, and it's the second that indicates the type. If the second digit is even, it's a production version. If it's odd, it's an experimental version. For example, version 1.2.0 is a production version and version 1.3.0 is an experimental version.

How Do the Two Trees Relate?

The two Linux version trees are related. They're done in tandem, with each tree starting at the same time. In fact, the appropriate x.y.0 versions are identical (e.g., 1.0.0 and 1.1.0 are the same, 1.2.0 and 1.3.0 are the same). From there, each tree grows individually with stable code added to the production version while the code still in the testing stages is added to the experimental version.

When Linus Torvalds determines that an experimental version has enough new features and is stable, he calls a *code freeze*. At that point, the stable experimental version becomes the new x.y.0 set, and development starts all over again in a new pair of trees.

History of the Version Trees

To get a feel for how Linux developed over time and how the version trees work, take a look at figure 1.2.

Fig. 1.2
The Linux version trees show the growth of the operating system.

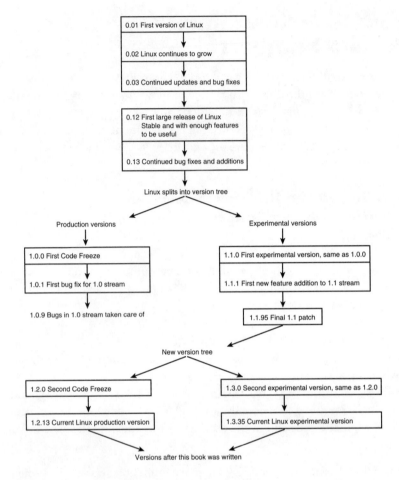

How To Register Your Site

All system administrators on the Internet must register their sites with InterNIC or with the appropriate agency for their part of the world. Site registration is the only centralized requirement on the Internet; a site cannot exist without it.

What Is Site Registration?

Site registration is a two part process. In the first part, you apply for the number of IP addresses you think your site will need. These addresses are then permanently assigned to your site for you to assign to your own machines as need arises.

IP addresses are made up of 32 bits of information, divided between network and host. *Network bits* are those that tell the Internet the particular site to which the IP address belongs. *Host bits* are those that tell your own network the particular machine to which the address belongs.

IP addresses are written in four pieces, separated by periods, for example, www.xxx.yyy.zzz. Each of these pieces contains eight bits of information. The way these bits are used depends on the class of the address involved.

Class A addresses are for large sites such as universities and huge corporations; a single class A address can be used to define millions of hosts. The chance of getting a class A address today is slim because of the shortage of address space. A class A address has 8 network bits and 24 host bits. For the address www.xxx.yyy.zzz, *www* contains the network information, and *xxx.yyy.zzz* defines the machine. The 8 network bits making up www is any number between 1 and 126. The host bits for xxx, yyy, and zzz are numbers from 0 to 255. An example class A address is 34.152.25.4, where 34 represents the site itself, and 152.25.4 represents a particular machine. In a class A address, this machine is one of many on a network within the site.

Class B addresses are for mid-size schools and companies. Each class B address can define thousands of hosts. These addresses are also difficult to get in today's address shortage. A class B address has 16 network bits and 16 host bits. For the address www.xxx.yyy.zzz, *www.xxx* contains the network information, and *yyy.zzz* defines the machine. The 16 network bits that make up www.xxx is any number between 128 and 191. The host bits for the yyy and zzz aspects are numbers from 0 to 255. An example class B address is 142.96.133.6, where 142.96 represents the site itself, and 133.6 represents a particular machine. This machine, just as with a class A address, is likely to be on one network among many within that same site.

Class C addresses are the largest addresses most sites are likely to get today unless they can prove sufficient need for an A or B. Each class C address has 254 or fewer hosts, but there are millions of possible class C network addresses. Some sites may find they can get multiple class C addresses instead of a single B or A address. A class C address has 24 network bits and 8 host bits. For the address www.xxx.yyy.zzz, *www.xxx.yyy* contains the network information, and *zzz* defines the machine. The 24 network bits that make up www.xxx.yyy are numbers between 192 and 223. The host bits that make up zzz is any number from 0 to 255. An example class C address is 214.130.78.10, where 214.130.78 represents the site itself, and 10 represents a particular machine. This machine may be on one network among many within that same site, or may simply be a machine on one large network.

Once your IP addresses are assigned, the second step of the registration process involves registering your site's domain name. The *domain name* is the part of a site's address that is the same for all machines. Once registered, it is linked to your IP addresses throughout the Internet's nameservers. You can assign machine and subnetwork names later (see chapter 5, "Setting Up Your Site up for General Use").

Because the registration process takes over six weeks, it's important to get things started. This registration process takes longer and longer because of the number of site registrations being submitted. Although your site does not have to be up when you submit the forms, it does have to be up when they are processed. Be sure that your site is up within six weeks from the time you submit the forms; otherwise, you may find yourself waiting another six weeks.

> **Tip**
>
> Some service providers do site registration; check into it because you may save yourself some work.

What Is the Process for Site Registration?

This section details the two step site registration process: applying for your IP address(es) and then your domain name.

It's important that you submit the forms for domain name registration after your IP address registration has been processed. Sending in the domain forms too early means you'll have to wait a lot longer for your registration to be complete because the IP information is needed to assign to the domain.

Getting Your IP Address

Before you get the appropriate IP address(es) assigned to your site, you need to decide how many of them you need. Let's take a look at how to determine the number of hosts you may eventually have and then see how to apply for the addresses.

How Large Might Your Site Get? The following are some questions to consider when deciding how many IP addresses you will need:

- Do you plan to be a large provider that might need an entire Class C address (254 possible hosts)?

- How far do you think your site will expand? Is it possible you might eventually need 100 or 150 hosts, or will 50 or even 20 be sufficient?

■ Will you need to use subnets? Reasons for using a subnet include the following:

> You will mix networking technologies (e.g., token-ring and Ethernet networks on the same site). This requires one subnet for each technology.

> You need to have one portion of your network set aside for extra security.

> There's a chance that part of your network will crash often, perhaps because it's experimental. You will want this part on a separate subnet so it won't take down your whole network.

> Your network will be too physically spread out to be all on one network because of cable length restrictions.

If you have to use a subnet, you lose the use of a number of possible IP addresses. For example, if you want a network with 2 subnets and you have a class C address, you would have two networks (subnets) each with 126 possible hosts. If you have 4 subnets, each could have at most 62 hosts. Setting up subnets is discussed in more detail in chapter 5, "Setting Up Your Site for General Use."

Address space is scarce on the Internet. If InterNIC feels that you're being overzealous during registration time, it will try to talk you down to lower numbers. If you need more IP addresses later, you can get them; they just won't be in sequence with the ones you already have.

Getting Your IP Addresses Assigned. To get IP addresses assigned to your site, you need to either write to InterNIC or to the appropriate agency for your country (see table 1.1). If you're unsure of where your country is covered, write to the service that looks likely for clarification. Any region not covered below is probably covered by InterNIC.

Table 1.1 IP Registration Services for Sites Outside the United States	
Country	**Service**
Asia-Pacific Region	AP-NIC E-mail: hostmaster@apnic.net Fax: +81-3-5276-6239

(continues)

Table 1.1 Continued	
Country	**Service**
Canada	CA*Net IP Registry E-mail: ipregist@canet.ca Fax: (416) 978 6620
Europe*	RIPE NCC E-mail: hostmaster@ripe.net Fax: +31 20 592 5090
US and remaining	InterNIC E-mail: hostmaster@internic.net Phone Number: 1-703-742-4777

* Europe *refers to requests from within the traditional European borders, as well as the former Soviet Union, Eastern Europe, Mediterranean countries, and parts of the Middle East. If you are unsure, contact RIPE NCC for clarification.*

Tip

If you want a block of addresses smaller than a class C, ask your provider if they will sign over some of their own reserved addresses. That can save you some hassle.

Now, the form you use to apply for your IP address(es) is determined by your location and your needs. These forms change on a regular basis. See the following minitable to find out the document you need to consult for the correct form information.

Covered by	**Form Location**
AP-NIC	ftp.apnic.net /apnic/docs/Contents
CA*Net IP Registry	rs.internic.net /templates/canadian-ip-template.txt
RIPE NCC	ftp.ripe.net /ripe/forms/netnum-appl.txt
InterNIC	rs.internic.net /templates/index

To register, just fill out the appropriate form and send it to the appropriate place. This chapter covers the InterNIC file for nonservice providers. If you're going to be a service provider, you need to fill out another form. At this time, the service provider form is `isp-ip-template.txt`.

The following are a number of the less self-explanatory exerpts from the general InterNIC IP registration form template (version 2.0 of `internet-number-template.txt` was the most current version at the time this book was written):

1. `2a.   NIC handle (if known)..........:`

If you have an NIC handle, include it here. If you have ever applied to InterNIC for something before, you were assigned a handle. If you have a handle and have forgotten about it, not including it is not a critical problem.

2. `3.   Network name...................:`

You need to make up a name for your network. It should end in "net," and be original. To get some ideas, think of what your network will be used for. Examples are GAMENET, PROVIDENET, HELPNET, or COMPANYNET.

Tip

When you come up with something, do a *whois search* on the network name (see the next section for more information on whois). If nothing for your network name comes up, that means no one's registered it yet.

---

3. `Justification`

`Host Information`

`6a.   Initially......................:`

`6b.   Within 1 year..................:`

You need to justify to InterNIC why you need the address space you've applied for. InterNIC wants to know how many hosts you intend to use when your site first starts up. In 6b, you need to predict the number of hosts you'll have in a year. If InterNIC doesn't feel you have sufficient reason to need a large block of addresses, it may offer you a smaller portion more in tune with your one-year projection. However, don't grossly overestimate what you think you need. Address space is scarce, but you can get more later if you need it.

Keep in mind that even devices such as printers can be hosts on some networks.

4.   Subnet Information

6c. Initially........................:

6d. Within one year.................:

Here, you need to tell InterNIC how many subnets you plan to have initially, and after one year.

5.   7a. Number of addresses requested...:

7b. Additional supporting

justification...................:

Here is where you actually request your IP addresses. In 7a, you tell InterNIC how many addresses you want. This can be a number of addresses, or a class, or multiple classes. For example, if you think you won't need more than 50 for quite a while, you can enter 50. If you think you'll need 4 class C's, you can enter that.

In 7b, if you're requesting a large number of addresses, you'll want to include more justification as to why you need all of them. If you're requesting more than 16 class C's, be sure to note the additional instructions in the template.

6.   8. Type of network..................:

Here, you need to tell InterNIC the type of network yours is, from the following choices: Research, Educational, Government-Non Defense, or Commercial.

Tip

Notice that InterNIC has included instructions at the bottom of the template.

Getting Your Domain Name

Once you have your IP addresses, you can apply for your site's domain name. Because of how long this takes, be sure you're not choosing a name that is already taken. You can use the InterNIC Whois service to look up the name you want to use. If you're not able to use whois from your own prompt, you can locate a list of registered whois servers via FTP at **rtfm.mit.edu** and get the file `/pub/whois/whois-servers.list`.

If you were looking for renaissoft, for example, type **whois \!renaissoft**

If you get something back, that domain name is taken. However, keep in mind that if its top level domain (e.g., com, net) is different from what you want to use, that may be okay. Be careful to avoid copyright terms because your domain name may be disallowed or could be taken away later by the owner of the copyright.

When you have chosen your domain name, go back to the location where you found your IP address forms. In the InterNIC case that I am using in my example, you are a non-service provider. If you want to have .us at the end of your domain name, use the form `us-domain-template.txt`. However, you're not trying for a .us top-level domain, so use the form `domain-template.txt`. When you've completed the form, send it to the appropriate organization.

Note

The .us domain is fairly new in the Internet's naming scheme. Sites outside the US are mostly used to having country extensions on their domain names, but sites in the US are still traditionally without a country extension. However, as new sites continue to appear, use of the .us country extension shows up more often.

Registration for the .us domain isn't handled through InterNIC. Therefore, this registration may go a bit faster. It also isn't subject to InterNIC's fees, although .us registration may eventually have fees associated with it. Another reason to register as a .us site may simply be to represent the United States on the Internet, as a US site.

Tip

If you're interested in registering for a local .us domain, ask your service provider who to contact.

Portions of this sample document (`domain-template.txt` version 2.0) follow:

1. `Technical Contact`

   `5a.  NIC Handle (if known)......:`

   You'll likely want to be the technical contact. InterNIC assigned you an NIC handle during the IP application process. Include that here.

2. Billing Contact

    6a. NIC Handle (if known)......:

    If the person handling the billing for your site is you, fill in the same handle you included in 5a. If you're not the billing contact, fill in the billing person's NIC handle.

3. Primary Name Server

    7a. Primary Server Hostname....:

    7b. Primary Server Netaddress..:

    Your site will have two nameservers. Generally, the primary nameserver is your own site's server. Include the hostname in 7a (more on choosing hostnames in chapter 5, "Setting Up Your Site for General Use"). In 7b, include the server's IP address.

4. Secondary Name Server(s)

    8a. Secondary Server Hostname..:

    8b. Secondary Server Netaddress:

    The secondary nameserver will likely be your provider's nameserver. If your own nameserver goes down for some reason, you still have access to your provider's. Fill the hostname of your provider's nameserver in 8a, and its IP address in 8b.

5. Stop where it says cut here. There are helpful instructions after this point, but the rest of it is for either changing already registered domain information, or for deleting a domain.

InterNIC Billing

InterNIC charges $100 for initial domain name registration. This fee covers the first two years your site exists. After that time, you have to pay $50 per year for domain name maintenance. You'll get an invoice to remind you, which will come through e-mail or postal mail, depending on what you selected on your domain name registration form.

It's important that you read the instructions involving where and when to send your payments, and that you meet these deadlines. If you're late, InterNIC will shut down your domain name. If you're seriously late, it will place your domain name back into the pool of names new sites are allowed to use.

Tip

A breakdown of current billing procedures can be found by FTP at **rs.internic.net**, in /billing/billing-procedures.txt.

If you intend to be a service provider that offers permanent connections, you may wish to apply for an account with InterNIC. Having an account would allow you to easily offer your users the extra service of registering IP's and domains, and make it simple for you to deal with user registration fees. The account application can be found by FTP at **rs.internic.net**, in /templates/account-template.txt.

Having an InterNIC account would enable you to get monthly statements from InterNIC to cover all your clients. You can then pay by credit card or check once a month rather than having to deal with a scattered payment schedule, which would occur as each site's anniversary came along every year. An initial deposit of $1,000 is required to open an InterNIC account.

## Chapter 2

What Kind of Hardware and Connection You'll Need

Equipment and connection types are important, but they become even more important when you set up a site. This is especially true if you make your site an Internet provider, in which case you need to seriously consider what you want to be able to provide with it early; it's much harder to make additions later. Keep in mind that as great as hardware updates are, adding one thing to a system seems to usually cause three other seemingly unrelated things to break. If you're going to provide service to outside users, it's an excellent idea to be as ahead of the game on hardware as possible. Users don't tend to be very patient when systems have to go down for upgrades and for unexpected glitches!

In this chapter, you learn how to:

- Choose necessary hardware

- Determine the connection type you need

- Find the best provider for your site

Choosing Your Hardware

Choosing hardware is mostly a matter of mixing technical understanding with common sense. The technical side is that each aspect of your computer's hardware affects the speed and efficiency of your services. The common sense side is to get the best hardware you can afford, focusing on which pieces will give you the most bang for your buck when it comes to what services you want to have available.

What hardware you need is subject to *many* variables. If you determine that what you need is more than you can currently afford to buy, decide what is most important to you in the beginning and where you can skimp for now. Some hardware is more easily upgraded or added to than others, for example.

Note

Because you're focusing on setting up an Internet service, some hardware is more important than others. For example, your main server's graphics capabilities can easily be next to nil. The only machines that will need to be able to display graphics are the ones you *want* to be able to display graphics (e.g., for Web page development). Other items that aren't necessarily important are:

- *Sound card*   Your main server likely won't need a sound card. Again, this hardware is only really necessary on machines where you want that capability.

- *CD-ROM drive*   The presence of a CD-ROM drive is entirely up to what you want to do with a machine. If you have a number of machines that you will occasionally want to use a CD-ROM with, one option is to get an external SCSI CD-ROM and SCSI cards in all machines where you may want to use it. Then, you could shuffle the drive to whichever machine you'd like it on at the moment.

- *Backup system*   You likely won't need a tape (or other type) backup on every machine on your network. You can use your tape backup on more than one machine on the network even if it's internally mounted on just your server! (Chapter 13, "Maintaining Linux," covers tape backups.)

For the services you offer, there are both server and client machines. The server machine provides the service in question (e.g., FTP, World Wide Web, X-Windows). The client machine accesses the server machine and utilizes its services (e.g., FTPing files, browsing the World Wide Web, using X-Windows). The server doesn't need to have all the capabilities necessary to run the service unless it's a client using the service as well. For example, a server that provides X-Windows to other machines doesn't need to have the graphics card and monitor to run X-Windows unless you need to run X-Windows on it.

However, be sure to provide yourself with a way of testing your services! If the server offering a particular service cannot use that service (e.g., provides X-Windows but doesn't have the graphics capability to use it), be sure you have a way of testing it. Once again, with the X-Windows example, be sure that you have at least one machine that is capable of using X-Windows. Otherwise, if you install X-Windows items for remote users, you'll have to trust that the server and software is working properly; you can't verify that they are.

> **Caution**
>
> Consult the Linux Hardware How-To (listed in Appendix F) for brands of hardware that Linux supports. Linux supports a wide range of makes and models, but drivers aren't always available—occasionally new items come out or specs are unobtainable. You can save yourself a lot of hassle by consulting the hardware how-to carefully.

> **Tip**
>
> For up-to-date information on the types of hardware available, check out the PC Hardware FAQ by FTP at **rtfm.mit.edu**, in the directory /pub/usenet/ news.answers/pc-hardware-faq. It comes in five parts.

How Your CPU Affects Performance

The speed of your CPU directly affects how quickly your computer can process. Think of the CPU speed as the baseline speed from which all other performance is measured. If you're going to run a site for yourself and one or two other users, and you're going to use your server as your primary console, you can get by with a 486DX33. However, even with a low load, this server may be a little slow (especially if you intend to use X-Windows). If you're going to have multiple machines, and you're going to use your server as a server and not as a console, a 486DX33's speed can be sufficient.

If you will have more than three or four users, you will likely want a faster server (see table 2.1). It becomes especially important as you get more users that your server be used as a server, not as a console, except for server maintenance. However, do keep in mind that important things like program compilation are heavily influenced by CPU speed. A compilation can take over an hour to do on a 486DX33, but only a few minutes on a Pentium. While you compile the program, everything else slows down (mail processing, mail writing, file editing, and whatever other things you may be trying to do).

> **Note**
>
> Using your server as a console on a regular basis means that you're taking up RAM that would normally be used for server functions for your other tasks. You're also using the server's hard drive, CPU, and so on. The combination of these things means slower server response for all the services handled by your main server. Compiling large programs is especially slow unless you severely *nice* the process (nicing processes are discussed in chapter 5, "Setting Up Your Site for General Use").

There are various types of motherboards on the market:

- *ISA, Intel Standard Architecture*   This motherboard is the old "standard." New machines don't typically come with this motherboard because the computer world is becoming more graphics intensive, and this motherboard is particularly slow with graphics.

- *EISA, aqSEnhanced ISA*   This motherboard is a faster version of the ISA motherboard, but still compatible with hardware that was built to work with standard ISA boards.

- *VLB, VESA (Video Electronics Standards Association) Local Bus*   This board is a modern version (as of the writing of this book) of the ISA/EISA board. Its makers concentrated on speeding up the graphics handling of the previous boards. If you're buying a machine that's below the speed of a Pentium, you want to get a VESA board.

- *PCI, Peripheral Component Interconnect*   Step up from VLB, used on Pentium machines and faster. This is the best motherboard architecture for Intel and Intel-compatible machines.

Table 2.1   CPU Requirements Relative to Number of Users

CPU	Usage
486DX33	Two users Mailing list
486DX-2 66	Five users Mailing list Small compilation
Pentium	Ten or more users Three mailing lists Two compilations

Note

The motherboard is the hardest part of your computer to upgrade, and the CPU is built into the motherboard. If you have to get a slower computer than you would like initially, be sure to get one that is easily upgraded to faster speeds.

A motherboard may require two basic types of RAM chips distinguished by the number of pins that connect the chip to the motherboard: 30-pin RAM, and 72-pin RAM. You should get a motherboard that uses 72 pin RAM, which is the newer type of chip and more technologically advanced (e.g., faster memory access).

The type of RAM a motherboard requires goes beyond pins. The time it takes the CPU to access the RAM in nanoseconds (ns) is also important. The higher the ns is, the slower the access. Also, the bus size (expressed in bits) is important, and equivalent to bandwidth. The more bits in the bus, the faster things pass through your RAM. Your motherboard manual will list the other important features your RAM must have, but I've discussed the ones that are important to look at when buying the RAM.

Tip

Be sure that your motherboard is easy to upgrade memory-wise. The fewer requirements on what kinds of combinations of chips you have to have, the more flexibility you have in buying RAM.

Tip

If you're being offered a "steal" on a Pentium, chances are that you're getting low-quality materials. Be sure that you're getting fast memory.

You *can* do a good number of things with a slower server, they will simply take longer—sometimes a *lot* longer.

How Your RAM Affects Performance

The amount of RAM your computer has is a significant factor in how many processes your server can handle at once, and how quickly it can chug through them. RAM can make the difference with things like:

- Processing mailing lists

- Handling your news server

- Processing multiple Web page requests

- Processing Gopher requests

- General X-Windows usage and using multiple processes within X-Windows

In all the above cases, the more RAM you have, the more items (Web pages, pieces of e-mail, Gopher files) you can load simultaneously. This means that multiple requests are processed faster, because instead of going through one at a time, they're going through 2, 5, or more at a time (see table 2.2). If you have a mailing list of 500 people, this can make *quite* a difference in how quickly the mail gets sent out.

You should have at *least* 8M of RAM for a site just for personal use. If you have a few users, and one server handling everything, you will likely want 16M of RAM. If you will have more than 4 or 5 simultaneous users, you may want more than 16M. This is especially true as the numbers get even higher.

How much you need as your number of simultaneous users rises depends often on what the users are doing on your system. Once you get past about 8 simultaneous users, one rule of thumb is 2M of memory for each simultaneous user. I stress *simultaneous* users because you don't need 200M of RAM if you have 100 users registered on your system. Instead, if you have 28 modems to cover these users, you need 28×2 or 56M.

If most of your users don't use applications that take up a lot of memory, you can do with less than 2M per user.

Table 2.2   RAM Requirements Relative to Number of Users and Usage Requirements

Users	Usage	Amount of RAM
Two	Mailing list Incoming news	8M
Five	Two mailing lists Incoming news Two Web page requests	16M
Ten	Three mailing lists Incoming news Six Web page requests Three Gopher requests	24M

> **Note**
>
> You may find that you can live with the results of having less RAM than recommended. RAM is simple to upgrade when it comes to your system, as long as the RAM works on your motherboard. There's no software reconfiguration required after the upgrade. Therefore, if you would rather skimp on the RAM for now and see how it does, it's not really a problem. If you have lots of users lined up already, simply be prepared to dash out and buy more RAM as payments come in. See chapter 15, "Upgrading Your System" for considerations on how to handle the upgrade.
>
> If you have to skimp on RAM, you can make up for it with swap space. Swap space is the space you assign on your hard drive to act as spare RAM, so that when you're using your RAM at full capacity, you still have room to do other things. For a more detailed discussion of swap space, see chapter 3, "Getting Ready To Install Linux from the CD-ROM."

How Your Hard Drive Affects Performance

For a site with one or just a few users, the hard drive isn't the primary consideration when it comes to performance. However, as the number of users and demand on services increases, the size and type of your hard drive becomes more important.

Choosing the Size of Your Hard Drive

The size of hard drive you should choose depends on how much you want to store. You will want a minimum of 200M for a full site Linux installation. Unless you're running a site only for yourself and don't intend to do much, you will want more space than that. With the prices of large hard drives dropping as they are, aim for a minimum of an 850M hard drive.

You can set disk quotas for your users. Often, 10M per user may be a good starting place (I have seen as low as 1M per user). Because there are few people on my system, I don't have quotas set and can get a bit excessive, up to 20M in the home directories. Drive space usage depends on how much mail and news people save, how many personal clients people install, and how many other programs and files folks keep lying around. Using quotas forces people to keep their home directories tidied and not to leave old stuff lying around.

Remember that the 10M per user doesn't cover mail storage, news storage (if you run your own server), POP storage, UUCP storage, and so on. You need to include space for storage of all these items (the ones you're using) in your estimates. Try to anticipate on the high side to save yourself some grief later.

> **Tip**
>
> If you're unfamiliar with POP and UUCP, see chapter 6, "Installing E-mail Server Software."

Choosing the Type of Hard Drive

As you get more users, the access speeds for your hard drive, and therefore the drive type, become more important. Even if you don't have a huge number of users, the drive type is important if you have a lot of traffic among services that are drive intensive. These services include:

- Electronic mail, mailing lists especially

- News, especially if you run your own server

- Web pages with a lot of pictures

The hard drives that most people buy with their computers are IDE drives (the standard internal hard drive most people own). These drives are great for most computer users, but they can access only one file at a time. If you'll be running a large site you should seriously consider getting a SCSI drive.

SCSI hard drives can access multiple files concurrently; get one of these drives if you want faster, more efficient file access. A SCSI drive speeds up mail and news processing immensely!

> **Tip**
>
> A fast SCSI drive also makes for faster swap space than an IDE drive.

Once your site has hundreds of users, consider buying a Redundant Array of Inexpensive Disks unit (RAID). A RAID unit contains a number of disks all working together in parallel. It acts like one huge drive, but instead stores your site's information on a number of disks instead of just one. When your site has thousands of users, one of these storage units is absolutely necessary.

How Your Monitor and Card Affect Performance

The monitor and video card are only important on machines where you will run X-Windows. You will want an SVGA card (if you can afford it, get an accelerated one) and a monitor that works with the card. Be sure to have enough memory on the card to handle the graphics modes you want to be able to use (this information should be available in the card's manual, or from the salesperson). This would be typically 1 to 2M of VRAM (Video RAM).

Of course, if you don't want to run X-Windows (or see graphics) on a particular machine, there's no need to have a high-end graphics setup for it. You only need to consider graphics capability on machines where you want to be able to use graphics.

Caution

It is imperative that you check with the Hardware How-To to be sure that Linux X-Windows supports your card and monitor.

Dealing with Power Outages

You don't want UNIX systems like Linux to just die with a power outage. Not only will all your users be rather unhappy, but you will lose all the partial files and bits of data sitting around in your system's memory that were supposed to be written to disk. One item you'll want to seriously consider for your site is an Uninterruptable Power Supply (UPS).

UPS's have power ratings on the packaging. Take a look at the power supplies on the backs of your computers, monitors, and any other devices you want to plug into the UPS. Add up the wattage listed on all of these and find a UPS rated for that many watts. If you will have a large number of machines, you may find that it's easier and more economical to buy a number of UPS's. There's nothing wrong with having more than one, and in fact it's a nice redundant safety measure.

The more items you have plugged into a UPS, the faster its battery will drain once power goes out, so it's not a good idea to put important equipment all on one UPS. You may want a single UPS for your main server and its monitor, and another one for peripheral machines.

A great feature to have on a UPS is a *network port,* which is a serial port going into the back of the device. You connect this to a serial port on one of the machines the UPS is connected to. You can then use the unipower package (the Hardware How-To lists where to get this item by FTP). This package watches the UPS's serial port. If it gets a signal from the UPS, it knows that the power has gone out and it needs to start a shutdown (you set the amount of time before it shuts down). If it gets a second signal before shutdown, the program knows that the power is back or it was just a spike, and cancels the shutdown. This gives your system a chance to save everything from its buffers.

Caution

Be sure to look in the Hardware How-To to make sure you get a UPS that has a driver available.

Tip

You need a nonstandard serial cable for the network port. Be sure to ask about the cable(s) when you go to buy the UPS(es).

Providing Dial-ins

If you intend to provide dial-ins for your users, you need to also provide modems for them to dial into. What method you use to provide these dial-ins depends on the number of people you want to allow to connect at once.

Small Number of Dial-in Users

If you want to only allow 16 or less dial-ins at one time, you can get multiport serial cards. See the Hardware How-To for what multiport cards have drivers available. Be sure to get the DB25 boards, which have cabling for external modem hookups.

These cards come with various numbers of ports, typically 4, 8, and 16. Remember, you will need an incoming phone line for each dial-in, and a modem to connect the phone line and the card.

Note

How many dial-ins should you start out with? Most service providers try to follow the rule of thumb of 1 modem for every 10 users. Once your system is up and running, have it keep track of dial-ins and use this formula to determine when you need to add more modems:

Total number of modems you need = (number of people trying to get in during your peak hours) × (average length of each connection in minutes) × (0.0238)

Chapter 5, "Setting Up Your Site for General Use," has more information.

Large Number of Dial-in Users

If you need more than 16 incoming connections, you should get a terminal server. You might be able to fit extra multiport cards into one machine, but it will be so slowed down by handling all the logins that your server won't be very useful for anything else. If you get a terminal server, it can handle the logins, and your site server can handle everything else.

> **Tip**
>
> Use the same formula as listed in the previous section to keep track of how many dial-ins you have.

The key to buying a terminal server is to buy one that has plenty of room to upgrade. Buy one that supports the number of dial-ins you feel you initially need, and with room to expand as far as you think you may need to in the near future. If necessary, you can always buy another terminal server.

For information on the terminal servers available, look in the following places:

- Your service provider may be able to give recommendations. However, they may not want the competition, so be careful if you intend to be their direct competitor at some point down the road. If they see you as a threat, they may not be eager to be helpful.

- Computer trade shows will likely have companies selling terminal servers.

- There are a lot of ads on the World Wide Web for high-end computer equipment, terminal servers included. Check out **http://www. infocom.net/~linuxisp/equip.html**, which is a list of Linux Internet service providers. You can follow a link to see what specific equipment these providers use for everything from servers to ISDN, to multiport cards, to terminal servers. There are links from there to the companies who make this equipment.

Choosing Your Connection Type

The speed, or *bandwidth,* of your connection makes all the difference in the world when it comes to how quickly your data will travel to and from the Internet. Think of your bandwidth as lanes on a highway. The wider the road, the more data can pass through.

If you think you may want something faster than a SLIP/PPP modem connection, check around with your local service providers and phone company to see what options you have, and what the costs are. Costs and availability of connections vary widely from place to place. There may even be alternative companies that can offer you faster digital connections.

> **Note**
>
> When I discuss numbers of users regarding bandwidth, I'm talking about the number of users who are using the Internet connection at the same time.

The bandwidth you need depends on your site's demands. Let's take a look at the options.

SLIP/PPP Over a Standard Voice Line

If you will have only a few users, a 28.8 kbps permanent connection is sufficient for most occasions. Also, this option is probably the least expensive you will find in your area. Make sure that the number you dial to connect to your provider is not a toll number because you'll use it all the time!

> **Note**
>
> If you want to move up to the next step faster in connections (ISDN, which is discussed in a moment), but it is far too expensive, another alternative may be to use two 28.8 KB modems and two standard phone lines. Using a technique called *EQL load balancing,* you can then use the two lines together to double your bandwidth (if your service provider supports this). If you consider this option, be sure to check into the cost of upgrading to ISDN and into the cost of permanent connections to the provider. You can then weigh the options and choose the least expensive. See the Net-2 How-To for more information.

ISDN

ISDN (Integrated Services Digital Network) doesn't use standard modems. Instead, it uses digital modems (or a computer designated to only be your *router,* turning your data into ISDN protocols). With this type of connection, you get 64 kbps speeds, and it still has a spare channel you can use for voice (and fax, and anything else you'd like to use it for) over the same line! If you don't want to use your ISDN line for voice communications, you can even combine the two primary channels (called *bonding*) to get 128 kbps! Small providers and businesses often use ISDN connections.

An ISDN line has two types of channels, labeled D and B. The D channel carries 16 kbps and is used for *signaling,* which means it carries all the control information necessary to handle the connections the data channels use. The B channel (the *primary* channel I referred to earlier) carries 64 kbps and is used for data transmission.

Often an ISDN connection comes with a D channel plus two B channels, giving you 16 kbps worth of control data transfer speed plus 128 kbps worth of data transfer. However, sometimes the phone company charges extra for the second B channel. This can be for a number of reasons, one being that phone company's lines might need to be upgraded before it can offer that high of a transfer rate to your location.

Unfortunately, ISDN is not available in some areas yet, because while it runs on standard copper phone lines, it doesn't *behave* like a standard phone line. The phone company has to be set up in your area to support its special behavior before it can offer ISDN. Some of the differences are:

- An ISDN line has no dial tone. It simply "connects" to the hardware at the other end.

- ISDN requires special 8-pin phone jacks at your end, instead of the standard 4 pin.

- ISDN requires 4-wire phone cabling instead of the standard 2, so your house or office would need to be rewired.

> **Note**
>
> The ISDN I'm discussing here, the one that works over copper wire, is technically *Narrowband ISDN.* There is another version that works over fiber optics lines, called *Broadband ISDN* (B-ISDN). Of course, fiber line is much faster for data transfer than copper. At the time this book was written, B-ISDN was still mostly in development stages, but you may want to ask your phone company how close it is to a reality in your area.

You need to buy extra equipment if you use an ISDN connection. You'll need at least one of the following:

- *Digital equipment*   Digital modem, phones, fax, and so on. Any equipment that used to work on your analog phone line will not work on the new digital setup. This is because the new setup won't have a dial tone. Keep in mind that you can have only one device per B channel.

- *Terminal adaptor (TA)* This piece of hardware can serve as an interface between your old equipment and the new line. You could then connect your computer via Ethernet to the TA, and your other devices directly to it as well without having to buy digital equipment.

- *Router* A dedicated router machine can feed your data to the Internet, plus serve as a terminal adaptor (if you buy a router, you may not have to buy a TA). Linux doesn't *require* a special routing machine, however, as it can handle routing itself.

> **Caution**
>
> Be sure that one of the units you buy to handle your connection also can provide power—a number of them are designed to do so. If they are, you don't have to add extra power outlets to your office. ISDN lines don't contain enough power in themselves to run your phones. If your power goes out, you will also lose phone service and your connection. A UPS may be helpful in giving you some time to shut things down.

Your phone company and service provider should be able to advise you of the best equipment options available at the time you're looking into buying. Shop around as much as you can, as rates can vary widely even within a small area. You may find that you can lease or rent the equipment you need.

> **Tip**
>
> You may want to pick up Que's *Special Edition Using ISDN* if you plan to use an ISDN connection. The WWW also has a great deal of information about ISDN.

Linux drivers for ISDN cards are still in the experimental stage. See the Net-2 How-To for up-to-date information on what's available. You'll need to keep in mind what equipment you can get drivers for when you make your purchases.

T1

T1 lines are even faster digital connections—1.544 mbps divided over 24 channels (which can be subdivided further) traveling along twisted-pair copper wires. These are serious, expensive connections that also require the phone company to lay a line to your location (which means you will need to discuss it with your phone company and find out the costs involved).

You will also need to buy or rent special hardware to run and maintain your connection, and find a provider that has the bandwidth to be able to feed your T1 connection to the Internet.

As with ISDN, a T1 is a digital line, with the same types of considerations involved (lack of dial tone, special digital equipment required). Often, you can lease or rent the necessary equipment for your end from your provider and/or phone company (e.g., a router machine to handle your Internet connection, phones, and so on).

With T1, you can use the software in the router to manage where each of the 24 channels goes. You can assign them to voice transmission (phones), video transmission, and so on and even change them dynamically according to your needs. The handy thing about the router is that you don't need special software or drivers on your Linux machines to use the T1 connection. You simply network the router to the rest via Ethernet and the router handles the rest.

Again, as with ISDN, talk to your phone company and your provider for up-to-date information on the hardware and software available. Shop around. Check out the Web—a number of companies are already offering hardware there.

The advantage of buying from your service provider, phone company, or a local computer consultant is that you can probably get your router preconfigured to the necessary settings. Then, you can simply take it, plug it in, and just do a little local setup. If you buy from a remote manufacturer, you may have to go through the headaches of getting all the settings from your phone company, provider, and so on. If you find you'd rather buy from a remote manufacturer, be sure to discuss what you will need to do when the machine arrives so that you're as prepared as possible.

> **Tip**
>
> You can get a router machine for ISDN connections as well. You don't need one, however, because of the availability of digital modems. Linux machines can handle routing themselves.

> **Tip**
>
> You might not be able to afford a full T1 line for your site, but you may be able to find an affordable FT1 (fractional T1) connection. These lines are generally offered in a multiple of 56 kbps, up to the full T1 bandwidth of 1.54 mbps.

Large corporations, universities, and large service providers generally use T1 lines and FT1 lines.

> **Tip**
>
> You can use parallel T1 lines to gain bandwidth. A provider I dealt with recently had around 8,000 subscribers, and was using multiple T1 lines.

T3

T3 lines are the cream of the crop, at 45 mbps (equivalent to 28 T1 lines) traveling along special cabling containing fiber optics. T3 connections are rare because of the expense and the special cabling.

An important thing to note about T3 is that no specific standard for all T3 lines exists. You'll need to ask your phone company about the specifics of how its T3 connections are set up. What they all have in common is that they are all high-speed digital lines. Therefore, again, you will need specialized equipment to handle the connection, the phones, and so on. Your phone company and/or provider can be of assistance with either leasing you the equipment, or with pointing you to a good manufacturer.

> **Tip**
>
> You can get a partial FT3 connection. In fact, you can get partial FT3 through T1 technology.

Only the largest sites will need and can afford T3 lines. If you find that no combination of T1 lines is enough for your site, it's time to move on to T3.

Cable Companies

Cable companies are slowly maneuvering themselves into the market of service providing. Their coaxial cable can handle up to 10 mbps, which makes it an excellent transmitter for voice, video, Internet data, and so on. Most cable companies are not yet poised to enter the providing market. There are some interesting experiments going on in various communities, however.

These experiments mostly involve the principle of the Information Super-highway, integrating video-on-demand services, video catalogs to browse, multiplayer games, home shopping, standard cable television, Internet access and more. The techniques and technologies used in the various test runs are different, as well as the services offered.

You may want to check with your cable company and see how far they are from offering such services in your area. The connections they offer are digital, requiring "cable modems" to handle the Internet connection, and special boxes often containing high-powered computer motherboards to handle the video aspects.

Phone Companies

Phone companies are also maneuvering into the Internet service providing business. Some are already there to a limited extent, while others are just entering the market. To find out what your phone company has available, contact its customer service department or if it has one, its technology or networking department.

Often, the networking services offered by the phone company are bundled with digital connections (e.g., ISDN, T1, and so on).

One new item to watch out for is a new method of high-speed communications over standard copper phone lines developed by AT&T Paradyne. It's called *GlobeSpan*; it's digital; and it gets an amazing 6 mbps!

Connection Summary

The connection's section contains a lot of important information to digest. In general, the speed of the connection you need is related to the number of simultaneous users you'll have on your site (see table 2.3). These are *simultaneous users*—users who are all logged in and taxing your connection at the same time.

Your mileage may vary. It's best to simply make sure that you have room to upgrade your connection if you need to.

Table 2.3 Which Kind of Connection You'll Need for Number of Users, Considering Usage Time			
Max Simult. Users	**Usage**	**Connection Type**	**Notes**
5	Low	28.8 Modem	
3	High	28.8 Modem	
20	Low	ISDN, 1B	If available in your area
12	High	ISDN, 1B	If available in your area

(continues)

Table 2.3 Continued			
Max Simult. Users	Usage	Connection Type	Notes
40	Low	ISDN, 2B	If available in your area
30	High	ISDN, 2B	If available in your area
100's	Low	T1	If available in your area, if you run into thousands of users you will eventually need more than one T1
100	High	T1	If available in your area

Note

By *low,* I'm referring to that number of users doing things that don't take up a lot of solid Internet connection time. These are things like using the Web (not a lot of graphics or FTP links), Gopher, IRC, and other nonbandwidth-intensive services.

By *high,* I'm referring to that number of users doing things that take up a lot of bandwidth. These are things such as using the Web and accessing a lot of Web graphics or FTP links.

Choosing Your Provider

It's important to shop around when you're looking for a provider to carry your site to the Internet. Your location will determine how many providers you have to choose from, and what services they can offer you.

Some things to consider in choosing your provider are:

1. *Expandability* How much do you think you will expand with time? Are you starting with a 28.8 SLIP connection and think one day you may need an ISDN or T1? Try to pick a provider that can support at least one step of growth. You don't want to have to tell InterNIC that you've moved too often because of the time it can take to get all your routing straightened out. You could end up in limbo if the Internet thinks it's supposed to send your packets to one location, but you're at another.

2. *Affordability*   Prices for services can vary widely. One local provider quoted me a setup fee of over two thousand dollars for a standard 28.8 SLIP permanent connection, while another provider waived the fee because it was a simple setup, and I could handle most of the setup on my own. Try to realistically assess how much assistance you want when discussing setup fees. I had set up such a connection before, so, for me, doing it myself wasn't a big deal. Setting up a much more complex connection where I'm unfamiliar with the technology involved might be something I don't have the time to fool with until I get it right. Sometimes, it's worth paying a setup fee to have the extra technical support. Some providers won't waive the setup fee because they assume that you will need their technical help at some point.

3. *Reliability*   Ask around, find out what other people in your area have to say about the available providers. Keep in mind that you will not be going through the provider's normal system. Basically, with a permanent connection (even a modem one at 28.8) you're connecting to a machine that goes straight to the Internet instead of going through the provider's internal network. Therefore, you probably want to try to find someone who has a permanent connection of the same type you want with the provider you're checking out (e.g., if you want an ISDN 2B connection, see if you can find someone else who has one, and ask him how reliable it is and about the technical support and customer service).

When it comes to permanent connections, providers will sometimes offer references in the form of other customers. You can also check on local newsgroups through another Internet account.

Note

If you're eager to get to the installation, you can get your server machine and install Linux there now. You don't *need* to be connected to your provider to set up the basic system or the servers themselves, but you won't be able to test the servers until you've got your system connected to your provider. Also, you don't need any other machines for your site until you have the server set up, because it's the machine that will run your entire network. Once you set up the server, you can install Linux on the other machines.

If you don't want to set up any extra machines until the server is fully functional, you can install client programs on the server to test it. However, if you don't want to bog down the server with such items, you may want to set up one additional machine, network it to the server, and test your clients on that machine. You should do this especially if you want to be able to test Web items with graphics, and don't intend to get a server that can handle graphics display.

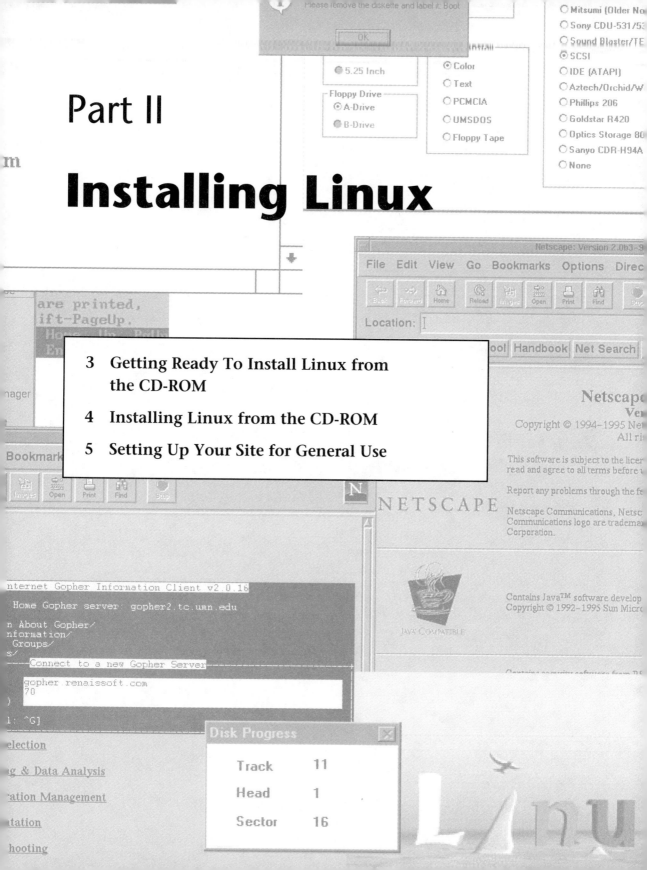

Part II

Installing Linux

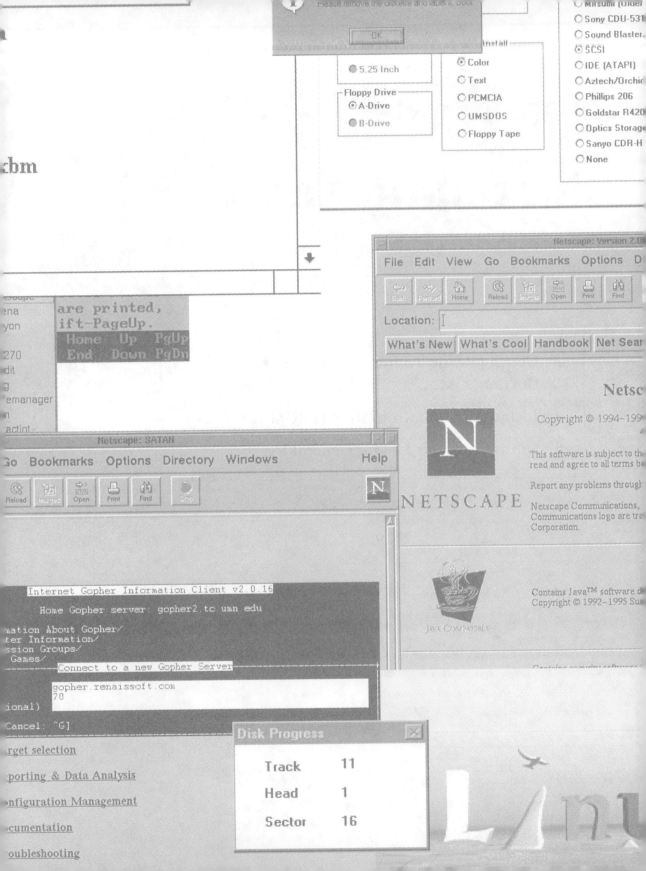

## CHAPTER 3

Getting Ready To Install Linux from the CD-ROM

Now that you've got the right equipment, the appropriate connection type, and a service provider to feed your site's data to the Internet, let's get down to business. The most important part of installing Linux, believe it or not, is preparation. Installing the operating system (which you'll do in chapter 7, "Installing Web Server Software") is the easy part and is fairly well-automated nowadays. First, however, you have to get set up properly.

In this chapter, you learn:

- How to make boot disks
- What size to make the partitions on your hard drive
- How to partition your hard drive
- How to create the file system

Preparations

There are a few things you need to do before you continue. Make sure to carefully go through this section if you want your Linux installation to go smoothly!

Have These Items Handy

Have the following ready to use before you go any farther:

- You need two MS-DOS formatted high density floppies, either 3.5" or 5.25". Both disks must be the same size, as the installation program will expect to use the same drive for both of them. It will not even check the other drive for the second disk.

- If the hard drive you're setting up will only have Linux on it (no MS-DOS), you'll need access to another computer that has MS-DOS. If you're partitioning the hard drive to run both operating systems, the MS-DOS partition on that drive will suffice.

- If you don't have a CD-ROM drive and plan to take the CD-ROM that came with this book somewhere else to copy it onto disks, keep in mind that you need one 3.5" disk for each distribution disk you want to install (except for the *a* series, which can be on either 3.5" or 5.25" floppies).

> **Note**
>
> It may seem that you cannot install from your CD-ROM drive if you don't have the operating system installed, because you don't have the drivers. However, when you select your *boot disk* later in this chapter, you will select the disk containing the appropriate drivers.

- You need all the information that you can find on the hardware in your computer, including brand names and exact versions.

Deciding How Many Disks You Need

The CD-ROM comes with a full set of Linux Slackware distribution disks on it. Slackware is a popular way Linux is distributed; it's a nice neat package containing everything you need to install and set up the operating system. Slackware has divided Linux into the distribution disks we discuss a bit later in this chapter.

If you're going to install from the CD-ROM, you need not worry about which disks you'll need at the moment. However, if you're going to copy the CD-ROM to floppies to install Linux, you can save yourself some extra work by deciding which disks you'll need. Remember, you'll need one floppy disk for each distribution disk.

The Slackware distribution included on the CD-ROM contains the necessary distribution disks for a full Linux installation. To help you determine which disk sets you might not need, here's a full list of what each set contains (the *a* series is not included here, since you *have* to install this one):

Set	Contents
ap	ash, bc, diff, ftape, ghostscript, gonzo, groff, ghostscript fonts, ispell, ispell, jed, joe, jove, jpeg, manpages, mc, mt_st, quota, sc, sudo, termbin, termnet, termsrc, texinfo, vim, workbone, zsh
d	binutils, bison, byacc, clisp, f2c, flex, gcc, gcl, gdb, gmake, libaout, libc, libgxx, m4, man2, man3, ncurses, p2c, perl, pmake, rcs, strace, svgalib, terminfo, tools
e	emacs
f	FAQ and HOWTO files
k	lx1213, lx1320n: bind, cnews, deliver, dip, elm, inn, mailx, netcfg, nn, pine, ppp, rdist, sendmail, smailcfg, tcpip, tin, trn, uucp
q	aaztcd, abare, acdu31a, acdu535, acm206, agscd, aidecd, amitsumi, aoptcd, asbpcd, ascsi, ascint, aha2940, asjcd, aztech, bare, cdu31a, idenet, cdu545, idecd, mitsumi, sbpcd, scsi, scsinet, xtt: tex
tcl	tcl
x	fvwm, rxvt, xwindows, xlock, xman, xpm
xap	xchess, ghostview, gnuplot, libgr, seyon, workman, x3270, xfig, xfileman, xfm, xfract, xgames, xgrabsc, xpaint, xspread, xv, xxgdb
xd	xd
xv	xv (xview)
y	abuse, bsdgames, doom, sastroid, tetris

Tip

If you're not sure which packages you want, or are concerned that you may accidentally overlook something you'll need, copy all of the disks. It's better to have too much than not enough!

Tip

If you're not going to install X-Windows, there's no need to copy any of the disk series that start with the letter X.

II

Installing Linux

Creating Your Boot and Root Floppies

In order to install Linux, you must create two floppy disks: one for the necessary boot information, and one for the necessary root information. After installing Linux, keep these disks handy for system emergencies that you may run into later.

Creating your boot and root disks is a simple but important step in the Linux installation process. You will use an MS-Windows program provided on the CD-ROM, called Lininst, to create it. Now, take one of your 3.5" or 5.25" disks and place it in the a: (or appropriate) drive. Then, in the File Manager, change to your CD-ROM (I will assume d:, but use the appropriate drive letter). Now, change to the \Lininst directory on the CD-ROM and double-click on the program Lininst (see figure 3.1 for what you will see at this point).

Fig. 3.1

The initial screen for Lininst from the CD-ROM.

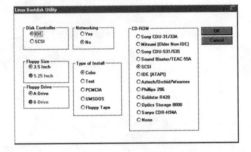

Now choose the appropriate options for the machine you're installing Linux on at this time. For example, my hard drive is an IDE, not SCSI, so I'll make sure IDE is marked under Disk Controller. I'm using 3.5" floppies for my boot and root disks, so I'll check 3.5 Inch under Floppy Size. Since I'm using a:, I'll click A-Drive under Floppy Drive. If you're installing using NFS (installing Slackware from another machine to this one), click Yes under Networking. If not, click No.

Now, choose the install program you want to use. I'll walk you through the Text installer in this chapter, because it gives you more complete error messages, and the Color install program doesn't work properly on a few types of systems.

Tip

If you would like to try the color installation program, you're welcome to. It works most of the time. You can click Text this time and then come back through this procedure and click Color the next if you like. This allows you to try the color installation, and if you find it too difficult or that it doesn't work, you can just erase what it installed and start over with the text install.

While the text and color installs do look quite different from one another, the thought processes behind making your choices are the same, so the walk-through in this chapter will still be useful.

Click on the type of CD-ROM you're using for your installation under the CD-ROM section. Finally, click OK to proceed with creating your boot and root disks. You'll be instructed to insert a blank, formatted floppy disk of the size you defined under Floppy Size, which in my case is a 3.5" disk. Do so, and then click OK.

Note

The boot disk is especially important because it contains the drivers that will allow you to install from your CD-ROM. Table 3.1 lists the types of boot kernels available with this Linux distribution for 3.5" drives. (If you're using a 5.25" drive and not using the installer program, look in the file d: \bootdsks12\readme.txt for information on the files available.) You'll quickly see that filling in what kind of hardware is in your computer system properly is important in helping the disk creation program choose which boot disk to use.

Table 3.1   Linux Boot Kernels for 3.5" Floppies

File Name	Hardware
aztcd.gz	IDE, SCSI, and Azetch/Okano/Orchid/Wearnes hard drives, non-IDE CD support.
bare.gz	Only IDE hard drive drivers.
cdu31a.gz	IDE and SCSI hard drives, and Sony CDU31/33a CD.
cdu535.gz	IDE and SCSI hard drives, and Sony CDU531/535 CD.
mitsumi.gz	IDE and SCSI hard drives, plus Mitsumi CD.***

(continues)

II

Installing Linux

Table 3.1 Continued	
File Name	**Hardware**
idecd.gz	IDE and SCSI hard drives, plus IDE/ATAPI CD-ROM.***
net.gz	IDE hard drive and EtherNet.
sbpcd.gz	IDE and SCSI hard drive, plus SB Pro/Panasonic CD and TEAC-55A CD.
scsi.gz	IDE hard drive, plus SCSI CD-ROM.
scsinet1.gz	IDE and SCSI hard drive, SCSI CD-ROM, and EtherNet.*
scsinet2.gz	IDE and SCSI hard drive, SCSI CD-ROM, and EtherNet.**
xt.gz	IDE and XT hard drive.

*   scsinet1.gz supports the following SCSI cards: Adaptec 152x/1542/1740/274x/ 284x, Buslogic, EATA-DMA (DPT/NEC/AT&T), Seagate ST-02, Future Domain TMC-8xx, 16xx.

**   scsinet2.gz supports the following SCSI cards: Generic NCR5380, NCR 53c7,8xx, Always IN2000, Pro Audio Spectrum 16, Qlogic, Trantor T128/T128F/T228, Ultrastor, 7000 FASST.

*** mitsumi.gz is not for the Mitsumi triple and quad-speed IDE/ATAPI drives. If you have one of these drives, you will want to use the idecd.gz disk.

You'll get a dialog box that shows you the progress made in writing the first disk, your boot disk (see fig. 3.2).

Fig. 3.2
The disk writing progress box for Lininst.

Once the process is complete, you'll get a dialog box instructing you to re-move the floppy you just wrote to from the drive, and label it as your boot disk (see fig. 3.3).

Fig. 3.3
Instructions to
remove the floppy
from the drive and
label it as Boot.

> **Caution**
>
> Make sure to label your boot disk clearly. Also, after you've used it for the installation process, put it somewhere safe. You may want to get a special disk box just for Linux items and keep the boot disk right up front. You'll need it if you ever have problems with your Linux system!

Set it aside in a safe place, as you'll need this disk in order to install Linux in your system. Click OK once you've done this. At the next dialog box, insert another formatted blank floppy of the same size as the previous one. Click OK.

> **Caution**
>
> Remember, you must use the same size disk for both boot and root! When you're booting into Linux, the computer will look in the same drive for both disks.

Once again, you'll get the disk writing progress box. Once this second disk, the root disk, is written, you'll get another dialog box instructing you to remove the floppy and label it as the root disk (see fig. 3.4).

Fig. 3.4
Instructions to
remove the floppy
from the drive and
label it as Root.

> **Note**
>
> The root disk contains the program you'll use to install Linux onto your machine. Table 3.2 lists the types of root images available with this Linux distribution. The root disk images are the same regardless of the size of the disk you're installing them to.

II

Installing Linux

Table 3.2 Linux Root Kernels

File Name	Method of Installation
color.gz	Root install disk for 1.44M floppy drives. Uses a new full-screen color install program. IMPORTANT NOTE: Although nice to look at, this install program has a few bugs and is not recommended until it's cleaned up. For example, it's not forgiving of extra keystrokes.
umsdos.gz	A version of color144.gz that uses UMSDOS. Allows you to install Linux into a directory or an existing MS-DOS partition. Not the fastest possible choice, but it works and won't require you to repartition your hard drive (discussed later in this chapter). For more information on this option, see the file d:\slakware\rootdsks\readme.uns.
text.gz	Root install disk for 1.44M floppy drives. Contains new versions of tty-based install scripts from previous Slackware releases of Linux. All new keymaps should be supported. Also gives more detailed error messages than color.gz during installation, so I use this one in my examples.
tape.gz	Installation from tape (semi-experimental). For more information on this option, see the file d:\slakware\rootdsks\readme_t.ape.
pcmcia.gz	Identical to the text.gz root disk, but used for installing via NFS to a laptop with a PCMCIA Ethernet card.

Click OK. Now you've created both of the disks you need to use in order to boot your system into Linux.

> **Caution**
>
> Be sure to label your root disk clearly as well!

> **Caution**
>
> Be sure that your computer's BIOS is set up to check for floppy disks at boot time! If you configured it to ignore disks in the floppy drives, you will not be able to use your boot and root disks.

Partitioning Your Hard Drive

The next step in the Linux installation process is partitioning your hard drive. Even if you plan to have only Linux on the drive, and not MS-DOS at all, you must partition your drive to create *swap* space. However, if you are using multiple hard drives in one machine that is used for Linux only, you don't need a swap partition on each drive. Only one swap space per Linux system is necessary.

> **Note**
>
> A swap partition is Linux's version of virtual memory. The less RAM you have in a computer, the more important the size of your swap partition is, as it serves as RAM.

> **Note**
>
> From this point, you no longer need MS-DOS capability unless you need to try another boot or root disk option. So, if you have MS-DOS on your drive but don't intend to use it, feel free to pretend that the drive is blank. For your piece of mind, however, you may want to make sure you have access to an MS-DOS system somewhere—just in case.

> **Caution**
>
> If you're installing Linux on a drive that you use for other work and have files you'd really like to keep, be sure to back them up! Repartitioning a hard drive can destroy data if something goes wrong. Back up everything you don't want to lose.

Choosing Partition Sizes

In chapter 2, "What Kind of Hardware and Connection You'll Need," I discussed various things that affect hard drive requirements. I seriously recommend that you get at least a 200M drive (not much of a worry since 200M is on the low price end of hard drives today) if you want to do anything with your site other than look at it. And the more space you have the better. As I know you've discovered, no matter how much hard drive space you have, you can find a way to fill it all.

> **Caution**
>
> Be sure to look at the physical hard drive space, and not compressed hard drive space. If you have your hard drive compressed (e.g., by Microsoft's DriveSpace), it looks to your computer like the data in that compressed drive is in one huge file. If you partition that drive, you will lose your data because the file will be broken in pieces.

Linux-Only Drive

If you're going to use only Linux on a machine, deciding partition sizes is fairly easy. You'll only need two partitions: main and swap.

I recommend that you make the total available memory at least 16M (your RAM plus your virtual memory should total 16M). Of course, even if you have a lot of memory on your machine, a server can often use even more. Decide how much space on your hard drive you can spare, and give yourself as much swap space as you can.

> **Note**
>
> The maximum size for a swap partition is 128M. If you want more than that, you can create several swap partitions, but no more than 16.

To find the size of your main partition, just subtract the swap size from the drive size. (For example, if your drive is 540M and your swap partition is 20M, your main partition is 520M.) If you have to use multiple swap partitions, total their sizes and subtract them from your hard drive space to see how much space you have left for your main partition.

> **Tip**
>
> One function of swap space is to handle overflow from your physical RAM, and this can be rather slow. If you find that your applications are consistently going into swap space because they have used up all of your physical RAM, you should consider purchasing more RAM for your server.

Linux Plus Other File Systems

If you want to install Linux on a drive that also contains MS-DOS and Microsoft Windows, you'll need to make three partitions: Linux, swap, and MS-DOS.

> **Note**
>
> Keep in mind that if you're going to switch between different operating systems, your machine will not be an Internet site when it's not running Linux. Using multiple operating systems is only recommended for secondary machines if you don't want to have to take your site down on a regular basis.

The size of each partition depends on the size of the hard drive and the following considerations:

- Decide how large you want your swap space to be. As stated in the previous section, your total memory (RAM plus swap) should at least add up to 16M. See the section, "Linux-Only Drive," for an in-depth discussion of the capabilities of swap space.

- Using an OS like MS-DOS 6.0 or higher that can run on a compressed drive is a factor in determining partition size. Keep in mind that if you drivespace your DOS drive, you won't be able to access that data from Linux. If you don't drivespace it, you will be able to access it. Software is in the works to enable Linux to read data from a drivespaced drive.

- Determine how much drive space you need for Linux based on the issues discussed in chapter 2, "What Kind of Hardware and Connection You'll Need." You'll want at least the minimum recommended: 200M.

- You might want to leave a blank partition for installing another operating system later. This will take some planning, as you'll need to determine how much space the spare partition will need.

> **Caution**
>
> If you plan to install Windows 95 after you've installed Linux, be prepared to use your boot and root disks. Windows 95 erases the boot sector (the very first sector) on your hard drive when you install it. You can avoid this problem by using a floppy disk to store the information you might otherwise store on your hard drive's boot sector (discussed in more detail in chapter 4, "Installing Linux from the CD-ROM").
>
> You will not have this problem in reverse. Win95 doesn't actually use the boot sector of your hard drive, so you don't have to worry about Linux causing you any problems there.

II

Installing Linux

> ### Caution
>
> If you've got a drivespaced drive (or it's compressed with another drive compression program), you're going to need to undrivespace it before you partition the drive. If the drive is almost full, you'll have to remove enough information to free space for decompressing the drive. If you have a tape backup, this would be a good time to back up your drive and then get the items you want off the tape when you're finished. No matter how you decide to do this, back up your most important files!
>
> You could also zip up the important files and copy them to disk if you don't have a tape drive. This will take you much less time than copying the files to disk without zipping them first.

Use the following method to determine the actual size of each partition that you want to create:

1. Look at your total hard drive space.

2. Determine the size of the swap partition(s) you would like to use.

3. Decide on a hierarchy of partitions (for Linux and your other operating systems), and allocate space accordingly.

4. Decide how large you'd like your primary partition to be.

5. Determine the minimum amount of space you'd like to have on the remaining partitions.

6. Add the amounts in steps two through five, and see if that sum fits into the total drive space.

7. If it fits, you're set! Just work the remaining space into partitions as you desire. If it's too large, go back over steps two through five, and trim partitions until they all add up correctly.

For example, let's say I've got a 540M drive and 8M of RAM, and I want both Linux and MS-DOS partitions on it. Following the process described above, my answers would be as follows:

1. 540M.

2. Minimally, I should have an 8M swap partition to make 16M of RAM. However, I'd love to have 30M of RAM available, so I'll first plan to create a swap partition of 22M.

3. Although I will do my word processing on my MS-DOS partition and use a few Windows programs there, I'll mostly use my Linux drive. Plus, I can drivespace my MS-DOS partition, so I can squeeze more space out of it even if I give it a smaller partition. Compressing my MS-DOS partition means I can't access DOS files from my Linux partition, but that is okay because I don't intend to move files back and forth and I need the extra space on my Linux drive.

Caution

You may find that you want to be able to move files between your MS-DOS and Linux partitions. While the server for my site is always in Linux, I switch my computer between Linux and DOS depending on what kind of work I have to do. If I want to take a word processing file and e-mail it to someone, I can't just copy it over from the Linux partition if I compressed my drive.

Tip

If you want to compress your MS-DOS partition, but still want to be able to transfer files between it and the Linux partition, you can create a small MS-DOS partition and not drivespace it. The small partition would be accessible by both MS-DOS and Linux. Don't make it too small, though. Remember, you have to be able to fit the files you want to transfer into the partition.

---

4. I at least want to have the minimum recommended 200M of space for my Linux drive. I don't want a massive news feed, but I tend to get a lot of e-mail due to mailing lists, and I would like to offer a few Web pages. Therefore, I'd like to have around 300M for my Linux partition.

5. Since I won't use my MS-DOS partition much (after all, I'd have to take my site down to get to it), it doesn't need to be huge—just large enough to hold MS-DOS, Windows, a word processing application, and a few other handy applications that I will need on that partition until equivalent programs are available in Linux. With drivespacing, I can get twice the room out of the partition, so 150M should suffice as it will turn into 300M with compression.

6. Let's see:

   22M of swap space

   300M for the Linux partition

II

Installing Linux

150M for the MS-DOS partition

472M total

My hard drive capacity is 540M. That means I've got a whole 68M to play with!

7. I have a few options. I could add more swap space, add more to my Linux partition, or add more to my MS-DOS partition. Better yet, if I wanted to be able to move files back and forth between my MS-DOS and Linux partitions, I could add a small MS-DOS partition and not drivespace it. That way, I could put the files that I wanted to transfer there, and copy them to the appropriate places.

> **Tip**
>
> If you're installing Linux on multiple machines that will be connected by EtherNet, and you're installing multiple operating systems on the second machine but not on the actual Internet server, you can set up your network so that you can use the Linux Internet connection from your MS-DOS partition. Thus, you can transfer your data between your MS-DOS partition and your Internet site via FTP instead of using an extra MS-DOS partition. More on this subject in chapter 5, "Setting Up Your Site for General Use."

In this case, the computer I'm setting up is my only one. I'll make a 10M MS-DOS partition, without compression, so I can transfer files around. That leaves me with 58M. I'll increase my swap partition from 22M to 30, my Linux partition from 300 to 340, and my MS-DOS partition from 150 to 170. That uses up the rest of my space.

Changing Your Partitions

If you're going to have MS-DOS and Linux both on the same hard drive, then what you will do next depends on whether your hard drive is already partitioned and how much of it is drivespaced.

If you're not going to have multiple operating systems on this drive, and it's already just one big partition that you intend to wipe clean, then skip to the next step in the installation process.

One MS-DOS Partition: Not Drivespaced

If you've got just one partition (MS-DOS) the first thing you need to do is clear it so that it fits, without compression, into the MS-DOS partition you're going to have. Then, run the DEFRAG program on your drive to make sure all of your data is together at the beginning of it. Once you've got your MS-DOS files all within the beginning of the hard drive, taking up less space than you plan for your MS-DOS partition, you're ready to continue.

> **Caution**
>
> There are methods of partitioning your hard drive that destroy your data. The one we use in this chapter doesn't destroy data, but just in case, you may want to back up your important files.

Before you partition your hard drive into one MS-DOS partition and one Linux partition, you need to do the following:

1. Create a bootable floppy disk with the MS-DOS command format a: /s (if your floppy drive is not a:, use the appropriate drive letter).

> **Caution**
>
> If you need special drivers, be sure to copy these to your bootable floppy! Especially if you're working with large hard drives. The best test is to make sure to reboot with the floppy disk and see if you can access the drive you want to partition. If you can't, be sure you have the drivers you need, and be sure to create a config.sys file on the floppy to load them. Each time, if you're not sure what to do, reboot with the floppy and see what you have access to and what you don't. Your config.sys file on your hard drive should be a good help in figuring out how to phrase the lines you need.

2. Go to the CD-ROM directory, `d:\install\fips`

3. Copy the files `restorrb.exe`, `fips.exe` and `errors.txt` to your floppy drive.

4. Reboot your computer with your MS-DOS bootable floppy in the drive to test it. Make sure you can access your hard drive after rebooting from the floppy.

5. Be sure that you've defragmented your hard drive and all of your information fits together at the beginning of the drive inside the space allocated for your MS-DOS partition.

II

Installing Linux

Now, it's time to repartition your drive! Do the following:

1. Reboot your computer again with the MS-DOS floppy in the drive.

2. Have a spare blank disk handy.

3. At the A:\ prompt, type **fips** (see figure 3.5 for what you'll see at this point).

Fig. 3.5

Fips, the program you will use to repartition your drive.

4. Fips will detect which operating system it's running under.

5. Fips will detect your hard drive(s). If you have more than one, it will ask you which one you want to partition.

6. Fips will look over the root sector of your hard drive and give you a table like table 3.3 in which there are three partitions on the hard drive. If you've only got one partition, then only the first line will have anything but zeros in it.

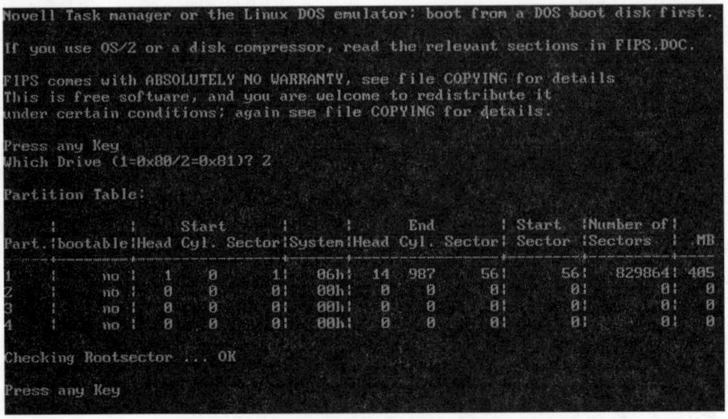

Fig. 3.6

Fips displays the initial partitions on your drive.

7. Fips checks the root sector for errors.

8. If you have more than one partition already, Fips will ask you which one you want to split.

9. Fips reads your root sector and gives you a list of information like:

Bytes per sector: 512

Sectors per cluster: 8

Reserved sectors: 1

Number of FATs: 2

Number of root directory entries: 512

Number of sectors (short): 0

Media descriptor byte: f8h

Sectors per FAT: 145

Sectors per track: 63

Drive heads: 16

Hidden sectors: 63

Number of sectors (long): 141057

Physical drive number: 80h

Signature: 29h

10. Fips makes sure this information is accurate.

11. Fips makes sure both copies of your FAT are accurate and will exit if they're not.

12. Fips looks for free space at the end of your partition

13. Now, you'll choose the size of your new partition (this size should be the size of your Linux partition plus the size of your swap space). You can use the right and left arrow keys to increase and decrease the cylinder count, which will change the size of the partition displayed. Just keep moving (to move through the cylinder counts more quickly, use the up and down arrows) until you get to the size you want for your Linux partition. When you're finished, press Enter.

14. Fips double-checks to make sure that the new partition is empty.

15. Fips calculates the changes to the root sector and shows you the appropriate table (see fig 3.7).

Fig. 3.7
Here is what fips set my partitions to once I gave it the sizes I wanted to use.

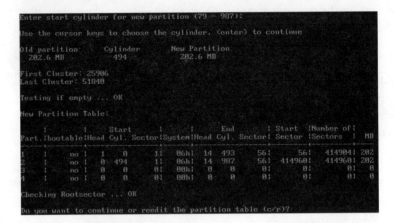

16. Type **c** to continue.

17. Fips displays the final disk information. Check it for accuracy and press a key.

18. Type **y** to save and exit.

19. Reboot from the floppy.

20. Run chkdisk to make sure that the old but smaller partition is still okay.

21. If there are no errors, remove the floppy and reboot normally.

One MS-DOS Partition: Drivespaced

If you're starting out with only one compressed MS-DOS partition on your drive, the first thing you need to do is decompress your drive. This can be a painful process if your drive is large and almost full, but you have to do it. Take the time to clear things out of the drivespaced drive (backup to disk, delete things you don't need or can reinstall) so you can decompress it in the room you've got. Once you've done this, follow the instructions in the previous section for non-drivespaced drive partitioning.

Preparing Your Linux Partition for Installation

Before you can install Linux on the new partition, you need to prepare that partition for the operating system. All of this fiddling with the hard drive may be a bit tedious, but remember, each step brings you closer to setting up your Internet site.

Setting Up the Linux Partition

It's time to boot your computer with Linux! Find the Linux boot disk you made at the beginning of the chapter, and put it in the floppy drive. Reboot and do the following:

1. Ignore most of the information scrolling past until you see Welcome to the Slackware Linux Bootkernel disk!

2. Press Enter at the first prompt, where you are given the option to enter extra parameters.

3. At the prompt, pop your boot disk out of the drive, insert the root disk (ramdisk), and press Enter.

4. Login as **root**.

5. A # prompt appears.

Now you're going to use Linux's fdisk program to finish with your drive partitions. Look below for the device names assigned to various hard drives.

/dev/hda First IDE Drive

/dev/hdb Second IDE Drive

/dev/sda First SCSI Drive

/dev/sdb Second SCSI Drive

Choose the appropriate device name, and then run fdisk using that device name (for example, fdisk /dev/hda).

Tip

To see the fdisk menu options, type **m** at the prompt.

Press **p** to look at your current partition table. If you don't want any MS-DOS partitions left (or if you have extras you want to delete), press **d** to delete a partition. Then, enter the number of the partition you want to delete, and press Enter.

Now, press **n** to define a new partition and **p** to make that a primary partition (one of the four partitions you were looking at using the fips program). Enter partition number **2** if you kept a DOS partition and the Linux partition is the second one on the drive. (If you don't have an MS-DOS partition, you'd enter **1**.) To keep from having to do a lot of math and count cylinders, I recommend you make your swap partition at the very beginning of the Linux partition. Therefore, enter the first cylinder number listed on your screen. Then, instead of having to calculate a last cylinder number, enter the size in megabytes of your swap partition, such as +30M.

> **Tip**
>
> If you get the message, `Warning: Linux cannot currently use XXXXX sectors of this partition`, ignore it. It's no longer valid for today's versions of Linux.

> **Note**
>
> Adjust the partition numbers if you don't have an MS-DOS partition. Basically, just subtract one from every partition number that I say to type in.

Now, type **t** to see a partition type, and enter the partition number you want to define. If your MS-DOS partition is one, your swap partition is two, and your Linux partition is three, then you'd first enter **2** for your swap partition. When it gives you the hex code, make sure it says 83 for a swap partition.

Now, you'll define your main partition. Follow essentially the same steps as before:

1. Press **n** to define a new partition.

2. Press **p** to say you want a primary partition.

3. For partition number, enter **3** for the Linux partition.

4. Enter the first cylinder number listed.

5. Enter the last cylinder number listed.

6. Type **t** to define the type of partition.

7. Enter **3** for the partition number.

8. Enter **82** for a Linux swap partition.

Just to double-check everything, press **p** to get a listing of the partitions on your hard drive. One should be listed as Linux swap, one as Linux native, and one as DOS if you've got a DOS partition. Now, write down the table on your screen. You'll need this information!

If everything looks okay, press **w** for write and quit. If something's wrong, go back and follow the instructions again, then exit as mentioned before.

Setting Up Your Swap Space

Now, you have to format your swap partition. Type **mkswap -c <partition name> <size of partition in blocks>** (you'll get the partition name and size from the table you just wrote down).

Tip

Partition name refers to the Device field of the table you copied down in the previous section (e.g., /dev/hda2). Size of partition refers to the size of the partition in blocks from the same table.

Once the swap partition is formatted, type **swapon <name of partition>**.

Creating Your Linux File System

Finally, all you really have to do is create the file system or format the drive. Type **mke2fs <name of partition> <size of partition in blocks>**. This time, the partition I'm referring to is your Linux partition itself—number three in my example above (the name of this partition would then be /dev/hda3).

Tip

I left out the -c option this time because it checks the drive for bad blocks and can take overnight on large drives. If you still want to use the -c option, you certainly can.

II

Installing Linux

Be sure to type **synch** before shutting your system off if you're going to shut it off between steps. This will make sure you don't lose any information that hasn't been stored to disk yet.

Now, you're all set to install Linux—yet one more step closer to setting up your Internet site!

Chapter 4

Installing Linux from the CD-ROM

You've finally made it to the last preliminary step before you can set up your Internet site. It's time to actually install Linux. Fortunately, this is the easier part of setting up the program. You already did the hard stuff! These days, the installation is largely an automated process; you make your choices and the software is installed for you.

In this chapter, you learn how to:

- Begin your Linux installation
- Make your Linux installation choices
- Install LILO
- Finish your Linux installation

Starting Your Linux Installation

All you have to do to begin setting up Linux is type **setup** at your prompt! From there, follow the choices you're given, and take your time answering the questions. You probably feel like rushing through this section so you can get your site up and running, but don't. You'll be much happier if you don't have to reinstall everything again because you missed something!

> **Tip**
>
> If you shut your system down between chapter 3 and now, remember you need to boot using your boot disk, then your root disk. Also, you can remove your root disk once you reach the login prompt.

The following are error messages to watch out for:

■ The installation program complains that there's a lock file already in place, and stops the installation process. Instead, it keeps going from disk to disk. Cancel (with Ctrl+C), reformat or erase the drive, and start over.

> **Note**
>
> A *lock file* is used to tell a program that something is in use. For example, in this case, the installation program tries to run itself and finds a file that tells it it's already running. Lock files are supposed to be erased by the programs that created them, but if they exit abnormally sometimes this will not happen.

■ If the error device full starts cropping up, your Linux partition is full. As I said, a full Linux installation takes up a lot of space. If you chose to make your main Linux partition close to 200M, you may find you don't have enough room if you install a large portion of the packages. Either repartition your drive for more space, or install fewer packages. Erase the installation you've done, and start from scratch.

Installing Linux

As I said in the previous section, take your time. You can always reinstall if you need to, so don't get nervous!

First, type **setup** at your Linux prompt. What you see from now on depends on which root disk you chose. I'll walk you through the Text installation because that's what I selected. However, both versions of the installation have the same goal and will produce similar results.

Note

If you use color, you'll get a menu-driven installation system. You'll have to consider the same items as you would with text, but they'll be presented differently. No matter which root disk you choose, there are sufficient instructions to walk you through the installation process. Just take your time and read everything that appears on your screen.

The reason the color installation isn't covered in this book is that it doesn't work on particular systems. Also, the text version gives more detailed error messages if you run into problems during your install.

As I discussed in chapter 3, feel free to try the color installation. The decisions you have to make are the same in both versions, just presented differently. You can always reformat the drive and start over if you need to.

After typing **setup**, you will go through a process similar to the following:

```
Welcome to Slackware Linux Setup (v. 3.0.0-tty)

Linux supports many different keyboard configurations. If you are
not using a US keyboard, you will probably want to remap your
keyboard.

Would you like to remap your keyboard?

1 - yes
2 - no
```

If you're not using a standard United States keyboard, then select option one. Otherwise, select two.

```
Slackware Setup has detected a swap partition:

/dev/hdb1        1    1    40    16772        82    Linux Swap
Do you wish to install this partition as your swapspace ([y]es,
[n]o)?



IMPORTANT NOTE:  If you have already made any of your swap parti-
tions active (using the swapon command), then you should not allow
setup to use mkswap on your swap partitions, because it may corrupt
memory pages that are currently swapped out.  Instead, you will
have to make sure that your swap partitions have been prepared
(with mkswap) before they will work.  You might want to do this to
any inactive swap partitions before you reboot.
```

```
Do you want setup to use mkswap on your swap partitions ([y]es,
[n]o)?
```

Since we already did swapon to activate our swap partition, type **n** here to avoid the memory problems warned of above.

Then, type **y** to be able to use your swap partition.

> **Note**
>
> The numbers that follow are an example. The numbers for your drive will be different.

```
The following partitions on your machine are available for Linux:

Device    Boot   Begin   Start   End      Blocks  Id   System
/dev/hdb1 1      1       483     202832   83      Linux native
/dev/hdb2 506    506     988     202860   83      Linux native
Which device would you like to use for your root Linux partition?
```

> **Note**
>
> The question Which device would you like to use for your root Linux partition? will not appear if you only have one root Linux partition set.

In my case, I will have two different Linux installations on this drive. I want my new Linux installation to be on /dev/hdb1, so that's the name I'll type in here. Hit Enter.

> **Note**
>
> In my case, I could also choose to write over the old Linux partition on /dev/hdb2. First I would have to go back to the end of chapter 3 and reformat it to make sure it's blank.
>
> I picked /dev/hdb1 because it used to be an MS-DOS partition on this drive, and now I'm going to install a new Linux version here. Normally, you won't have two Linux versions on the same drive, I'm just being redundant because I need access to the older one for now.

```
If this is the root partition of an existing Linux system, you may
add more software to the existing system, or you may reformat the
partition and install from scratch.

Would you like to [a]dd more software, or [i]nstall from scratch?
```

Type **i** unless you're just adding more software packages at the moment, then hit Enter.

```
There are two main filesystem types that are used for Linux. There
are the xiafs filesystem, and the second extended filesystem
(ext2).
If you are adding new software to a system that has already been
installed, you must enter the filesystem type it currently uses.
If you're installing to a new system, you can try either filesystem
type.
```

> **Note**
>
> By either filesystem type the installation program is referring to the filesystems xiafs or ext2.

```
Which of these two filesystems to use is one of those things that
some Linux users like to argue about needlessly. Both are good
filesystems, and it's hard to say whether either one has a
significant speed or reliability advantage. Ext2 does have one
nice feature to it that xiafs doesn't have yet—as an ext2
partition is unmounted, a clean bit is written to it. When the
machine is rebooted, checking is skipped for any partitions that
have the clean bit on them. For this reason, ext2 systems boot faster
than xiafs systems, unless you disable the automatic filesystem
checking in /etc/rc.d/rc.S. If you use xiafs for your root
partition, you'll see some warnings when you shut the system down.
These are harmless and can be ignored.

What filesystem do you have (or do you plan to use) on your root
partition (/dev/hdb1), [e]xt2fs or [x]iafs?
```

Note that the last sentence refers to the root partition you defined a couple of steps earlier. Now, if you have any preferences, go ahead and follow those. I recommend ext2fs due to the reasons given above, such as a faster booting system, so I will type **e**. If you would like to use the xiafs file system, type **x**.

```
Since you've chosen to install Linux from scratch, we want to be
sure you know how to proceed, and we also want to give you one
last chance to change your mind. When using this option, you must
install to a blank partition. If you have not already formatted it
manually then you must format it when prompted.

Enter [i] again to install from scratch, or [a] to add software to
your existing system.

Install fresh, or add software to your current system? ([i]nstall,
[a]dd)?
```

Once again, if you're installing a brand new version of Linux, type **i**. If you're adding more software to your setup (for example, perhaps you realize later you wanted a package that you said no to before), type **a**.

```
Would you like to format this partition ([y]es, [n]o, [c]heck
sectors too)?
```

If you followed the steps in the previous chapter completely and formatted your Linux partition, feel free to type **n** for no. If you'd rather err on the side of caution, go ahead and type **y** for yes. I don't recommend **c** for check sectors unless you want to wait quite a while, as it can take hours to check every sector of a larger hard drive.

> **Note**
>
> If you have more than one Linux native partition on your drive, you'll be given the opportunity to mount large directories on another partition at this point. If you'd like to split some things up between different partitions, that's not a problem. It's best to do it through the install program if you're going to do it at all, because a lot of packages won't work or won't work properly if you move them to anything other than your root partition.

Now, the install program checks to see if you have any extra FAT partitions for DOS (FAT) or OS/2 (HPFS). If you do, you'll be given the option to make these partitions visible from Linux. If you'd like to be able to access them, type **y**. If the non-Linux partition is compressed (which means Linux cannot access it), or if you don't want people to be able to get to your other partition without rebooting, type **n** to not be able to access it.

```
SOURCE MEDIA SELECTION

1—Install from a hard drive partition
2—Install from floppy disks
3—Install via NFS
4—Install from a pre-mounted directory
5—Install from CD-ROM

From which source will you be installing Linux (1/2/3/4/5)?
```

If you're installing straight from the CD-ROM that came with this book, type **5**. If you put the installation material on floppy disks and are installing from disk, type **2**. If you're installing from one of the other methods listed above, type the appropriate number. You'll be asked to indicate where precisely you're installing Linux from (which drive, for example). Answer the questions appropriately.

If you choose **5** for CD-ROM, you are given the following list of models to choose from:

```
INSTALLING FROM SLACKWARE CD-ROM

1—SCSI [ /dev/scd0 or /dev/scd1 ]
2—Sony CDU31A [ /dev/sonycd ]
3—Sony 535 [ /dev/cdu535 ]
4—Mitsumi [ /dev/mcd ]
5—SoundBlaster Pro (Panasonic) [ /dev/sbpcd ]
6—Aztech/Orchid/Okano/Wearnes with interface card [ /dev/aztcd ]
7—Most IDE/ATAPI CD-ROM drives
8—Scan for your CD-ROM drive automatically

CD-ROM type (1/2/3/4/5/6/7/8)?
```

```
CHOOSE YOUR INSTALLATION METHOD

With Slackware, you can run most of the system from the CD-ROM
if you're short of drive space or if you just want to test
Linux without going through a complete installation.

slakware    Normal installation to hard drive

slaktest    Link /usr->/cdrom/live/usr to run mostly from CD-ROM

Which type of installation do you want (slakware or slaktest)?
```

You are creating a full Internet site, so you definitely want to type **slakware** here.

Now, it's time to tell the install program which disk sets you want to use. If you're using text, you get a list of the disk sets, as shown in chapter 3, "Getting Ready To Install Linux from the CD-ROM," and a list of what package each disk set contains. If you're using color, you'll be asked a list of questions about whether you want to use various packages.

The items you definitely want to install are:

Item	Description
A	Necessary system disks. You *must* install this set.
AP	General Linux applications that don't require X-Windows.
D	Development tools. You may not feel you need these because you don't see yourself as a programmer. However, as a system administrator you have to compile applications and do a bit of programming work, so it's important to have the proper tools installed.
E	The Emacs editor. You will likely want to use this editor on your system.
F	FAQ and HOWTO files. These will help you if you want to do things that aren't covered in this book.

(continues)

(continued)

Item	Description
N	Network utilities. Considering you are setting up an Internet site, you will want network utilities!
Y	Games that don't require X-Windows, if you want them.

If you want X-Windows, you'll at least want:

X   The X-Windows system itself.

XAP   X-Windows applications.

XV

For the rest, take a look at them. Remember, you can go back and install other packages later if you're not sure you want them now.

Once you've told the install program which disks you want to use, follow the prompts to install everything, choose Prompt mode so you can select the specific packages you want to install on each disk set. Then, when given the option to use special tagfile extensions, press Enter to use none, since we're not using any custom installation files.

If you're installing from CD-ROM, the next part is minimal effort. If you're installing from disk, hang in there with the disk switching!

Install anything on the disks you selected that has the priority **Recommended**. It will use a bit more disk space than it might otherwise, but it takes some experience to know which packages you want for what you want to do and which you don't for your needs.

When it comes to packages marked as priority **Optional**, I recommend you install the following:

■ getty: Handles login sessions, etc. You need this to handle such things for your site!

■ ghostscr: Postscript interpreter. Useful not only for documents but for faxes.

■ gsfonts1: Some ghostscript fonts for your system.

■ JPEG: JPEG viewer if you would like to be able to view pictures in this format.

- workbone: Program that allows you to listen to CDs on your system through your CD-ROM.

- gsfonts2:   More ghostscript fonts. If you are concerned about disk space, you may want to skip this one. Fonts packages are large.

- ispell: Emacs spell-checking program.

- gcc270:   GNU C Compiler. You definitely want this so you can compile some of the servers and clients we will use later in the book.

- gxx270:   GNU C++ Compiler. If you intend to develop in C++ or compile programs written in C++ install this package. If you are concerned about disk space, you can skip this one for now and wait for when you may need a C++ compiler one day.

- svgalib: Libraries for use with Super VGA graphics. Install if you have computers with this graphic capability on your network. Without it, you cannot use graphics outside of X-Windows.

- perl: Script language becoming popular among Linux system administrators.

- dip: Necessary to run SLIP connections, whether you use it to connect to your provider, or allow people to dial in and connect to SLIP accounts on your machine.

- elm: Commonly used mailreader.

- smailcfg: Configuration package that tells the setup program to help you choose which initial sendmail configuration file you want installed on your system.

- tin: Commonly used newsreader.

- inn: News server software (configured in chapter 9).

- nn-nntp/nn-spool: Commonly used nn newsreader. If you use a remote news server, install nn-nntp. If you have your own news server, install nn-spool. If you are unsure, install nn-nntp for now and you can change it later if you change your mind in chapter 9.

- pine: Commonly used mailreader. Supports sending attachments.

- trn-nntp/trn: Commonly used newsreader. Same considerations as the nn-nntp/nn-spool options.

- x312doc: Documentation for X-Windows 3.1.2 (the version used in this Slackware release).

- ■ xgames: Games for X-Windows if you want them.

- ■ workman: X-Windows version of the workbone CD player.

Once the system disks have been installed, you have the option of creating a boot disk. This boot disk will be specific to the configurations you choose, while your original boot disk is more generic.

> **Tip**
>
> This boot disk must be the same size as the other boot disk you made. This is because you must be able to use it with your root disk, and both the boot and root disks must be of the same size. Your system looks for both disks in the same drive.

Therefore, go ahead and create another boot disk, and label it something like "Boot Disk, After Installation." Keep this in a safe place with your other boot and root disks (you'll use the new boot disk in emergencies, but having the other one around can be handy if something goes wrong with your new one).

Next in the text progression, the install program offers to install the following devices in this order:

1. Modem

2. Mouse

3. CD-ROM

For each device, answer **y** if you want to install it and **n** if you don't. If you answer yes, you'll be asked for detailed information. Just take your time, and make sure you answer the questions correctly so you don't have to turn around and fix things later.

> **Note**
>
> As I discussed in chapter 3, since the boot disk you choose contains your CD-ROM driver, you are able to install from the CD-ROM. Much faster than installing from disk!

You next get the chance to try out some custom screen fonts. If you want to give them a try, type **y**. I find that the standard fonts are easier on the eyes, so I stick with them. You can certainly take a look at the options and choose for yourself. If you'd like to stick with the standard screen fonts, type **n**.

If you installed Ftape, a tape backup program, you'll next get a prompt asking you if the Ftape module should be loaded at boot time. If you want to activate Ftape at boot time so you can back up your system, type **y**. If you don't intend to back up your system to tape, type **n**.

> **Note**
>
> If you purchase a tape backup system in the future, or find that you want to install another package off the CD after installing, you don't have to go through the install process again. To install something from the CD, do the following:
>
> 1. Log in as **root**.
>
> 2. Go to /slakware/ap1 on the CD-ROM.
>
> 3. Copy the appropriate **.tgz** file (ftape.tgz) to the / directory (same thing as .tar.gz).
>
> 4. Uncompress the file with the command **gunzip ftape.tgz**. You will get a file with the same package name, but a .tar extension.
>
> 5. Untar the file with **tar -xvf ftape.tar**. This will unpack the file and place it in the appropriate directories, relative to the / directory. It will also set the appropriate permissions.

Next, you're given the opportunity to set your default modem speed. You can change this value later, so don't worry too much if you're not exactly sure what you want to use. Select the option your modem can best support (if you're using a modem) and press Enter.

Installing LILO

At this point, you've installed most of your Linux system. Now you need to decide if you want to install LILO. LILO is the Linux Loader, a program that lets you tell your computer what operating system or kernel to boot with.

> **Caution**
>
> Be sure to have boot disks available for any other operating systems you may have on this drive. If something goes wrong with your LILO installation, your boot disk will be the only way to get back to that OS until your LILO setup is fixed.

The LILO installer gives you the following options:

1. Start LILO configuration with a new LILO header

Start a new LILO. If you have an old one, this will overwrite it when you save. However, if you don't have a LILO configuration set up yet (perhaps from a previous version of Linux), this won't erase anything.

2. Add a Linux partition to the LILO config file

Start to configure LILO to know how to boot up your computer into Linux.

3. Add an OS/2 partition to the LILO config file

Start to configure LILO to know how to boot up your computer into OS/2, if you have an OS/2 drive or partition.

4. Add a DOS partition to the LILO config file

Start to configure LILO to know how to boot up your computer into MS-DOS, if you have an MS-DOS partition.

5. Install LILO

Save your LILO settings.

6. Reinstall LILO using existing lilo.conf

Your LILO data is in /etc/lilo.conf. If you install Windows 95 after installing Linux (which erases your boot sector and thus gets rid of LILO), you can select this option to copy your LILO settings from the file to the boot sector of your hard drive.

7. Skip LILO installation and exit this menu

If you decide you're not sure you want to install LILO at the moment, select this option to exit without saving.

8. View your current /etc/lilo.conf

Take a look at what you have so far in your LILO settings.

9. Read the Linux Loader HELP file

Read the online help for LILO.

Since this is your first time using LILO, pick option one. First, you'll be given the chance to enter any extra parameters you need to use at boot time. These are the same parameters you had to consider when booting with the boot disk you made in chapter 3, "Getting Ready To Install Linux from the CD-ROM," (your first boot disk). If you have any extra parameters, enter them here. Many people won't have any and will just hit Enter.

> **Tip**
>
> Whenever you're at the LILO main menu, you can choose option eight to see what your current LILO settings are.

Next, you'll select where you want to install LILO. Recommendations are given, such as where to put it if you're using OS/2's boot manager. Also, if you're nervous about overwriting the master boot record of your hard drive (which isn't really as dangerous as it sounds; it just means that you need to take your time and not forget any of your existing partitions) you can install LILO to a floppy.

Keep in mind that as long as you can get into your Linux partition with your (newer) boot disk later, you can change your LILO settings and fix any problems. For most people (except those with OS/2), you'll want to go ahead and install it on your master boot record. Select the option you want, and press Enter.

> **Tip**
>
> If you're concerned about your boot sector getting overwritten, install LILO to a disk as well. Mark it clearly and insert it in the drive before you turn on your computer to use it. Setting the length of time it should wait (discussed next) to 0 will tell it to just boot straight into Linux.

Choose how long you want LILO to wait before it starts it's default boot. I'd recommend at least five seconds because if you're upgrading kernels, you can use LILO to boot into a new kernel to test it without losing your old kernel. Once you've selected the option you want, hit Enter and you'll go back to the main LILO menu.

Now, you'll want to add your partitions to your LILO config file. I'll walk you through adding the Linux partition, which is option two:

1. Select the Linux partition you want LILO to boot with by typing the device name (i.e., /dev/hdb1).

II

Installing Linux

2. Enter the name you want to type in when you're booting with Linux (as LILO recommends, "linux" is a nice, easy-to-remember choice).

3. Return to the main LILO menu.

If you have an MS-DOS partition, then select option three. Using "dos" or "msdos" for telling LILO to boot with MS-DOS is a good choice because it's easy to remember.

If it would make you feel better, select option eight to double-check your LILO settings. When you're finished, select option five.

Tip

If you installed LILO to a floppy disk, be sure to label it clearly and keep it with your other important Linux disks!

Finishing Your Linux Installation

Now that you've got LILO installed, we can finish the installation. If you think this takes a while, think of how long it took before the installation program was available! It's nice to be able to just make your choices and let the program do the rest.

You'll be given a chance to configure your network. You should choose **y** for yes since you're going to be running an Internet connection. The network configuration section asks for the following information, in this order:

1. Your host name. This is just the name of this particular computer, and doesn't include your domain name. For example, my computer is known to the Internet as **catherine.renaissoft.com**, but the host name I'll enter is "catherine."

2. Your domain name. This is the name by which the Internet knows your network. In my case, this is **renaissoft.com**.

3. Whether you want to use TCP/IP for anything but loopback (a closed system). Choose **n** for no since you are setting up an Internet site, so you'll be using your TCP/IP for more than just loopback. You would choose yes for an isolated system.

4. Your machine's full IP address. My machine's is 199.60.103.2.

5. Your machine's gateway IP address. The gateway is the server your machine goes through to get to the Internet, the server itself. It will end with a 1 (e.g., 199.60.103.1). If you've only got one machine, its address will be the gateway address as well.

6. Your netmask. This will be 255.255.255.0 for a class C address (like mine), 255.255.0.0 for a class B, and 255.0.0.0 for a class A.

7. The installer creates the necessary files, and then asks if you'll be accessing a nameserver. Answer **y** for yes.

8. If you're setting this up on a computer that is not your server, enter the IP address of your server (e.g., 199.60.103.1). If you're setting this up on your server, enter the IP address of the computer it looks to on your provider's end for nameservice.

9. The installer saves the remaining information for your network configuration.

Tip

As the install program points out, you can type **netconfig** at your Linux prompt later to change these settings if you realize you set something incorrectly.

The installation process continues as you're asked if you'd like gpm installed. This is a program that allows you to cut and paste between virtual windows in X-Windows. I highly recommend you install this option if you're going to use X-Windows; it's great for transferring information from one place to another. If you want gpm to run when you boot, type **y** for yes. If you don't, type **n** for no.

At this point we're at the sendmail configuration section. Sendmail is one of the programs available to you to handle your e-mail. Here's what the install program will want to know for your sendmail configuration:

1. If you want a sendmail configuration file created for you, press **y** at the prompt. Since you will use sendmail as your mail server, choose yes.

2. You're offered a choice between three different configuration files (pick option one since your site will be on the Internet), or you can change your mind and not install the config file. I recommend you go ahead, though you can certainly come back to it later per the instructions on your screen.

Finally, the Linux installation program lets you configure your time zone, as follows:

1. You're given the option to configure your time zone. Go ahead and press **y** for yes.

2. A list of time zone choices is displayed. Type in one of them and press Enter. For example, I entered Canada/Pacific.

That's it! Congratulations, you've installed Linux. Go ahead and reboot to take a look (hitting the Alt or Ctrl key when LILO shows up on your screen). If you find you're not happy with some of the choices you've made during the installation, or your disk space is low, you can certainly wipe the disk clean and start over.

Setting Up Your Site for General Use

5

Now that you've got Linux installed, you need to do a bit of fine-tuning. Once that's done, you'll be able to use your Linux system, and then you can get on to the fun stuff of setting up all of the tools for your site!

In this chapter, you learn how to:

- Do general system setup
- Mount remote drives
- Create accounts
- Handle connections

General Site Preparations

Let's take a bit of time to get familiar with your system before proceeding to deal with adding users and other system administrator tasks.

> **Note**
>
> You may find that you need to recompile your kernel before you continue. With Slackware, the default kernel you end up with can take up a good chunk of your system's memory. If it takes up a big enough chunk of your RAM, that forces your system to go into swap space that much earlier.
>
> (continues)

> (continued)
>
> The kernel is stored as a compressed file, and loaded into memory as your system boots. The file is /zImage or /vmlinuz (only one of these will exist on your system). To see the file size, type **ls -l *filename***. The compressed file is expanded, and then loaded into memory, so if it looks like the size you see will take up more memory than you'd like, imagine how much it might take up when expanded.
>
> For information on replacing your kernel, see chapter 16, "Upgrading Your Software."

Booting Your System

The first thing you need to do before proceeding is to reboot your Linux system if you haven't done it yet. When you see the LILO prompt, press either the Alt key or the Ctrl key. Then, at the prompt, enter the name you assigned to Linux in your LILO setup (e.g., **linux**).

Tip

If you can't remember what you called your Linux session, just press the Tab key. That will list your options.

Now, you can watch screens and screens of messages flash by as Linux boots, telling you what's happening in the process. Finally, you should get to the following (note that your machine name will appear in place of catherine):

```
Welcome to Linux 1.2.8.
catherine login:
```

Note

If you didn't set your machine name during the installation process and instead are using the defaults, you can edit the file /etc/rc.d/rc.M. Find the lines in this file that refer to hostname and change it from the default to the name of the computer you're setting up (e.g., catherine).

Linux and Drives

Unlike MS-DOS and Macintosh systems, UNIX systems look at drives (hard drive, floppy drives, and so on) as directories in their filesystem. The general format of the command used to mount a device is:

```
mount device_name location_to_mount_to
```

For example, if you wanted to mount a data CD, and your CD-ROM is defined as /dev/cdrom (all of your devices are listed in the /dev directory), and wanted to mount the CD at /mount/cd you would use:

```
mount -t iso9660 /dev/cdrom /mount/cd
```

This breaks down as follows:

mount	Command you're running
-t	Tells your system the next item defines the filesystem type
is09960	Filesystem type for IDE CD-ROM
/dev/cdrom	The device you're mounting
/mount/cdrom	The location for the item you're mounting. To access anything on the CD-ROM, the path of the file would start with /mount/cdrom.

If you wanted to mount a floppy disk using the filesystem ext2, at device /dev/fd0 (the A drive in MS-DOS terms), and to /mount/floppya, you would use the following:

```
mount -t ext2 /dev/fd0 /mount/floppya
```

When you're finished using the filesystem you mounted, you can't just remove the disk, CD, etc. You need to first *unmount* the drive. This tells your system to finish writing any data that's left, and that the path you mounted it to no longer exists. To unmount something, use:

```
umount device_name
```

To unmount the CD-ROM in the first example in this section, you would simply use:

```
umount /dev/cdrom
```

Linux and File Permissions

While most UNIX users are familiar with file permissions, it is important to understand them as a system administrator. It's through setting your file permissions appropriately that you will keep your system secure. The easiest way to make an insecure system is to have permissions that make an intruder's work easy.

File permissions are broken down into groups to determine the access for the file's owner, the owner's group, and everyone.

t   rwx   rwx   rwx

The structure of file permissions is, reading the line above from left to right:

t	The type of file
rwx	Permissions related to the user
rwx	Permissons related to the user's same group
rwx	Permissions related to everyone (other)

The first item in the permissions values describes the file type. It can be one of the following:

–	Average ordinary file (e.g., text file, program)
d	Directory
l	Symbolic (soft) link
b	Block device (e.g., hard drive)
c	Character device (e.g., modem, keyboard, tty)

The following three sets of three each have the same permission options:

r	The ones the permission is defined for (user, group, or everyone) can read the file. This item can only be in the first position.
w	The ones the permission is defined for can write to the file, plus delete and rename it. This item can only be in the second position.
x	The ones the permission is defined for can execute the file, or enter it if it's a directory. This item can only be in the third position.
–	Permission is not given for the item defined in that particular position.

For example, the file permissions:

```
-rwxrw-r--
```

The preceding permissions define a normal file. Its user can read, write, and execute it. The user's group can read and write it, but not execute it. Anyone outside the user's group can only read it.

Now, to set these permissions, you use the command chmod. Since each item (except for the type definition) is either on or off, either blank or with a letter, permissions can be expressed with the binary numbering system.

In the case of permissions, the binary usage is 1 for "allowed," and 0 for "disallowed." However, instead of using binary to enter the permissions, you'll use the decimal versions. Each variation on permission combinations has its own decimal value, which is the sum of the binary components (see table 5.1).

Table 5.1 Decimal Equivalents of the Permission Combinations

Permission Set	Binary	Decimal
–	000	0
–x	001	1
–w–	010	2
–wx	011	3
r–	100	4
r–x	101	5
rw–	110	6
rwx	111	7

Let's break down the example from above, –rwxrw–r–:

- The leading - is the file type. This doesn't factor into the numbers used with chmod in general. Using a filetype other than - is discussed in a moment.

- The first triple is rwx. According to the table above, this is a 7.

- The second triple is rw–. According to the table, this is a 6.

- The final triple is r––. This is a 4.

To set the above permissions, you would use:

```
chmod 764 filename
```

If you want to set the file to run as something other than the standard, you can do this with chmod as well. In particular, you can set this file to run as SUID (set user ID), or SGID (set group ID). By doing this, you tell the file to run as though it's a member of the particular group or owner.

Setting a file to SUID or SGID simply requires adding an extra digit to the permissions you use with chmod. Technically, if you don't use anything, it assumes a leading 0.

Decimal	SID Setting
0	Standard file. Runs as the user who invokes it.
2	SGID: File runs as a member of its group.
4	SUID: File runs as its owner.
6	Both SUID and SGID.

The example we've been using in this section would be permission set 0764. If it were 2764, it would look like -rwxrwsr--. 4764 would be -rwsrw-r--. 6755 would be -rwsrwsr--.

Linux and Environment Variables

When you log into an account, it starts up a shell. This shell runs in an environment, with its own variables that define your preferences and settings. There are two types of environment variables, exported and local.

Exported environment variables exist outside of your shell script. They're mostly defined in your startup script, which is .login or .profile. To get a list of your current environment variable settings, type **env**. Some examples of environment variables and their settings for the user fred might be:

```
HOME=/home/fred

SHELL=/bin/tcsh
```

The export environment variable people are most likely to want to change will be the PATH statement. Just as with an MS-DOS path statement, this variable defines all the paths the system automatically searches when you enter a command. You can modify your PATH statement in your `.login` or `.profile` file.

How you set an environment variable as exported depends on the shell you're using:

- `Root` typically uses the `sh` shell. In this shell, to set an environment variable as one to be exported, define it with the `setenv` command. For example, `setenv NNTPSERVER news.provider.com`.

- Users typically use the `csh`, or `tcsh` shells. In these shells, to set an environment variable as one to be exported, define it with the `export` command. For example, `export NNTPSERVER=news.provider.com`.

Local environment variables are only used within the shell script. When the script is finished running, the variable no longer exists. Keep in mind that your `.login` or `.profile` script actually runs the entire time you're logged in. Local environment variables are mostly used in scripts written for specific purposes, where you don't need the values set to last past the running of the script. To set a local environment variable regardless of the shell type, simply use the format:

```
VARIABLE=value
```

For example, `TERM=console` tells your system that you typically log in from the actual console instead of dialing in.

Mounting Remote Home Directories

If you're running a large site you will likely want to have user home directories on their own drive. This is because home directories can take up a *lot* of space, depending on whether or not you set disk quotas, and how large those disk quotas are per user. Remember, space tends to fill.

If you haven't set this hard drive up for use yet, there are a few things you need to do:

1. Make sure your computer's BIOS recognizes this hard drive, and take note of which hard drive it shows up as (1, 2, 3, etc.).

2. In Linux, take note of the last hard drive name you have assigned (`hda`, `hdb`, etc.).

II

Installing Linux

> **Tip**
>
> If you're not sure what exactly you've already set up, type **mount** (as root) to get a list of the drives your system is set to use.

3. Use fdisk to add another disk to your Linux setup (using fdisk is covered in chapter 3, "Getting Ready To Install Linux from the CD-ROM").

> **Caution**
>
> Don't forget to format the drive for Linux!

Now, to turn this disk into /home. To turn your extra drive into the home directory, do the following:

1. Log in as **root**.

2. Back up your home directory!!! Change it to something like home-original for now, by typing:

   ```
   mv /home /home-original
   ```

> **Caution**
>
> Make sure to do this drive switch when no one is *using* your system! See chapter 15, "Upgrading Your System" if you are making this change after your system is already up and running with users.

3. To ensure that the filesystem on the new drive is set up properly, run fsck manually (it usually checks the filesystem during bootup). If, for example, your new drive was hdc, then you would type the following to force an immediate check:

   ```
   fsck -f -y /dev/hdc
   ```

4. Edit the file /etc/fstab

5. Now we'll tell your system how to mount the new drive. The format of an fstab line is:

   ```
   devicename    mount location       filesystem type    options
   ```

The general options available are:

rw	Read-write filesystem
ro	Read-only filesystem
suid	(Default) SUID access is allowed
nosuid	No SUID access is allowed
noauto	Don't automatically mount this particular filesystem (default is to mount)
usrquota	Use of user quotas are allowed on this filesystem
grpquota	Use of group quotas are allowed on this filesystem

You can use multiple options separated by commas, or just the word `defaults` if you don't want to set anything special.

For example, if your main partition is `/dev/hda1`, and you're using the `ext2` filesystem, this drive's entry would look like:

```
/dev/hda1      /             ext2          defaults
```

For the new drive (I'll use `/dev/hdc1` as an example), the entry might be:

```
/dev/hdc1      /home         ext2          defaults
```

This tells your system to mount the new drive partition as its `/home` directory.

6. Shut down your system (shutting down is covered later in this chapter) and reboot.

7. Change into the backup of your home directory (as `root`). In my case, this would be `cd /home-backup`

8. Move the contents of this directory to the new home "directory" with `mv * /home`

Caution!

If you're concerned with something happening to your files during the move, you may want to make a backup of the backup directory just in case.

Adding Machines to Your Network

Once you get your main server set up, you can start setting up the other machines in your network (if there are other machines). You can add all or some of them now if you want to be able to install some servers on separate machines, or have at least one machine other than the main Internet server from which to test your services. Or, you can proceed and get your main server completely set up, and then come back and set up some or all your other machines. The order you work in when it comes to adding machines to your network really depends on your personal preferences and needs.

The work you will need to do when adding machines is identical regardless to *when* in the site setup process you decide to add them.

> **Note**
>
> You need to go back to chapters 3 and 4 to install Linux on each machine you'll add. However, keep in mind that these other machines are not your main server. You won't need to install any of the main services on these machines, because they will use clients and look to your server instead. Other differences will be addressed in this section, so be sure to read it before you begin setting up the added machines.

> **Caution**
>
> Be sure to pick your Ethernet cards from the list in the Hardware How-To. Also, be sure to get the proper cable types.

Telling the Server About Other Machines

When you add a machine to your network, you have to tell the server that it exists. This ensures that the main server knows how to route each machine's packets to and from the Internet, and within your own network. Fortunately, since the Linux setup utility takes care of storing the network information required for the other machines, all you have to worry about is adding them to the server.

To add these files to your server, log in as **root** and edit the file /etc/hosts. For each machine—and each incoming modem line, and each device you want people to be able to connect to such as printers—you'll need to enter two pieces of information: the IP address and a list of name aliases.

Assigning IP Addresses

Assign each machine and device its own IP address from within those assigned to you. There's no *necessary* order of what numbers to use where. Most simply choose one number up as they add machines to the network.

Tip
It's helpful to put physical labels on machines, and especially modems. On a machine, use the IP address and name. On a modem, use the IP address and its phone number. This will save on running around time when dealing with technical problems.

Caution
If you're setting up subnets, be sure to read ahead in the section "Setting Up Subnets" before proceeding.

Assigning the Alias List

This alias list includes the actual full domain name plus host name for the machine, plus any aliases you want to add, all separated by spaces. Aliases might include:

■ The host name itself, so people can telnet in without having to type in the full host plus domain name.

■ Alternate host names, or alternate host plus domain names. You can use this to assign more than one name to a machine. For example, often if you go to a Web URL of the format www.site.com, you're really going to an alias for another machine. This both disguises which machine the service is actually on, and makes it easier for people to find your Web server and FTP server.

Note
Many sites like to name their hosts on a theme. It's much more interesting to the sysadmin than looking at a list of meaningless host names like machine1, machine2, and so on. If you have a favorite hobby, sport, genre of movies or books, or time period, you can use it to come up with related host names. Just make sure not to pick something that will run out of options too quickly!

An example of an entry (pulling an IP address and domain name out of the air, both may actually exist on the Net) for a machine is

```
195.85.231.5      baseball baseball.sports.net
```

Your main server might have a longer entry, for example

```
195.85.231.1      fencing fencing.sports.net www.sports.net➥
ftp.sports.net
```

Setting Up Subnets

If the discussion of subnets in chapter 1, "Why Create Your Own Site with Linux?" led you to determine that you need to use subnets within your site, follow this section carefully. If you don't intend to use subnets, go ahead and skip to the next.

Typically, you'll see the number 255.255.255.0 and be told that this is your *netmask* (on a class C address, on class B it would be 255.255.0.0 and class A it would be 255.0.0.0). However, this can become your *subnet mask*.

In order to tell your site what your subnets are, you need to assign a subnet mask. In order to assign a subnet mask, you need to think of IP addresses in terms of bits. An IP address is made up of 4 sets of 8 bits.

```
11111111.11111111.11111111.00000000
```

The decimal for the first set is

128+64+32+16+8+4+2+1=255

So, these bits all together form the class C netmask:

```
255.255.255.0
```

When you assign subnets, you use the last set of 8 bits to tell your site how many subnets you're going to have. Because of this, if you want a number of subnets that doesn't quite work out in binary, you'll need to estimate the next step up. Let's say you want 6 subnets. You need to look and see how many binary combinations you have to use to get this number of subnets.

Binary Digits	Possibilities	Subnets
One	0 1	Two
Two	00 01 10 11	Four
Three	000 001 010 011 100 101 110 111	Eight

To get six subnets, you need to start with eight subnets and use only the first six combinations: 000, 001, 010, 011, 100, 101. The last two combinations aren't used: 110 and 111.

As you can see, you will need to waste a bit of address space to get six subnets. Now that we know how many binary digits we need to get six subnets, we need to figure out the final IP decimal to use.

The netmask we're using for six subnets is:

        11111111.11111111.11111111.11100000

The decimal for 11100000 is 128+64+32=224.

So, if you wanted six subnets, your netmask would suddenly become 255.255.255.224. In fact, if you wanted seven or eight subnets you'd use the same netmask.

Each of the six subnets will be within a particular IP range. To determine these IP numbers, we have to go back to the bit format. In figure 5.3, we determined which bits our six subnets would start with. From there, we can determine the IP ranges for each of these subnets.

II

Installing Linux

Subnets	Bit Format	IP Range
000	00000001-00011110	1-30
001	00100001-00111110	33-62
010	01000001-01011110	65-94
011	01100001-01111110	97-126
100	10000001-10011110	129-158
101	10100001-10111110	161-190
110		193-222
111		225-254

00000001 is the lowest valid host; 00000000 is reserved. 255 (11111111) is also reserved.

So, if you had the IP assigned 235.23.42, a machine in subnet one might be 235.23.42.13. A machine in subnet three might be 235.23.42.68.

Telling Your Nameserver About Your Machines

Your nameserver—since you're providing your own primary nameservice—needs to know about the other machines on your network as well, so it can translate them into the appropriate IP numbers for the rest of the Internet.

As root, edit the file /etc/named.rev. Now, for each machine and incoming modem line, plus any devices you want people to be able to access from outside your network, you need to make a nameservice entry. This entry is in four parts:

- The distinguishing IP numbers for the machine. For example, if your network's assigned IP address begins with 195.85.231, you would only need to include the host-specific number. If the host you're setting up is 195.85.231.5, you'd enter a **5** as the first item in the nameservice definition.

- The second entry will be the letters **IN**. This defines the entry as a DNS (Domain Name Service) resource record.

- The third will be the letters **PTR**. PTR stands for Pointer, which tells your nameserver that this entry is used to convert a host IP address to a host name.

- The final entry is the full host plus domain name for the machine you're defining. For example, baseball.sports.com.

Putting this entry together, it would look like:

```
5     IN     PTR     baseball.sports.com
```

Mounting Directories by NFS

Network File System (NFS) is a method of mounting directories across a network as though they were on your local machine. There are two aspects to NFS mounting. You have to set up the machine whose directory is being mounted to allow it, and you have to set up the machine's access to the directory to do so.

Setting the NFS Server To Allow Access

The machine whose directory is mounted is the NFS server for that particular directory. There are a few files you need to attend to in order to set a server up to allow other machines to access its files via NFS.

First, you need to edit the file /etc/exports (create it if it doesn't already exist). Each line in this file contains two pieces of information. The first is the path for the directory you're allowing other machines to access. The second is a list of machines who are allowed to access the directory, and their permissions. An example (rw stands for read and write permissions):

```
/home     hockey (rw) baseball(rw) soccer(rw)
```

Make sure that the file /etc/rc.d/rc.net1 has the following components in place:

- In the beginning of the file, where the environment variables are defined, make sure the following variable definitions are present: NFSD=/etc/rpc.nfsd and MOUNTD=/etc/rpc.mountd.

- Lower in the file, there are a series of if/then statements. Right after the INETD if/then, make sure the following two statements are present:

```
if [ -x $NFSD ]; then
        echo -n " 'basename $NFSD'"
         $NFSD -f /etc/exports
fi
if [ -x $MOUNTD ]; then
        echo -n " 'basename $MOUNTD'"
         $MOUNTD
fi
```

Setting Other Machines To Access NFS Mountable Directories

The machines NFS mounting the directories are clients. Sometimes you'll have a machine being both server and client, if it needs to both offer and mount NFS directories. Make sure if a machine is performing this dual function that you do both the server and client setup.

There is one file you need to attend to in the machines you want to have mount an NFS directory. This file is /etc/fstab (covered in depth in the

section on adding hard drives), which is loaded at boot time and conse-
quently mounts the appropriate directories.

An example of mounting the /home directory on the server machine (let's call
it referee) to /home on the local (client) machine is:

```
referee:/home /home nfs
```

This breaks down as follows:

referee:/home	The machine to mount from, plus the directory to mount
/home	The directory to mount it to
nfs	The type of filesystem being mounted

Creating Accounts

Since it's not a good idea to do anything except system administration tasks
from root, now's a good time to create some accounts on your site. It's also
important to set up some accounts aside from root so you can use them to
test your servers as you get them set up. It's important not to assume that
because your software works for root, it will work for everyone!

Creating User Accounts

To create an account by hand, type **adduser** at the prompt. You'll get the
following sequence of prompts:

```
Login to add (^C to quit):
Full Name:
GID [100]:
UID [501]:
Home Directory [/home/username entered in first prompt]:
Shell [/bin/bash]:
Password [username entered in first prompt]:
Information for new user [username entered in first prompt]:
Home directory:  Shell: you entered at  [shell you entered
[home directory]   the earlier prompt]  earlier]
Password:  UID:  GID: [password you entered earlier]
   [UID you entered earlier]        [GID you entered earlier]
Is this correct? [y/n]:
```

Note

The UID is the User ID. This tells Linux what User group the particular account belongs to when it files permissions.

The GID is the Group ID. This tells Linux what Group the particular account belongs to when it files permissions.

For example, I'll set up an account for myself, answering the prompts as follows:

1. Login of **dee**

2. Full name of **Dee-Ann LeBlanc**

3. GID of **100** (100 is the default in the Slackware distribution for a general user.)

4. UID of **501** (500 is the user root; 501 is mine because I was the next account added, and the number will go up from there with each user.)

5. Home Directory of /home/dee (There's no rule that says you have to chose /home/<username>, it's simply tradition and it makes it easy to keep track of where everyone's directories are.)

6. Shell of /bin/bash (Bash is common for root, but less experienced users often find /bin/tcsh more friendly.)

7. Password of…(Well, I'll come up with something!)

Caution

When you choose a password, try not to pick a standard dictionary word, and use a combination of upper- and lowercase letters. Adding numbers is even better. You'll learn more about the need to have hard-to-get passwords in chapter 12, "Security."

Tip

Don't forget to give root a password! As root, type **passwd**, and follow the prompts. Root's initial password is blank, so when you're asked to enter the old password, just hit Enter.

II

Installing Linux

> **Note**
>
> You can set up a skeleton directory to mirror what you want your users' directories to look like (particular files you know everyone will need). Just create the directory `/etc/skel` and put everything in there that you want to be in all user directories by default.

It's common practice to send a standard form letter piece of electronic mail to a new account when you set it up. If you write your own account setup program or a special script, you can configure your system to do this for you automatically so you don't have to remember to send the mail each time. A simple example script I'll call `newuser` calls the adduser program, and afterwards sends the mail you want (invoke this script by typing **newuser newusername**):

```
#!/bin/sh
/needpathfor/adduser
mail -s 'Subject line for the mail' $1 < /path/file_to_send.txt
```

The lines in this script do the following:

1. `#!/bin/sh`

   Tells Linux to run the `/bin/sh` shell, which interprets everything that comes after that.

2. `/needpathfor/adduser`

   Runs the adduser program for you. Fill it in just like you filled it in before.

3. `mail -s 'Subject line for the mail' $1 < /path/file_to_send.txt`

   Invokes the mail program. The `-s` states that the next item is the subject of the mail, which you'll put inside single quotes. The `$1` refers to the username (the `newusername` mentioned above) to send the mail to. The `<` tells the script to include what follows in the mail. The item `/path/file_to_send.txt` refers to the full path and filename of the text file you want included in the new user e-mail.

For example, if I typed **newuser dee**, I would first go through the adduser program as described earlier in this section, and then the script would send `dee` e-mail containing the text file I created for this purpose.

Keeping Track of Usage Time for Accounting Purposes

If you're running a site that requires you to bill for SLIP line usage, you'll need to recompile your kernel and say yes to the IP accounting option (see chapter 16, "Upgrading Your Software" for more on compiling a new kernel).

Check out the Linux Documentation Project Web pages for pointers to accounting programs (see appendix C for a listing of URLs for the LDP pages).

Informing Users of Internet Etiquette

It is the responsibility of system administrators to be sure that users know where to find resources explaining Internet etiquette. This is partially to ensure a good reputation for your site, especially if it is a large one. You don't want a reputation for having clueless users who consistently don't appear to have any idea of what they're doing!

You can't force people to read documentation, or be sure they read it even if you put in safeguards that requires them to say they did. However, you can provide an explanation of why it's important to understand a bit of how the Internet works (most people don't want to look clueless) and pointers to recommended reading. The best way to do this is through including this information in the initial e-mail you send to users as their account is set up (more about this in a moment).

There are a number of excellent resources on the Internet regarding Internet etiquette (netiquette). On UseNet, these resources (which you may want to require your users to read) are:

- **news.announce.newusers** Periodic postings (twice a month) to aid new users to UseNet. Includes technical explanations of how things work, and netiquette advice.

- **news.newusers.questions** A place where users new to UseNet can ask questions and get answers from more experienced users.

Also, if your users want FAQs for almost any newsgroup, they can find them by FTPing to **rtfm.mit.edu** and going to /pub/usenet.

Acceptable Use Policy

It's important to set up an Acceptable Use policy for your site. This policy should detail:

II

Installing Linux

- Any time limitation policy you might have, such as not allowing users to camp on your lines 24 hours a day, 7 days a week.

- Any service limitation policy you might have, such as not using your FTP server to transfer items that are illegal where your site is located.

- Any general Internet abuse policies you have, such as not harassing other people on the net and not spamming newsgroups.

- The actions that can be taken if your rules are broken.

- Any other rules you feel you need to state.

The basic idea of your Acceptable Use Policy is to state the rules for using your site up front. This helps new users to understand a bit of what is unacceptable behavior, and also gives you the room to deal with problem users without getting sued. If they break one of the rules in your AUP, you can point to it and show them exactly which rule they broke, and exactly where you said how that infraction would be dealt with.

Some tips on putting together an Acceptable Use Policy are:

- Look at the policies the other providers in your area put together. They should be available on the providers' Web pages.

- If you plan to run a large site, you may want to show your policy to a lawyer.

- Think through the things you don't want people using your site for, or that you would consider excessive use of your site.

Keep in mind that if you develop serious problems with a user that affect a good portion of the Internet, the other system administrators may put a lot of pressure on your site to deal with them. It's important to have the legal backing of your Acceptable Use Policy so you can deal with someone who's flooding UseNet, or otherwise abusing the Internet.

Assigning User Disk Quotas

If you're concerned that your users will overrun your site's hard drive space through their home directories, you can assign quotas to keep them limited to a particular amount of drive space.

There are two types of quotas you can use, *hard* and *soft*. If you are seriously hard-pressed for disk space, you may want to use hard quotas. With hard quotas, the system will not allow the user to exceed the quota you assign, which can cause whatever they're doing at the moment to crash. They won't be allocated any more disk space until they clean their usage down below the quota.

However, if you have a little leeway in your space, you may want to assign soft quotas. When a user reaches his limit with a soft quota, he can exceed that limit temporarily. This allows the user to finish the particular task he's working on, and then clean out some space. If the user doesn't clean out space, and leaves his disk usage higher than his quota, each time he logs in he will be warned. If the user persists in not cleaning out the space, he won't be allowed to use any additional disk space until he cleans his home directory back down below the quota.

Setting Your System To Use Disk Quotas

Before you can assign user disk quotas, you have to tell your system that you intend to use them. First, however, you need to decide what particular directories you want to apply the quotas to. If you just want to assign user quotas, /home is a good choice, as all of the user home directories inside it would be affected.

To set your site up to handle disk quotas, do the following:

1. Log in as **root**.

2. Edit the file /etc/fstab.

3. To tell your system to expect quotas to be applied to, for example, /home and everything beneath it (with your home directories being for this example on /dev/hda1 using the filesystem ext2), enter the following:

   /dev/hda1 /home ext2 rw,quota

   This sets the home directories to both readable and writable, and tells the system they'll have quotas assigned to them.

   > **Tip**
   >
   > If you mounted home directories from a separate drive, you can change the default entry to rw,quota instead of adding a new line.

4. Save and exit the file.

Setting Up User Quotas

Now we'll set up the quotas themselves. To set a quota for all users, do the following:

1. Change to `/home`.

2. Type **touch quota.group**. This creates the data file that handles user quotas, and the rest of the quota system needs it to be there before you proceed in defining those quotas. You could also use `quota.user`, but then you'd have to create a new quota every time you assigned a new user account!

3. Type **chmod 600 quota.group**. This changes the file's permissions to only readable and writable by the owner, `root`.

4. Type **edquota -g users**. This invokes the command that will handle setting your quotas for you, making sure files are in their proper places and to their proper settings.

> **Note**
>
> The `edquota` command is used to assign disk quotas to users and groups. Its general format is:
>
> ```
> edquota -flag who_to_assign
> ```
>
> The `edquota` flags are:
>
> | | |
> |---|---|
> | u | You intend to define a user quota |
> | g | You intend to define a group quota |
> | p | Use a "prototypical" user quota definition to simply copy to the users you are assigning. When using this flag, the format of the `edquota` command becomes `edquota -p username_of_protouser username_to_be_defined` |
> | t | You want to edit the soft time limits for each of the filesystems that have quotas assigned. |
>
> `Edquota` then opens a temporary file where you can define how you want the quota handled. The format for the definition line is:
>
> ```
> fs /filesystem_to_have_the_quota blocks (soft=number_of_blocks,➥
> hard=number_of_blocks) inodes (soft=number_of_inodes,➥
> hard=number_of_inodes)
> ```
>
> An example follows.

5. Once the `temporary` file comes up, add the line that defines the quota space you want to assign to your user home directories. For example, if you wanted to set your limits to a soft of around 10M, and a hard of around 20:

```
fs /home blocks (soft=10000, hard=20000) inodes (soft=0,➥
hard=0)
```

> **Tip**
>
> One block of disk space is one kilobyte (k, or 1024 bytes) of disk space.

> **Note**
>
> Every file needs 1 inode. The *inode* contains the filesystem information about this file. Unless you want to limit the number of actual files someone can have, set the inode limit to 0, which disables that limit option. This way, the user can have as many files as he wants as long as he stays within the limits.

6. Save and exit the file.

7. Type **quotaon -a**. This tells your system to use the quotas you've set, and to use all quotas you've defined.

Handling Connections

As an Internet site, you need to handle connections to other machines. These come in two forms. First, there is the connection between you and your provider. This is, of course, important because if you're not connected, you're not on the Net! The other type of connection is that of your users dialing into your site (if you have dial-in connections).

Connecting to Your Provider via Modem

To connect to your provider using a modem (an analog or digital modem), you'll use the dip program. This package is part of the Slackware distribution disks on disk set n. If you didn't install it and you need it, go ahead and do so now.

Tip

For especially high grade connections, e.g. T1, your provider or the people you purchase/lease your equipment from may recommend another connection method.

Once you have the binary installed, you need to make a login configuration file. Where you put it is your choice, since you include the path to the file when you call the dip program. It's important that you first find out from your provider the sequence of commands you'll need. You should be familiar with modem login scripts, but I'll provide an example of a dip login script here to show you some tips:

```
init:
        print Initializing...
        get $local host.domain.com
        port cua1
        speed 38400
        send atz1\r
        wait OK 5
        send AT&C1&D2&K3&R1&S0\r
        wait OK 5
        if $errlvl != 0 goto modem_trouble

dial:
        sleep 3
        print Dialing Internet Direct...
        send atdt5551234\r
        if $errlvl != 0 goto modem_trouble
        wait BUSY 10
        if $errlvl != 0 goto login
        print BUSY
        send \r
        wait CARRIER 5
        send atz\r
        wait OK 5
        goto dial

login:
        print Login prompt...
        wait gin: 30
        if $errlvl != 0 goto login_error
        send rsoft\r

        print Password prompt...
        wait word: 30
        if $errlvl != 0 goto password_error
        send blort\r
```

```
    wait session 30
    if $errlvl != 0 goto prompt_error
    get $rmTip remote 30
    if $errlvl != 0 goto prompt_error
    wait to 30
    get $locip remote 30

done:
    print Host is $rmTip
    print You are $locip
    get $mtu 1006
    default
    mode CSLIP
    goto exit

prompt_error:
    print Timeout waiting for IP login to fire up...
    goto error

login_error:
    print Trouble waiting for login prompts...
    goto error

password_error:
    print Trouble waiting for the password prompt...
    goto error

modem_trouble:
    print Trouble occurred with the modem...
    goto error

error:
    print CONNECT FAILED to Internet Direct

exit:
```

Tip

You may want to write a script that checks occasionally to make sure your connection is up, and if it's not up, reconnects your site automatically.

Tip

If you don't want to use dip, you can use slattach. There is more on dip and slattach in the Net-2 How-To.

II

Installing Linux

Users Connecting to Your Site via Modem

If you have users dialing in for SLIP connections, you need to have a program waiting to pick up the phone. The program I recommend for this task is sliplogin. You can find this program by FTP at **sunsite.unc.edu**, **/pub/ Linux/system/Network/serial/sliplogin-1.5.tar.gz** (the version number may be different when you go to fetch the file).

This program has a number of configuration files associated with it. These files contain all the information necessary for it to run all of your incoming SLIP connections, and some of them require some alterations. The ones requiring changes are discussed here.

> **Note**
>
> You can set up accounts that only allow people to use SLIP through your machine. The sliplogin program documentation spells out in detail how to set up these accounts.

The slip.hosts File

In the slip.hosts file, you define types of logins and how they're treated. The following is an example of this file.

```
# login  local-addr    remote-addr  netmask      slipmode   opt2 ...
#
# valid slipmodes: normal,compressed,ax25,6bit,auto
#
slip    199.60.103.1  DYNAMIC      0xffffff00   normal
cslip   199.60.103.1  DYNAMIC      0xffffff00   compressed
bob     199.60.103.1  DYNAMIC      0xffffff00   normal
susan   199.60.103.1  DYNAMIC      0xffffff00   compressed
```

I'll walk you through the slip definition line. The IP number given is that of the site's server. Then, when you tell it DYNAMIC, it knows that you want to dynamically assign IP addresses as people dial in. The hex 0xffffff00 (you would need to use the appropriate hex for a non-class C address) is 255.255.255.0, which tells sliplogin to replace the last digit in the server's IP number with the appropriate digit for the line. Finally, you define the connection type as either compressed (using CSLIP compression) or normal.

The slip.tty File

In the slip.tty file, you define what IP addresses to use for which tty's during dialin. This tells your system which address to use for DYNAMIC definitions. An example of this file follows. As you see, a definition in this file contains the name of the device, then the IP address assigned to that device.

```
# slip.tty    tty -> IP address mappings for dynamic SLIP
#
/dev/ttyS0    199.60.103.4
```

The slip.login File

The slip.login file is what's run when someone logs in via dial-up as just slip. There is only one change you need to make in this file, which is the hardware address for your Ethernet card. To get this address, type **ifconfig**. The Ethernet address in the example below is 00:20:AF:6E:E1:47.

```
#!/bin/sh -
#
#   @(#)slip.login  5.1 (Berkeley) 7/1/90
#
# generic login file for a slip line.  sliplogin invokes this with
# the parameters:
#       1       2       3       4       5       6       7
8-n
#   slipunit ttyspeed pid loginname local-addr remote-addr mask
opt-args
#
/sbin/ifconfig $1 $5 pointopoint $6 mtu 1500 arp -trailers up
/sbin/route add $6 $1
#in case you have an ethernet card this will announce the slip
client
#xx:xx:xx:xx has to be replaced by your hardware address
/sbin/arp -s $6 00:20:AF:6E:E1:47 pub
echo $4 > /var/run/$6
exit 0
```

Accessing the Internet from Winsock on the Same Network

If you have machines on your local network on which you switch between Linux and Windows, or on which you only use Windows, you can use them to access the Internet over Ethernet even if they're not in Linux. Just configure your Winsock program to use a *direct connection* instead of SLIP or PPP, and set the appropriate network values.

Using Your Virtual Consoles

One wonderful feature of UNIX that Linux shares is that of having virtual consoles. By *virtual consoles*, I mean that you can be logged in to the system more than once and through different accounts.

II

Installing Linux

You have twelve virtual consoles by default. You switch between them by holding down the Alt key and the appropriate function key. For example, right now you're probably on Alt+F1. Hold down the Alt key and press F2. You'll find yourself at another login prompt. Keep doing that on Alt+F3 through Alt+F12; they're all new login prompts. You can do completely different things with each terminal. For example, you can log into all of them with the same account or with all different accounts.

Shutting Down Your Linux System

With Linux, you really don't want to just shut the computer off right away. There may be important data stored in the buffers that won't get saved if you just turn the machine off, or you may be shutting off a process that you didn't notice, before it finishes what it's doing.

To shut down your system, do the following:

1. Log in as **root**.

2. Type **shutdown [-hrf] [time]**

3. Watch and wait.

> **Note**
>
> The "h" stands for hard shutdown: The computer will shut down all processes and then sit and wait for you to hit reset or shut it off.
>
> The "r" stands for restart or reboot: The computer will automatically reboot once all processes are shut down. A restart shutdown is particularly useful if you intend to reboot and use LILO to access another operating system.
>
> The "f" stands for fast shutdown: The computer writes the fastboot file as it goes down so that when it comes back up it knows it doesn't have to check the filesystem.

I commonly use **shutdown -h now**. That tells my system to immediately shut down all processes, and then sit and wait for me to either shut the power off or hit the reset key.

If you want to tell it to shut down in a certain amount of time, give the time in minutes. For example, type **shutdown -h 5**.

Now you're all set up and ready to start installing your servers!

Part III

Setting Up Your Internet Site

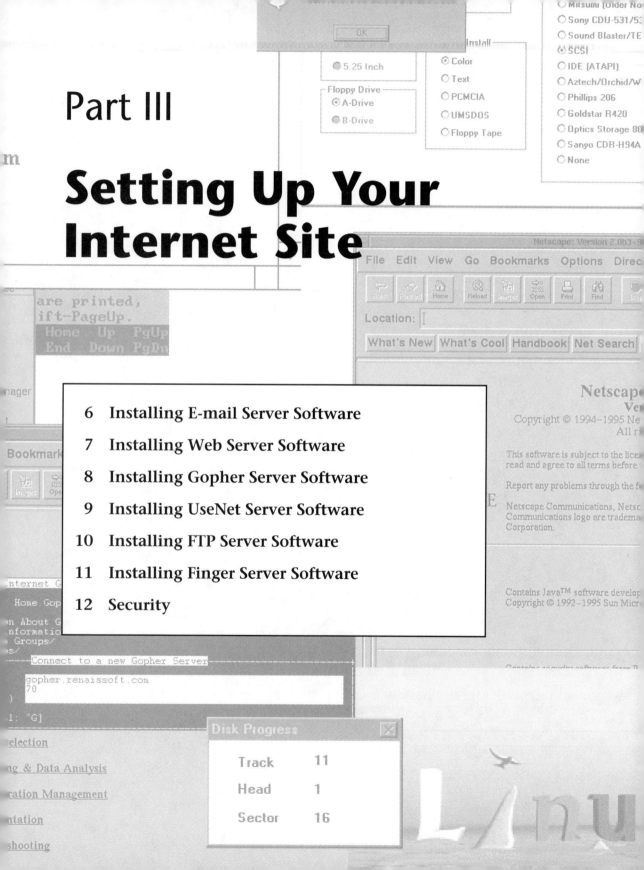

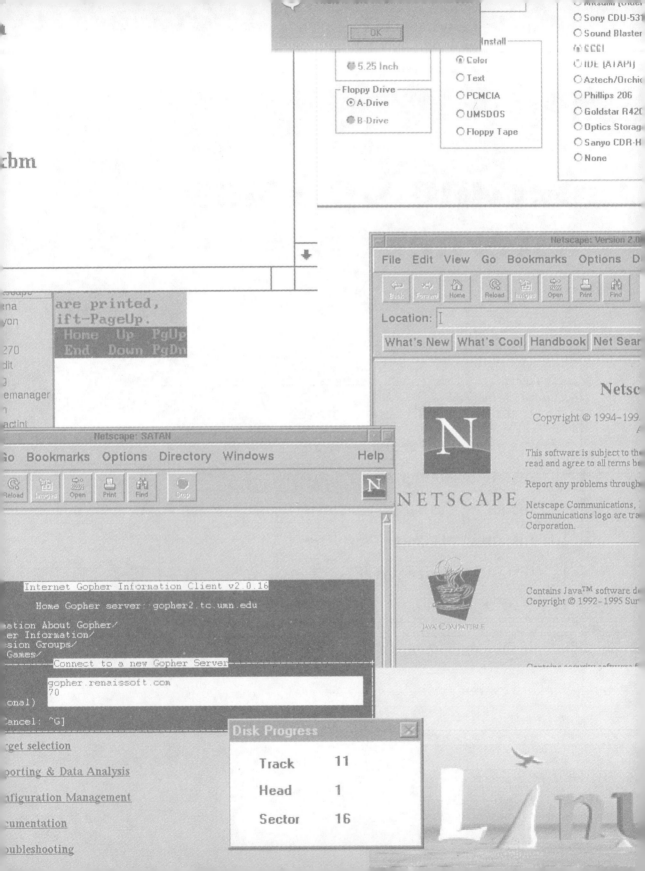

Chapter 6

Installing E-mail Server Software

Now that you've got Linux installed and accounts created, you can move on to getting your servers set up. Start with the one that's often the most necessary and useful: your electronic mail server. After all, e-mail is the most used tool on the Internet other than, perhaps, Ping!

There are three e-mail servers you may want to install. One is the *Sendmail* server, which will handle your SMTP mail to and from the Internet. *Simple Mail Transport Protocol* (SMTP) is the standard method for transmitting electronic mail from one site to another.

The second is a *Post Office Protocol* (POP) mail server. A POP server holds mail for people just like a post office box. Users can connect to the POP server as they wish and it will transfer their mail to them. Some POP servers can also send mail out to the rest of the Internet.

Finally, there is a *Unix-to-Unix Copy* (UUCP) server. UUCP, in a way, is between SMTP and POP. It gets and sends out its files in batches at regular intervals, and doesn't require a permanent connection as long as it's connected during its file transfers. Many sites are more likely to have their users using UUCP from home to get and send their mail, than to use it for their own mail transfer. This server is useful for more than e-mail, it also can transfer news. Chapter 9, "Installing UseNet Server Software," has more about setting up this function.

In this chapter, you learn how to set up:

- Sendmail for local mail

- Sendmail for Internet mail

- Sendmail for UUCP mail

- A POP mail server

- A UUCP mail server

Setting Up Sendmail

The Sendmail server was conveniently installed during the Linux setup process that you went through in chapter 4, "Installing Linux from the CD-ROM." This includes a basic Sendmail configuration file (`sendmail.cf`). Although the basic configuration file was set up during the installation process, there is more work to be done to configure it for your particular needs.

> **Tip**
>
> If you have not installed Sendmail, log in as root and type **setup**. Add a package; the Sendmail items are on disk set N. To save a little time, choose the option that sets up your sendmail.cfg file.

Although there are entire books on the subject of Sendmail, I'm going to show you how to set up your Sendmail server for the basic tasks that you need to be able to perform. In the section, "Setting Up Sendmail for Local Mail Delivery," you'll learn how to configure your mail server to handle the following functions:

- Mail within your local system

- Mail to the Internet

- UUCP mail

> **Caution**
>
> Don't get the Sendmail files confused with the *smail* files. Smail is a completely different mail server!

Note

Smail is an older program that was written so people wouldn't have to deal with the complexity of Sendmail. However, because you can now start with a generic sendmail.cf file and simply modify it, Sendmail has become much easier to use (you used to have to do it all from scratch). So, smail is not so necessary anymore.

Additionally, smail is only really suited for small use. Sendmail is necessary for running a full Internet site.

Tip

Anything that you do in this chapter, you'll do from your root account.

Setting Up Sendmail for Local Mail Delivery

You're already equipped for basic local mail delivery if you chose to let the Linux installation program set up your sendmail.cfg file (see fig. 6.1). You'll need to take care of a few items, though, to make sure things run smoothly.

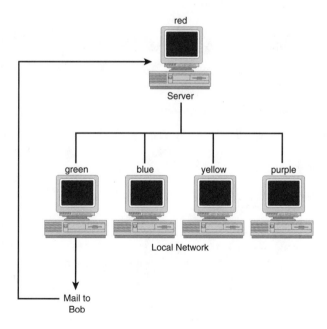

Fig. 6.1
Local mail delivery.

III

Setting Up Your Site

Setting Sendmail To Start as a Daemon

First, you need to make the Sendmail daemon launch at boot time. A *daemon* is a program that runs in the background and watches for the items it's supposed to handle, in this case, mail. If you don't have your Sendmail daemon running, it won't be sitting and waiting to process incoming and outgoing mail.

To make sure the Sendmail daemon is loaded, do the following:

1. Go to the directory /etc/rc.d.

2. Open the file rc.net.

3. Look for the following lines of code toward the bottom of the file:

```
if [-f /usr/lib/sendmail ]; then
(cd /usr/spool/mqueue; rm -f lf*)
/usr/lib/sendmail -bd -q1h; echo -n 'sendmail' > /dev/console
fi
```

4. If you find these lines, you can close the file. If you don't, then add them in the section where the other daemons are started. You can easily recognize them because each item that starts a daemon looks similar to the Sendmail code in step 3.

> **Note**
>
> The code for the Sendmail daemon is not as complicated as it looks. It breaks down as follows:
>
> 1. The first line looks to see if the file /usr/lib/sendmail exists.
>
> 2. The second line changes to your mail queue directory and removes any lock files that might be left over if you had to reboot while your system was processing mail.
>
> 3. The third line actually starts the Sendmail daemon. The switches that you use mean the following:
>
>   - -bd tells your system to run Sendmail as a daemon, which will sit on port 25 and wait for mail to process. You need to use this option, because otherwise Sendmail won't be listening to mail coming in from the Internet. If you don't run it as a daemon, you can only send mail out; you won't receive it.
>
>   - -q1h tells your system to process the mail queue once an hour. If you want it processed more often, every 30 minutes for example, enter -**q30m**. The rest of this line simply tells your system to put the word sendmail on your screen (/dev/console).

How often you have the mail queue processed depends on how much mail goes out of your site. If it's a lot, you may want to process the queue more often because it will take up smaller chunks of your CPU time and bandwidth than doing it in large pieces. If your site sends out a lot of mail—especially if it has mailing lists—you may want to process the queue as often as every 15 minutes.

4. The final line just ends the if/then statement.

Setting Aliases

Now, set a few aliases for Sendmail to make life a little more convenient and to make your system a little more in tune with the other sites on the Net.

To set the aliases, do the following:

1. Open the file /etc/aliases.

2. Add the aliases you want; it doesn't matter where you put them in the file. I recommend that you keep them together and add comment lines to remind yourself what the aliases are for. An example of what I might add at this stage is as follows:

```
#sendmail aliases
postmaster: root
admin: root
info: dee
rob: rjl
steven: stephen
```

3. Save the aliases file.

4. Type **newaliases** to activate the aliases you just added.

The following are some general alias ideas:

■ If there's a userid that people keep mistyping, you can add a line for it. For example, people often type **rjl** for **jrl**, so I'd add the line jrl: rjl

■ If you have accounts on other systems with different userids than the one you use on your own site, you may want to add an alias for them as well in case people assume you use the same userid on all sites. For example, if you're fred on your own system, but fdt2351 on another, you may want to add: fdt2351: fred

■ If there are generic userids you want people to write to at your site, you can simply make aliases for them rather than create a whole new e-mail address for each. Examples of these are `postmaster`, `admin`, `webmaster`, and `info` in the list above. Personally, I'd rather have items like these go directly to my root or personal mailbox than have to remember to check five different sets of e-mail.

- You can also define aliases for people's real names. For example, some people who don't know my full e-mail address might try to write to me at **dleblanc@abc.com**. I could add a line that said `dleblanc: dee` in the `aliases` file.

- If you offer mailing lists and intend to have one person as the maintainer of all lists, you may want to add a `listmaster` alias (e.g., `listmaster: dee` or even `listmaster: admin`). If you have a different admin for each list, you can use aliases such as `owner-list1: rjl`.

- You can even make an alias that contains more than one account: `admins: dee, rjl`, for example. This is similar to setting up a small mailing list, as every time someone sends mail to **admins**, that mail will go to everyone listed under the `admins` alias (see fig. 6.2).

Fig. 6.2
Aliasing an address to multiple userids.

admins: root, admin, dee, rjl, postmaster

Setting Up Sendmail To Handle Internet Mail

Setting up your mail server to handle mail to and from the Internet is a little more complicated than processing local mail (see fig. 6.3). In this section, you'll learn to use the `sendmail.cf` file. Fortunately, you've got a sample `config` file already on your system that's preset to meet your TCP/IP and UUCP needs, so your work's been started for you!

Finding Your Way Through a sendmail.cf File

The following are a few tips to keep in mind when you're digging your way through a `sendmail.cf` file:

- The file is divided into specific sections, and each section is labeled to tell you what it contains. (These labels are indicated by the pound (#) sign.)

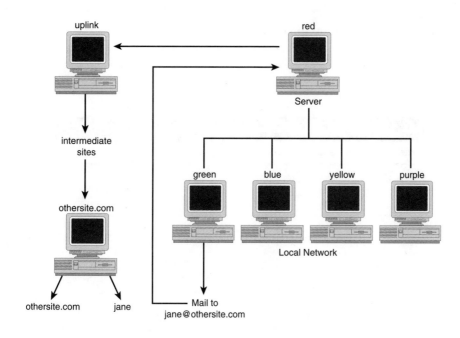

Fig. 6.3
Sending mail out
to the Internet.

- Anything that's specific to the machine you're working on is probably at the beginning of the file.

- Commands are grouped according to type, so the commands that are similar will be in the same area of the file.

- Most of a `sendmail.cf` file is made up of *rewrite rules*, which are used to rewrite e-mail addresses if you need to have this done.

- The end of the file is probably made up of mailer definitions and their associated rewrite rules. *Mailer definitions* tell Sendmail where mail should go and whether it's to a user or a program.

- The first character on a line is the command for that line, as Sendmail variables and commands are only one character long.

Fortunately, there's really little you have to change at first if you chose the appropriate default file during your Linux installation. As you add more services—especially such services as electronic mail to fax—you'll need to get a bit more technical with your `sendmail.cf` file.

III

Setting Up Your Site

Commands in a sendmail.cf File

It takes a little getting used to, but just remember that commands are only one character long in your sendmail.cf file, and the first letters on the line are the commands, as shown in table 6.1.

Table 6.1	Commands Used in sendmail.cf	
Command	**Use**	**Syntax**
D	Defining macros	D[macro][value]
C	Defining class macro	C[class][word1][...]
F	Defining class macros from files or pipes	F[class][filename]
H	Defining headers	H[?flag?][name]:[format]
M	Defining mailers	M[name],[field]=[value]
O	Defining options	O[option][value]
P	Defining delivery priorities	P[name]=[value]
R	Defining rewriting rules	R[lhs][rhs][comment]
S	Declaring new ruleset starts	S[number]
T	Declaring trusted users	T[user1][user2][...]

The following are some examples and a more in-depth discussion of the two straightforward sendmail.cf commands:

- The P command is used to set mail priorities. Whether you use mail priorities is your choice. As more mailer programs and people out there start using mail priorities, it may be worthwhile to define them in your sendmail.cf file. The main problem with defining priorities is coming up with the right terms. For example, you may want to use something like the following:

```
Purgent=100
Pjunk=-100
```

The larger the number, the higher the priority. The smaller the number, the lower the priority. Just keep in mind that you need to use priority names that are used in the mailer clients that send e-mail to your system if you want to take full advantage of mail priorities.

For example, the e-mail program Eudora uses the following priorities: Highest, High, Normal, Low, Lowest. So, you may add the following list of definitions:

```
Phighest=100
Phigh=50
Pnormal=0
Plow=—50
Plowest=—100
```

■ The T defines a *trusted user*—a user who is allowed to send mail as another user (a *normal user* can only send mail as coming from their own account, while a *trusted user* can send mail as coming from wherever). The standard trusted users are root, daemon, and uucp. You will likely find these three users already listed as trusted in your sendmail.cf file, as follows:

```
Troot daemon uucp
```

You will probably not want to have any other users defined as trusted. After all, root should be trusted to do everything on your site, being the system administrator. Daemons need to be trusted so they can send mail when it's one of their tasks, and that mail shouldn't go out as coming from the daemon itself, but from the user assigned to it. UUCP should be trusted because it needs to be able to shuttle mail around. Other than that, you don't want people on your site being able to pretend to send mail as other people from other accounts.

The rest of the Sendmail commands have their own extra parameters, and there are entire books on how to use them properly. Instead of going into an exhaustive discussion about what each parameter can do, I will recommend the changes that you should make.

Recommended Changes to Your sendmail.cf File

All these changes are at the beginning of the sendmail.cf file, where the machine and site information is stored (the macro definition section). When multiple machines are mentioned—and there are different changes to make to different machines—I am referring to the individual sendmail.cf files on each machine. I recommend you make sure the following lines exist:

1. DSyour.main_server.name

This line defines your *smart relay host,* telling Sendmail to send anything it can't handle with its own rule sets. For example, I'm setting up a server on ABC company's network where there are the following computers: red, green, blue, and yellow. Their domain name is **abc.com**. Our main server is red, and the other three go through it to the Internet. On green, blue, and yellow, I would put in their sendmail.cf files the line:

```
DSred.abc.com
```

ABC's feed site is **direct.ca**. On red, I use the location of my provider's mail server instead of my own:

```
DSmail.direct.ca
```

2. `DRyour.main_server.name`

This line determines where mail to *unqualified names* goes, telling Sendmail where to send e-mail that's going to someone who doesn't exist. On the three machines that aren't ABC's main server, I would use the line:

```
DRred.abc.com
```

On the main server, I would use *nothing*. That resolves it to the same server that the sendmail.cf file is on, which would be the main server, **red.abc.com**.

3. `DHyour.main_server.name`

This determines where all local e-mail traffic goes. If you are using a centralized mail server, you'll want to use the same settings as in the DR section. If you're using a separate mail server, you'll use the name of that server on all the machines.

4. `DMyour.site_domain.name`

You use this line to have all of your site's e-mail *masquerade* as though it were coming from a particular common area. In all the sendmail.cf files on all the computers in ABC's network, I have:

```
DMabc.com
```

This means that if someone sends e-mail to **user@domain**, it won't be rejected because it's missing its host name. For example, people can write to me at either **dee@abc.com** or **dee@green.abc.com**, and the message will get to me. If I hadn't set the DM value, the people sending me e-mail at **dee@abc.com** would have their mail bounced back.

When you log into a specific computer on the network, if they've all mounted the same mail spool (mounting directories across computers is covered in chapter 5, "Setting Up Your Site for General Use"), it doesn't matter if something is just sent to **user@domain.com** or not. If all the machines are mounting the same mail directory, they're all going to see the same list of mail, even if it isn't directly sent to each of the machines.

5. CEusername

This tells Sendmail which userids shouldn't be masqueraded. For example, root isn't the same person at all of our machines. Therefore, if someone wrote to just **root@ abc.com** they may not be writing to the proper person. Instead, I will include the following:

    CEroot

Now, root@abc.com will not be treated as a valid userid even though any other userid@abc.com would be just fine. To write to the admin of the machine green, for example, they would have to write to **root@green.abc.com**.

If one person is in charge of all the machines on your site and is root at all of these machines, then *do not* include the CEroot in your sendmail.cf files.

Setting Up Sendmail to Handle UUCP Mail

If you're using UUCP as well, there really aren't any changes you have to make as long as you used the sendmail.cf that includes UUCP capability. However, only your main server (in ABC's case red) should have the UUCP version of this file. The other computers' sendmail.cf files should *not* have UUCP capability (see fig. 6.4).

> **Note**
>
> You may not want to send or get mail by UUCP, but you may have dial-in users sending and getting mail by UUCP. If this is so, you still need to have UUCP defined in your sendmail.cf file.
>
> If you need to install UUCP on your site, you can find it on the n disk set.

Fig. 6.4
Sending out UUCP
mail.

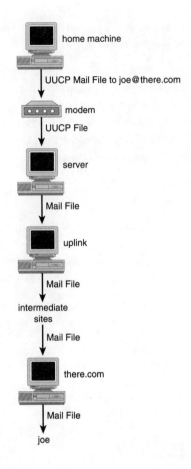

Now, if you don't intend to offer POP mail, you're finished setting up your mail server! Move ahead to the next chapter. If you do intend to offer POP mail, read the next section.

Setting Up POP Mail

To offer POP mail, you need to set up your POP mail server (see fig. 6.5). However, this is such a simple task, you won't even realize you've done any more work! Simply do the following:

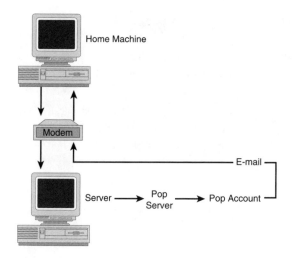

Fig. 6.5
Getting POP mail.

1. Log into root on your main server.

2. Edit the file /etc/inetd.conf.

3. Find the section of the file that allows and disallows various services.

4. Add the following line (or delete the # sign in front of it if it already exists and is commented out):

```
pop3   stream   tcp   nowait   root   /usr/sbin/tcpd   /usr/sbin/in.pop3d
```

> **Tip**
>
> A line is *commented out* in these files if it begins with a number sign (#).

5. If there's a similar line with pop2 in front of it, make sure there's a # sign in front of it to comment it out.

6. Go to the other machines on your network and comment out anything referring to pop2 or pop3 by putting a # at the beginning of each of the lines. You only want the main server to handle POP connections.

III

Setting Up Your Site

> **Note**
>
> POP2 is simply an older version of the POP server than POP3. When people refer to POP servers in general, they're referring to POP3. Some sites simply haven't upgraded to it.
>
> If you want to allow people to use the Eudora e-mail client from a Windows or Macintosh machine to access your POP server, you need to get the server QPOPPER. It's available via FTP at **sunsite.unc.edu /pub/Linux/system/mail**.

Running Mailing Lists

One thing many Internet sites run is mailing lists. With mailing lists, you can have a centralized distribution point to send a piece of mail to a small or large number of people. You can have them for all of your users, for people interested in a particular hobby or discussion topic, or really anything else you might want a number of people to be able to talk about together.

In a way, a mailing list is like a members-only newsgroup. Everyone sees the posts that go to the list, but only if they're subscribed to it through the list software.

You can find majordomo on the FTP site **ftp.greatcircle.com**, in the directory /pub/majordomo. The first file you should look at is majordomo-1.93.README (the version number may be different when you go to download the file). It walks you through the installation process. The file itself is majordomo-1.93.tar.Z. You also may want to take a look through the other text files in this directory, such as the CERT file and the SECURITY file.

> **Tip**
>
> You may want to wait until you've installed some of the servers in this book before installing majordomo if you are new to compiling programs.

Some tips on running mailing lists:

■ In the stock "Welcome to the list" message, you should have a list policy stated. This is a lot like an Acceptable Use policy, in that you define what is acceptable behavior on the list, the list's purpose, acceptable subjects for the list (and how closely you'll try to keep it to those subjects).

- You can set majordomo to put a small line at the bottom of every post that points people to where to get help with the list. This can cut down on headaches with people posting to the list asking for help.

- Majordomo comes with a standard help file. However, you can customize it to fit your needs. If you find you have a problem with people always asking you the same question about the list, add the solution to the question to either the help or welcome file. Be sure to keep these files up-to-date.

- Only moderate lists if you feel they need to be moderated. If you moderate a lot of your lists and personally set yourself up as the moderator, you're going to have a lot of work to do! Many lists really don't need a moderator, as you can still step in and remove someone if it becomes necessary.

Verifying that Your E-mail Works

Once you get a server installed, it's time to test it. With Sendmail, this is simple! Just send two pieces of mail. The first you should send to yourself. Mail the second to someone on another site on the Internet. Then, get the person to write you back (or write to an autoresponder that will write you back immediately).

If the mail you sent to yourself doesn't come back, check `root`'s mail (or `post-master` if you gave it a different account). An error message was likely sent there telling you where things might be misconfigured. If there's no mail in `root`, type **mailq** as `root`. If the mail you sent was stuck in the queue, then it will be listed along with its status. You can then force it to process (flush) the queue by typing **sendmail -q**.

If the mail you sent to yourself comes back, but the mail you sent out to the Internet doesn't arrive there, once again first check `root`'s (or `postmaster`'s) mail for any error messages. Also, check the mail queue again. If it's not in the queue, you can look in your system's logs for sendmail statements. If there's not a listing for that piece of mail stating `Accepted for delivery`, your uplink server (say, your provider's mail server) hasn't accepted the mail. If it wasn't accepted, there will be an error message—if you keep getting `deferred` as an error you may need to talk to your provider and see if it's having problems with its mail system.

If the first two tests worked, but the incoming mail doesn't arrive, first check root/postmaster's mail to see if there's an error message. Also, your logs will show a connection from the mail server it was coming from, but you won't see any messages about errors with the transfer. Other than that, you'll need to find out from the sender of the note if the mail bounced back, and what kind of error it bounced back with.

Chapter 7

Installing Web Server Software

One of the hottest services available on the Internet right now is the World Wide Web. Everyone seems to be creating home pages and reveling in the multimedia experience of it all. If you'd like to offer Web pages from your site, you must have a WWW server running to handle the page requests. If you don't intend to run a WWW server, feel free to skip ahead to the next chapter.

Why wouldn't you want to run a Web server? Primarily, if you don't intend to offer Web pages, there is no reason to run a Web server. You and your users can still look at Web pages outside of your site without a Web server. Some reasons to not offer Web pages on your site might be:

■ You have limited bandwidth and disk space and can't afford to strain it with the added service of providing WWW pages.

■ Neither you nor your users are interested in offering WWW pages at the moment.

■ Your provider stores Web pages for free or at virtually no cost, and you'd rather use their bandwidth for access than your own.

In this chapter, you learn how to:

■ Compile your Web server

■ Configure your Web server

■ Select server scripts

■ Move all of your server files to the proper places

- Start up your Web server

- Test your Web server

Compiling Your Web Server

With Linux, you'll find that, more often than not, you're going to have to compile source rather than fetch binaries. There's no need to panic, however! You'll get plenty of practice in this book at setting up systems. Your programming skills will especially improve over time as you fulfill your duties as system administrator.

> **Note**
>
> I'll go into a discussion of HTML and browsers later in the chapter. First, let's get the server set up! If you need extra help and have access to a Web browser (or want to jump ahead and install X-Windows and Netscape), you can go to **http://hoohoo.ncsa.uiuc.edu** for online assistance with this process.

Finding and Decompressing the Server Source

The Web server you're going to use is the NCSA's (National Center for Supercomputing Applications) httpd version 1.4.2. This is a daemon, which runs in the background and waits for Web page requests to come in.

Locate the file /contrib/httpd.tgz on the CD-ROM and copy it to a directory, such as /usr/src. To deal with the .z (which means the file is compressed and can be taken apart with gunzip), type **gunzip httpd.tgz.**

> **Tip**
>
> A good habit to develop is keeping source code around when you can. Putting it into /usr/src means it's immediately where you can find it at a later date. If you update your libraries later, you'll need to recompile it.

Note

There are precompiled binaries available of httpd, but I highly recommend you compile the server yourself. For one thing, as a sysadmin you're going to have to compile a lot of programs as time goes by, so the more experience you get in the beginning, the better. For another, the risk of getting precompiled binaries instead of source is that they may not be compiled for a system that's set up the way you have yours set up. It may be compiled for a different set of source libraries than you have, and in this case the binaries don't come with some of the nice extra scripts that the source does.

If you want to try the binary, you can find it via FTP on **ftp.ncsa.uiuc.edu** in /Web/ httpd/Unix/ncsa_httpd/httpd_1.4/ httpd_1.4.2_linux.Z. While this file does contain the source code, it also contains a precompiled binary.

Then, to get rid of the .tar (a utility that groups items together, but doesn't compress) type **tar –xvf httpd_1.4.2_source.tar**.

Note

Some tarred files are set to create a particular directory for themselves, and some are not. If they create their own directory, you want to untar them straight in /usr/src. However, if they don't, you'll end up with a bunch of files directly in /usr/src instead of a subdirectory. I know httpd creates its own directory. If you're not sure about a program, you may want to create a directory for it, untar the file inside that directory, and if it creates its own directory move the tar file back to /usr/src and erase the untarred version. You can then untar it again and let it create its own directory.

Tip

In Linux, you'll use tar to cluster items into one file and then gzip (or the UNIX command compress) to compress the file. These two commands are like PKZip in the MS-DOS world.

III

Setting Up Your Site

Compiling Your Web Server

Now you can actually compile the server. With any luck, it will be a painless process, but you may have to use some of your programming skills to put it together. Yes, programming skills. As a system administrator, you will find that if you don't have them, you will slowly develop them as a necessity.

First, make sure that your Makefile is in your current directory. Then, type **make linux** to begin the compilation, and watch what happens. Don't worry too much about the warnings unless there's an overwhelming number of them. If any serious errors occur, the compilation will stop.

> ### Note
>
> When you see an error kill your compilation that claims that a particular header file with an .h extension doesn't exist, that's often not true. Take a look in /usr/include and /usr/include/linux (for example), and see if you can find that particular file somewhere else.
>
> When you find the file that was missing, you'll need to edit the source file (with a .c extension) referenced when the error was displayed and change the call to the file so it's correct.
>
> If you get an error that says something about an *undefined function*, a particular function is probably in a different .h file than it used to be in. Instead of looking through every header file you can find, go to directories like /usr/include and /usr/include/linux and type the following:
>
> **grep 'string you are searching for' *.h**
>
> For example, if I were looking for the function foo(), I would type **grep 'foo' *.h** in each directory until I found what I was looking for.

Now the initial installation is complete!

Configuring Your Web Server

Now that the server is compiled, you need to configure it to suit your system and needs. Once you finish with this process, it's not something you'll have to worry about again until you have a need to change your configurations. You may need to change your configurations if you decide to offer a different set of features, or change your system in a significant way.

> **Note**
>
> It's become common practice for people to alias their site's Web server to
> www.your.domain_name. This is because it makes it simple for people to guess at
> the URL for your site's main Web page. If you don't want people to be able to easily
> locate your site's main Web pages then you probably don't want to alias it to
> www.your.domain_name. In fact, if you only want key people to be able to access it,
> you may want to alias it to an obscure machine name that others won't guess.
>
> As I covered in chapter 5, "Setting Up Your Site for General Use," you can set aliases
> for a machine in the `/etc/named.d/named.hosts` file by simply adding the new
> machine name right after the other ones in its list. Then, after you've added the new
> alias, you need to kill your *named* process and restart it. For example, if the process
> ID for your named is 210, type **kill --HUP 210**. HUP tells your system to reload the
> config files without actually killing the process.

General httpd Configuration File Rules

There are three configuration files you need to set up. All of them observe the
following rules:

- The only place where case matters within these files is in file paths
  and names.

- To comment out a line, use a pound (#) sign.

- When you use the `directive` command (discussed in the next section), you can only have one directive per line.

- To make your directive and following data statements easier to follow at a glance, you can include extra white space. It will be ignored
  by the Web server.

Setting Up the Server Configuration File

The first configuration file you'll set up is for your Web server. Use the file
`httpd.conf-dist` (listed here) as a template for suggestions, but you won't
want to use it as is.

```
# This is the main server configuration file. It is best to
# leave the directives in this file in the order they are in, or
# things may not go the way you'd like. See URL http://
# hoohoo.ncsa.uiuc.edu/
# for instructions.
# Do NOT simply read the instructions in here without understanding
# what they do, if you are unsure consult the online docs. You have
# been warned.
```

(continues)

(continued)

```
# NCSA httpd (comments, questions to httpd@ncsa.uiuc.edu)
# ServerType is either inetd, or standalone.
ServerType standalone
# If you are running from inetd, go to "ServerAdmin".
# Port: The port the standalone listens to. For ports < 1023, you
will need httpd to be run as root initially.
Port 80
# StartServers: The number of servers to launch at startup. Must be
# compiled without the NO_PASS compile option
StartServers 5
# MaxServers: The number of servers to launch until mimic'ing the
# 1.3 scheme (new server for each connection). These servers will
# stay around until the server is restarted. They will be reused as
# needed, however. See the documentation on hoohoo.ncsa.uiuc.edu
# for more information.
MaxServers 20
# If you wish httpd to run as a different user or group, you must
# run httpd as root initially and it will switch.
# User/Group: The name (or #number) of the user/group to run httpd
# as.
User nobody
Group #-1
# ServerAdmin: Your address, where problems with the server should
# be e-mailed.
ServerAdmin you@your.address
# ServerRoot: The directory the server's config, error, and log
# files are kept in
ServerRoot /usr/local/etc/httpd
# ErrorLog: The location of the error log file. If this does not
# start with /, ServerRoot is prepended to it.
ErrorLog logs/error_log
# TransferLog: The location of the transfer log file. If this does
# not start with /, ServerRoot is prepended to it.
TransferLog logs/access_log
# AgentLog: The location of the agent log file. If this does not
# start with /, ServerRoot is prepended to it.
AgentLog logs/agent_log
# RefererLog: The location of the referer log file. If this does
# not start with /, ServerRoot is prepended to it.
RefererLog logs/referer_log
# RefererIgnore: If you don't want to keep track of links from
# certain servers (like your own), place it here. If you want to
# log them all, keep this line commented.
#RefererIgnore servername
# PidFile: The file the server should log its pid to
PidFile logs/httpd.pid
# ServerName allows you to set a host name which is sent back to
# clients for your server if it's different than the one the
# program would get
# (i.e. use "www" instead of the host's real name).
#
# Note: You cannot just invent host names and hope they work. The
# name you define here must be a valid DNS name for your host. If
# you don't understand this, ask your network administrator.

#ServerName new.host.name
```

Build your personalized config file, `conf/httpd.conf`, and fill it in, following the same order as the example above. The following is a walk-through of the choices I made for my server configuration file:

1. `# ServerType is either inetd, or standalone.`

When reading this line, it's easy to think you want `inetd` because you'll be running a site on the Internet. However, you want to use `standalone` because you will have a lot less CPU load by letting httpd handle itself than you will if `inetd` has to take care of it. Therefore, the first line in your `conf/httpd.conf` file is the following:

        ServerType standalone

2. `# Port: The port the standalone listens to.`

The standard httpd port is 80. Generally, you'll want to stick with standard ports, as doing this will make it easier for people to access your services. So, your second line reads as follows:

        Port 80

3. `# StartServers: The number of servers to launch at startup.`

Although there is a compiled default for the number of server processes that initially fork off, it's best to go ahead and set a number anyway so you *know* what you're using. If you accept the defaults, you won't know what settings you're using unless you dig through the source code to find what they are.

I chose to use the same number of servers (five) used in the example configuration file. My system can easily handle five HTTP requests simultaneously without having to use extra resources to start up more httpd processes. Also, five idle daemons won't hog your resources. Therefore, the next line in your configuration file is the following:

        StartServers 5

4. `# MaxServers: The number of servers to launch until mimic'ing the`
`# 1.3 scheme (new server for each connection).`

Once again, there is a compiled default available to you, but I recommend that you include a value for this variable in your configuration file as well. The value included in the sample config file is 20. This may seem like a lot of servers to run at once, but remember that the more inline image, bullets, etc., on a Web page, the more server processes are needed to load that page. So, for example, if you have a page with three pictures, five bullets, and text, it would need a total of 9 server processes to send all of that information to the person accessing the page. I'll stick with the default, so my next line is:

```
MaxServers 20
```

5. `# User/Group: The name (or #number) of the user/group to run httpd as.`

The defaults for ownerships for httpd are nobody and nogroup. However, some people prefer to have it run as owned by another known process, such as FTP. To set mine up to run as user ftp and group bin, my next two lines are:

```
User ftp
```

```
Group bin
```

> ### Caution
>
> Be sure that the user and group you select exist in your /etc/passwd file.

6. `# ServerAdmin: Your address, where problems with the server should`
   `# be e-mailed.`

Make it easy for people to contact you about your services. It is, of course, great to hear positive comments, but it is also a good idea to make it simple for people to complain or offer "constructive" criticisms. If it takes users a while to figure out how to contact you to make a complaint or comment, they tend to be more irate than they might otherwise have been.

Therefore, include the e-mail address of the person in charge of maintaining your Web services. If this person may change often, then you might want to go back to your aliases file (discussed in chapter 5, "Setting Up Your Site for General Use") and add an alias for an address like **webadmin** or **webmaster**, so you don't risk forgetting to change it in the httpd config file later. I used the following:

```
ServerAdmin webadmin@renaissoft.com
```

7. `# ServerRoot: The directory the server's config, error, and log`
   `# files are kept in`

Here you tell your system where it can find your httpd files. Where you keep them really depends on your preferences, but instead of making up something like /servers/httpd, stick with the default so you become familiar with Linux file organization:

```
ServerRoot /usr/local/etc/httpd
```

8. Now tell your system where it can find your httpd log files. If you don't start the paths with a slash (/), it is assumed that the directory starts in the directory assigned by ServerRoot. The log files are as follows:

- ErrorLog keeps track of clients that take time out, scripts that produce no output, .htaccess files that try to override items they don't have the permissions to override, serious server bugs (producing segmentation faults or bus errors), and problems with user authentication.

- TransferLog keeps track of the following information on accesses: client host, identd info offered, user authentication if used, date and time of access, first line of the HTTP request, server status code, and the total number of bytes sent.

- AgentLog keeps track of the client agent software that is used. This is mostly employed for gathering statistics and for tracking which clients follow protocol that cause errors in your server.

- RefererLog keeps track of the documents that referred people to your links.

  There is a variable associated with this log file called ReferIgnore, which overlooks references to particular referring links. You use it if you don't want to record every time someone looks at one of your pages following a link on your own site, for example. Because I have www.renaissoft.com set up, I'd tell it to ignore that host.

- PidFile keeps track of your server process ID numbers.

You can choose to keep your logs in some sort of central log area. Because I decided that I want to keep my logs with the other htppd items, the next few items in my config file will be the following:

```
ErrorLog logs/error_log

TransferLog logs/access_log

AgentLog logs/agent_log
```

```
RefererLog logs/referer_log

RefererIgnore www.renaissoft.com

PidFile logs/httpd.pid
```

9. ServerName tells your system another name for the location of your Web server. Once again, a good example of this is our site, where the real name of the server is **davinci.renaissoft.com**, but we like the world to see it as **www.renaissoft.com** for simplicity's sake. So, for the last line of the server configuration file, I'd have:

```
ServerName www.renaissoft.com
```

Setting Up the Resource Configuration File

The second configuration file you'll set up is used to tell your Web server where to find documents, scripts, and aliases. Use the file srm.conf-dist (listed here) as a template for suggestions as you did with the server configuration file, but don't use it as is.

```
# With this document, you define the name space that users see of
# your http server.
# See the tutorials at http://hoohoo.ncsa.uiuc.edu/docs/tutorials/
# for more information.
# NCSA httpd (httpd@ncsa.uiuc.edu)
# DocumentRoot: The directory out of which you will serve your
# documents. By default, all requests are taken from this
# directory, but symbolic links and aliases may be used to
# point to other locations.
DocumentRoot /usr/local/etc/httpd/htdocs
# UserDir: The name of the directory which is appended onto a
# user's home directory if a ~user request is received.
UserDir public_html
# DirectoryIndex: Name of the file to use as a pre-written HTML
# directory index
DirectoryIndex index.html
# FancyIndexing is whether you want fancy directory indexing or standard
FancyIndexing on
# AddIcon tells the server which icon to show for different files
# or filename extensions
AddIconByType (TXT,/icons/text.xbm) text/*
AddIconByType (IMG,/icons/image.xbm) image/*
AddIconByType (SND,/icons/sound.xbm) audio/*
AddIcon /icons/movie.xbm .mpg .qt
AddIcon /icons/binary.xbm .bin
AddIcon /icons/back.xbm ..
AddIcon /icons/menu.xbm ^^DIRECTORY^^
AddIcon /icons/blank.xbm ^^BLANKICON^^
# DefaultIcon is which icon to show for files which do not have an
# icon explicitly set.
DefaultIcon /icons/unknown.xbm
# AddDescription allows you to place a short description after a
```

```
# file in server-generated indexes.
# Format: AddDescription "description" filename
# ReadmeName is the name of the README file the server will look
# for by default. Format: ReadmeName name
## The server will first look for name.html, include it if found,
# and it will then look for name and include it as plaintext if
# found.
## HeaderName is the name of a file which should be prepended to
# directory indexes.
ReadmeName README
HeaderName HEADER
# IndexIgnore is a set of filenames which directory indexing should
# ignore Format: IndexIgnore name1 name2…
IndexIgnore */.??* *~ *# */HEADER* */README*
# AccessFileName: The name of the file to look for in each directory
# for access control information.
AccessFileName .htaccess
# DefaultType is the default MIME type for documents which the
# server cannot find the type of from filename extensions.
DefaultType text/plain
# AddType allows you to tweak mime.types without actually editing
# it, or to make certain files to be certain types.
# Format: AddType type/subtype ext1
# AddEncoding allows you to have certain browsers (Mosaic/X 2.1+)
# uncompress information on the fly. Note: Not all browsers support
# this.
#AddEncoding x-compress Z
#AddEncoding x-gzip gz
# Redirect allows you to tell clients about documents which used to
# exist in your server's namespace, but do not anymore. This allows
# you to tell the clients where to look for the relocated document.
# Format: Redirect fakename url
# Aliases: Add here as many aliases as you need, up to 20. The
# format is Alias fakename realname
Alias /icons/ /usr/local/etc/httpd/icons/
# ScriptAlias: This controls which directories contain server
# scripts. Format: ScriptAlias fakename realname
ScriptAlias /cgi-bin/ /usr/local/etc/httpd/cgi-bin/
# If you want to use server side includes, or CGI outside
# ScriptAliased directories, uncomment the following lines.
#AddType text/x-server-parsed-html .shtml
#AddType application/x-httpd-cgi .cgi
# If you want to have files/scripts sent instead of the built-in
# version in case of errors, uncomment the following lines and set
# them as you will. Note: scripts must be able to be run as if they
# were called directly (in ScriptAlias directory, for instance)
# 302 - REDIRECT
# 400 - BAD_REQUEST
# 401 - AUTH_REQUIRED
# 403 - FORBIDDEN
# 404 - NOT_FOUND
# 500 - SERVER_ERROR
# 501 - NOT_IMPLEMENTED
#ErrorDocument 302 /cgi-bin/redirect.cgi
#ErrorDocument 500 /errors/server.html
#ErrorDocument 403 /errors/forbidden.html
```

Build your personalized config file, conf/srm.conf, and fill it in following the same order as the example above. The following is a walk-through of the choices I made for my server resource configuration file:

1. `# DocumentRoot: The directory out of which you will serve your`
`# documents.`

With this variable, you specify the main directory that your server will show files from. As usual, I am going to stick with the standards (though if you prefer to keep all of your log files in one central place, you can certainly change this to suit your needs), so this configuration file will start with the following:

`DocumentRoot /usr/local/etc/httpd/htdocs`

2. `# UserDir: The name of the directory that is appended onto a user's`
`# home directory if a ~user request is received.`

This directive is used to assign a directory that will exist in user directories where the users can keep their own HTML files for Web access. The standard is the directory `public_html`: any time someone follows a link to, say, **http://www.server.com/~user,** they would actually be going to **http://www.server.com/~user/public_html**. It's mostly a way of keeping things tidy and keeping the proper security, so outsiders can't get into user directories.

The next line in my config file, because I'm using the default, will be as follows:

`UserDir public_html`

3. `# DirectoryIndex: Name of the file to use as a pre-written HTML`
`# directory index.`

With this directive, you can set an assumed file name when an outside user follows a link into someone's home directory. In the example URL's above, note that there were no file names listed. That is because a default file name is set, so the server looks at that file first (generally, `index.html`). I'm going to use the default once again, so my next line will be:

`DirectoryIndex index.html`

4. `# FancyIndexing determines whether you want fancy directory indexing`
`# or standard.`

FancyIndexing refers to showing directories and files with icons and file sizes. If you want to display your files and directories in this fashion, turn this option on. If not, set it to off. My next line, setting it to on, is as follows:

```
FancyIndexing on
```

5. `# AddIcon tells the server which icon to show for different files`
`# or file names. extensions`

You can use this directive to define what icons your Web server will use to display the types of files in a directory. This is simply a way to jazz up your directory displays a bit. There are no defaults, so if you don't define something, no icons will be used.

The path you use to the icons will be taken to be inside the value of the DocumentRoot variable that you defined at the beginning of this configuration file (which I set to be /usr/local/etc/httpd/htdocs). Therefore, the first variable refers to the directory you want to keep the icons in, and this directory will be inside your DocumentRoot directory. So, for example, if you want the icons in /usr/local/etc/httpd/htdocs/icons, just enter **/icons** for the directory.

The next item is the particular icon. While there are no defaults, the server does come with icons you can use, which are in the /icons subdirectory of your server files. The icons available are shown in figure 7.1.

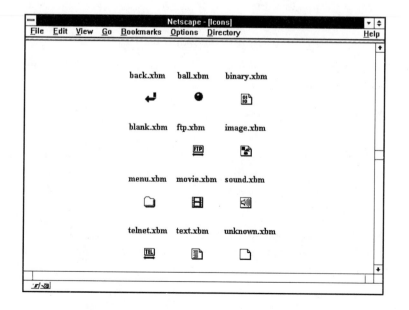

Fig. 7.1

You can use these icons to show what kind of file is in a directory listing.

For example, if I wanted to use the icon `sound.xbm` for my sound files, I'd add `sound.xbm` to the path statement, making it `/icons/sound.xbm` (which would really refer to `/usr/local/etc/httpd/htdocs/icons/sound.xbm`).

Finally, the last piece of the icon statement is where you'll identify which file types to use the icon with. In the case of our sound file example, I would now add `*.au`. This makes the entire statement `/icons sound.xbm *.au`.

Other examples of icon definitions are:

```
AddIcon /icons/dir.xbm ^^DIRECTORY^^

AddIcon /icons/image.xbm .gif .jpg .xbm
```

6. `# DefaultIcon determines which icon to show for files that do not`
   `# have an icon explicitly set.`

Here, you tell the server what icon to use for file types that you didn't define. A pretty standard one is the unknown icon that comes with the other default icons. I'll use this one, so the next line in my config file is as follows:

```
DefaultIcon /icons/unknown.xbm
```

7. `# AddDescription allows you to place a short description after a`
   `# file in server-generated indexes.`

If you want to add a line of description for specific files, you'll use this directive. Say you have the file `dogs.txt`, and you want to make *sure* people read it. You might add the following:

```
AddDescription "Description and discussion of various breeds
➥of dogs" dogs.txt
```

8. `# ReadmeName is the name of the README file the server will look`
   `# for by default.`

You can use this directive to define the HTML file that will contain a list of descriptions of the files in the current directory. These file descriptions would be displayed right next to the file names in the directory listing, even though they were stored in a separate file.

You will need to create the HTML file containing the descriptions at a later date. Just to make my life easy, I'll name mine `readme.html`, so the line I'll add to my resource config file is as follows:

```
ReadmeName readme
```

Note that I didn't include the `.html`. When you don't include the extension, the server will first look for `readme.html`, and then look for the plain text file `readme`.

9. `# HeaderName is the name of a file that should be prepended to`
`# directory indexes.`

You can use this directive to define the HTML file that will contain a custom header for the current directory. The header will be displayed at the top of the directory listing. You will need to create the HTML file containing the header at a later date. To make things easy to remember, I'll name mine `header.html`, so the line I'll add to my resource config file is the following:

```
HeaderName header
```

Once again, note that the `.html` extension is assumed first, and if it can't find `header.html`, it will look for `header` without an extension.

10. `# IndexIgnore is a set of file names that directory indexing should`
`# ignore.`

If you don't want certain files to show up in directory listings, use `IndexIgnore`. For example, if I want to disregard the `readme.html` and `header.html` files (they're used by the server itself, and users don't need to access them by hand), I would use the following line next in my resource configuration file:

```
IndexIgnore readme.html header.html
```

When you test this, you may find that there are other files you don't want displayed. Just come back to this line and add them to the `IndexIgnore` list. For example, you may want to use `IndexIgnore readme.html header.html # ~`.

Now, all emacs autosave and backup files are no longer included.

11. `# AccessFileName: The name of the file to look for in each`
`# directory for access control information.`

This directive refers partially to the next section, "Setting Up the Access Configuration File." It tells your server where to look for *access control files*, which are the files you'll configure to set up what directories people need higher than generic guest access to get to, etc.

I'm going to stick with the default file for this one, so my next resource config line is the following:

```
AccessFileName .htaccess
```

12. `# DefaultType is the default MIME type for documents that the`
`# server cannot find the type of from file name extensions.`

You can use this directive to assign a default file type when your server cannot determine the actual file type. I will stick with the default setting on this one for now, and see if I consistently run into another file type that I should use here instead. My next line will be the following:

```
DefaultType text/plain
```

In this case, `text` refers to the file *type* (standard file type), and `plain` refers to the *subtype* (what MIME calls the file type).

13. `# AddType allows you to tweak mime.types without actually editing`
`# it, or to make certain files to be certain types.`

If you want to assign a particular type to files with certain extensions, you'll use this directive. The types you assign here override the types already listed in your *TypesConfig* file. This file already contains a list of file types and corresponding MIME types.

Although you may want to take a look at it (you can find it in `conf/ mime.types`), you shouldn't need to edit this file. Instead, make your changes by using the `AddType` directive here.

Let's say, for example, that I intend to use the extension `.help` a lot, and all `.help` files will be text files. I would therefore add the following to my resource config file:

```
AddType text/plain help
```

14. `# AddEncoding allows you to have certain browsers (Mosaic/X 2.1+)`
`# decompress information on the fly.`

If you want to enable your server to decompress files as it sends them (so you can use less drive space storing the files), use this directive. For example, let's say I want my server to be able to decompress UNIX compressed (`.Z`) files and gzipped (`.gz`) files (as shown as an example in the resource configuration file listing). I would enter the following in my config file:

```
AddEncoding x-compress Z
```

```
AddEncoding x-gzip gz
```

15. `# Aliases: Add here as many aliases as you need, up to 20.`

If you want to add an alias that you can use for paths later in your HTML files, use this directive. To alias the path /ftp/pub/docs to /docs, you would add the following line to your resource config file:

```
Alias /docs /ftp/pub/docs
```

Setting Up the Access Configuration File

The third configuration file that you'll set up is used to tell your Web server which clients can get to which directories and which services are available in other directories. Use the file access.conf-dist (see below for file listing) as a template for suggestions as you did with the server configuration file, but don't use it as is.

```
# access.conf: Global access configuration
# Online docs at http://hoohoo.ncsa.uiuc.edu/
# I suggest you consult them; this is important and confusing
# stuff. /usr/local/etc/httpd/ should be changed to whatever you
# set ServerRoot to.
<Directory /usr/local/etc/httpd/cgi-bin>
Options Indexes FollowSymLinks
</Directory>
# This should be changed to whatever you set DocumentRoot to.
<Directory /usr/local/etc/httpd/htdocs>
# This may also be "None", "All", or any combination of "Indexes",
# "Includes", or "FollowSymLinks"
Options Indexes FollowSymLinks
# This controls which options the .htaccess files in directories
# can override. Can also be "None", or any combination of
# "Options", "FileInfo", "AuthConfig", and "Limit"
AllowOverride All
# Controls who can get stuff from this server.
<Limit GET>
order allow,deny
allow from all
</Limit>
</Directory>
# You may place any other directories you wish to have access
# information for after this one.
```

Build your personalized config file, conf/access.conf, and fill it in following the same order as the example above. In a way, this is your most important configuration file because it controls access to your system, so take your time. The following is a walk-through of the choices I made for my server access configuration file:

1. `# /usr/local/etc/httpd/ should be changed to whatever you set`
   `# ServerRoot to.`

```
<Directory /usr/local/etc/httpd/cgi-bin>

Options Indexes FollowSymLinks

</Directory>
```

Rather than just being a one line item, the `Directory` directive is a statement. It begins with setting the directory. Just take a look in your server configuration file and see what you set `ServerRoot` to, in case you changed it from `/usr/local/etc/httpd/`. Then, add `cgi-bin` after it. In my case, I left it at the default, so I'll just enter:

```
Directory /usr/local/etc/httpd/cgi-bin>
```

Now, tell your server the features available in this directory (Options). Your choices are the following:

- `None` enables no features in this directory. This is the ultimate security, as someone using your Web server would be completely unable to do anything in this directory.

- `All` enables all features in this directory. Don't use this one unless you really want to give users access to *everything* in the particular directory, including users' home directories. In fact, if a `simlink` is created from a user's home directory to a directory that you don't want outsiders to be in, this option will let outside Web users employ that link.

- `FollowSymLinks` enables the server to follow `simlinks` out of this directory. Watch out, though, because if the `simlink` is in a user's home directory, a link may be created to something that you don't want outsiders to access.

- `SymLinksIfOwnerMatch` enables the server to follow `simlinks` out of this directory if the file the link points to is owned by the same person who made the link. This one takes care of part of the `simlink` problems mentioned above. Outsiders won't be able to follow a link unless the file it's linked to is also owned by the user.

- `Indexes` enables the server to let people request indexes of the current directory and lets outside users get HTML indexes of the directory they're in. If you don't use this option, outside users won't be able to get HTML indexes, but would be able to load any other index files in this directory. If you intend to offer HTML file indexes with descriptions, use this option.

- `Includes` enables the server to let users offer information on the fly, such as the date a file was last modified.

After taking a look at the options that are available, and knowing that I have full control over this directory as root, I choose to have the following as my next line:

```
Options Indexes FollowSymLinks
```

I'm not too worried at the moment about simlinks in user home directories because this isn't one.

Now, I end this particular item with the following:

```
</Directory>
```

2. # This should be changed to whatever you set DocumentRoot to.

```
<Directory /usr/local/etc/httpd/htdocs>
```

This Directory directive is also a full statement rather than a one line item. Follow the same pattern as before, but this time in reference to the directory you used for ServerRoot (I used /usr/local/etc/httpd/ htdocs). My first line for this section will be the following:

```
<Directory /usr/local/etc/httpd/htdocs>
```

In this case, I have full control over the directory again as root, and I want people to be able to access all of the documents here. I'll use the following option:

```
Options All
```

Now enter the term that will control which .htaccess options the server can override in individual directories. Although you have a number of options available, I highly recommend the following:

```
AllowOverride All
```

This way, if you *want* to override something, it will be in the .htaccess files. If not, nothing is overridden.

Now set the limits on who can get files from the server, as follows:

```
<Limit GET>
```

You can both deny and allow. Tell your server which list to look at first: the *deny list* or the *allow list*. Notice that there is no space between deny and allow in the following code:

```
order deny,allow
```

Unless you actually *do* want to deny any hosts access, all you need to add now to finish this section is the following:

```
allow from all

</Limit>

</Directory>
```

3. Now set user home directory access.

Tip

If you want to set permissions for other directories, just add a new directory statement for each one after the one you just added.

Instead of doing an individual statement for every user's home directory, focus instead on /home. The first line of the directory statement is the following:

```
<Directory /home>
```

In this case, you don't want any .htaccess files to override anything because a user could just create one and weaken your security. So, instead of allowing anything to be overridden, specify none as follows:

```
AllowOverride None
```

Now, set what kinds of files people can access in the home directories. I recommend using the Indexes option and the Includes option (in case a user would like to write a small script to keep track of access numbers, date last modified, etc.)

The only other items in users' directories that outsiders will be able to access through the Web servers will be pages in their public_html directories (unless you changed public_html to another directory name). So, the next lines (as this is the end of this section) are the following:

```
Options Indexes Includes

</Directory>
```

Pat yourself on the back. You have *finally* finished configuring your server!

Selecting Server Scripts

There are a number of scripts that come with the Web server software that allow you to personalize your setup a bit. Even if you don't want to use any of these scripts, they can serve as examples. The cgi-bin directory of your server files contains a number of sample scripts, which can provide useful lessons on how to write your own.

The Date Script

The script date is a simple but useful one for seeing how httpd scripts work.

```
#!/bin/sh

DATE=/bin/date

echo Content-type: text/plain
echo

if [ -x $DATE ]; then
        $DATE
else
        echo Cannot find date command on this system.
fi
```

This script breaks down as follows:

1. `#!/bin/sh`

This runs the sh shell to interpret everything that follows in this script.

2. `DATE=/bin/date`

Setting the variable DATE to the full path for the program that determines the date.

3. `echo Content-type: text/plain`

This code displays Content-type: text/plain on your screen.

4. `echo`

This shows a blank line on your screen.

5. `if [ -x $DATE ]; then`

`$DATE`

If there is a program at the location assigned to DATE, the program is run, and the output is displayed.

6. `else`

   echo Cannot find `date` command on this system.

   `fi`

   If there isn't a program at the location assigned to `DATE`, `Cannot find date command on this system.` is displayed, and the program ends.

If you want to make a script to run other small programs similar to `date` (which require no input and have plain text output), all you need to do is replace the appropriate terms and you have a new script!

The Finger Script

The `finger` script is useful to see how forms are handled.

```
#!/bin/sh

FINGER=/usr/ucb/finger

echo Content-type: text/html
echo
if [ -x $FINGER ]; then
    if [ $# = 0 ]; then
        cat << EOM
<HTML><HEAD><TITLE>Finger Gateway</TITLE></HEAD><BODY>
<H1>Finger Gateway</H1>

<ISINDEX>

This is a gateway to "finger". Type a user@host combination in your
browser's search dialog.<P>
EOM
    else
        echo \<PRE\>
        $FINGER "$*"
        echo \</PRE\>
    fi
else
    echo Cannot find finger on this system.
fi
cat << EOM
</BODY></HTML>
EOM
```

Once again, let's take this script apart. Notice the similarities to the `date` script:

1. `#!/bin/sh`

   This command runs the `sh` shell, which will interpret the rest of the script.

2. `FINGER=/usr/ucb/finger`

This sets the variable `FINGER` to the full path where the `finger` program is found.

3. `echo Content-type: text/html`

`echo`

This displays `Content-type: text/html` and a blank line on your screen.

4. `if [ -x $FINGER ]; then`

This code looks to see if there's really a program where the value of FINGER claims there is. If nothing is found at this location, the script proceeds to item 15.

5. `if [ $# = 0 ]; then`

This starts a statement that prints out a header for the `finger` program if no arguments (`$# = 0`) were entered. If arguments were entered, the script jumps to item 11.

6. `cat << EOM`

The script displays what it sees until it reaches the letters `EOM`, then continues normally.

7. `<HTML><HEAD><TITLE>Finger Gateway</TITLE></HEAD><BODY>`

`<H1>Finger Gateway</H1>`

This assigns an HTML header, title, and smaller (`H1`) header line to the results page.

8. `<ISINDEX>`

A precursor to the HTML `<FORM>` command, this will provide an input form block where the user can enter an account to finger.

9. `This is a gateway to "finger." Type a user@host combination in your browser's search dialog.<P>`

This is another HTML formatted statement for the results page.

10. `EOM`

This marks the end of this `if` statement. The script jumps to `fi` if no parameters were entered.

11. `else`

This begins the statement that will happen if item 5 did find parameters.

12. `echo \<PRE\>`

This displays "<PRE>" on the screen. The slashes (/) are necessary to tell the script that you want to actually print the brackets (< and >).

13. `$FINGER "$*"`

This executes the program the `FINGER` variable points to. The `$*` refers to the parameters passed to finger.

14. `echo \</PRE\>`

   `fi`

This displays `</PRE>` on your screen then ends the inner `if` statement.

15. `else`

This continues with the portion of the program that handles the absence of a FINGER program.

16. `echo Cannot find finger on this system.`

This displays `Cannot find finger on this system.` on the screen.

17. `fi`

This ends the outer if/then statement.

18. `cat << EOM`

The script displays everything it sees until it comes to `EOM`.

19. `</BODY></HTML>`

This closes the body of the results page.

20. `EOM`

This command ends the script.

Note that the first four items of this script are virtually identical to the `date` script. You will start every script in a similar way.

The source for the other sample scripts is available in the cgi-bin directory. Take a look at them to see what kinds of programs you can write.

Moving Server Files Where They Need To Be

Now for a bit of cleanup work: you've got everything set up, but your files are still sitting in the directory that you decompressed them to.

Look in your server configuration file and remind yourself of what you used for `ServerRoot`. Now, move all of the following into the appropriate directory (in my case I used `/usr/local/etc/httpd`):

- The file `httpd`

- The `conf` directory

- The `logs` directory

- The `support` directory

- The `cgi-bin` directory

Make sure your `logs` directory's permissions and ownerships are set so it can be written to by whoever the Web server is set to run as. In my case, this user is `ftp`, and the group is `bin` (set with the `User` directive in the configuration file).

Starting Your Web Server

Here's the final step: actually *starting* your Web server! You may want to find a friend out on the Internet to help you test it when it's up.

Set things up so that the server will automatically start every time you boot your system. To set this, do the following:

> **Tip**
>
> If you configured your server as `standalone` instead of `inetd`, you don't need to follow this process.

1. Edit the file `/etc/services`.

2. Add the following line:

```
http            80/tcp
```

III

Setting Up Your Site

You don't have to use port 80, but it's the standard http port, and people will have to use the port number in the URL's going to your links if you use another number.

3. Save and exit /etc/services.

4. Edit the file /etc/inetd.conf.

5. Add the line:

```
http    stream  tcp     nowait ftp /usr/local/etc/httpd/
➥httpd httpd
```

> **Tip**
>
> First, look to see if this line already exists. It may already be there.

> **Caution**
>
> If you didn't use /usr/local/etc/httpd/httpd, be sure to use the proper path.
>
> If you didn't use FTP for the user the server runs as (remember, I used FTP), be sure to replace it with the proper user.

6. Close and save /etc/inetd.conf.

7. Log on as **root**.

> **Tip**
>
> Type **su** at your prompt if you're not already root, and then type your root password.

8. Type **ps aux**.

9. Find the process number for inetd.

10. Type **kill <process#> –HUP**.

> **Note**
>
> You may see some warnings about unsupported features (such as max servers) as your httpd starts up. However, if it starts and works okay otherwise, don't worry about it. I ran into this myself and had no problems.

> **Caution**
>
> If you used su, remember to type **exit** to leave the superuser mode at this point.

From now on, one of the processes that starts automatically when you reboot your system will be httpd.

Setting Up X-Windows

Before we can proceed to setting up Web clients, we'll want to set up X-Windows. There is a non-graphics oriented Web client (lynx), but the beauty of the World Wide Web is in the graphics! X-Windows is to Linux what MS-Windows is to MS-DOS: a graphical interface.

> **Note**
>
> Remember, you need to have purchased the proper monitor and graphics card to run X-Windows (see the Hardware How-To for which hardware is appropriate).
>
> Also, you need to have at least 8M of RAM on the machine you're running X-Windows on, and at least another 8M of swap space. If you're one to do 5 things at a time while using a GUI (Graphical User Interface, like MS-Windows), you'll likely want 16M of RAM.

Setting Up the XF86Config File

The main part to setting up X-Windows is the XF86Config file. Follow the instructions in this section carefully. If you find you're getting confused or are unsure of what to do, consult the documents in /usr/X386/lib/X11/doc.

> **Caution**
>
> Read through this whole setup section before you proceed.

To set up your XF86Config file, do the following:

1. Log in as **root**, then go to the directory /usr/X11R6/bin.

2. Type **SuperProbe**. This program will take a look at your video card and tell you the details you need to know. Write this information (chipset, memory, and RAMDAC) down for use while running the next program.

3. Type **xf86congfig**. This will start a program that makes your life much easier. It configures most of your X-Windows items for you, especially the graphics-intensive ones! Hit Enter to continue and follow the instructions. I'll walk you through the items I entered during my configuration.

4. First is the mouse configuration. I have a Logitech mouse that's Microsoft compatible, so I'll choose the Logitech MouseMan (Microsoft compatible) option—number 6. As a side note, I also select Yes to ChordMiddle, which lets my middle mouse button (it's a 3 button mouse) function as a double-click from the right button. I then say No to Emulate3Buttons because I already have a three button mouse. Finally, I enter my mouse's device name, which is /dev/mouse.

5. Next is keyboard configuration. I don't need International character support for my keyboard, so I select No.

6. Now we reach the monitor section. You'll need your monitor manual for this, unless your monitor is in the following file: /usr/X11R6/lib/X11/doc/Monitors. If it's in this file you can find the numbers you need there. In either your manual or the Monitors file, find the Horizontal and Vertical synch rates your monitor is capable of.

> **Caution**
>
> Don't select a synch rate for either horizontal or vertical that's higher than your monitor can support! You can potentially damage your equipment this way.

You're given a table with ranges to choose from for the Horizontal synch rate. Pick the item in the table that best suits your monitor and card. In my case, I chose 31.1 - 64.3; Monitor that can do 1280×1024 @ 60 Hz. I chose this option because my monitor manual tells me that I can go as high as 64 khz horizontally, and vertically 50 to 90 Hz. The numbers from my manual fall into both of the ranges listed, and my monitor is capable of 1280×1024.

> **Note**
>
> If your monitor doesn't match at all with the Horizontal options offered, you can enter your own numbers (same goes for the Vertical options).

7. Now I choose my Vertical synch rate from a table. Once again, make sure you don't overstretch what your monitor can do! My monitor falls into the option 50 to 90 Hz.

8. Now you need to assign the following information to your monitor:

- *Identifier string*   Give a name to the monitor. It can be technical (Exact type of monitor), or nontechnical (Dee's Monitor).

- *Vendor*   The manufacturer of your monitor. This is displayed, but not actually used by X-Windows.

- *Model*   The model of your monitor. Once again, this is simply for display.

9. Next you configure the video card. You have the option to look through a database, and I chose to do so. Let's say my card is a Paradise/ WD 90C33, I look through the table and find Paradise/WD 90CXX. I choose this option.

> ### Tip
>
> If you're not sure, you can either call the vendor where you bought the machine, the manufacturer who made the card, or pick the generic VGA option.

The program now gives you information about your card, and tells you which server you need to use. It tells me that I'm using the XF86_SVGA server, which is the generic VGA server.

10. Let the program install the server it recommended after you gave it the card information. Let it set up the symbolic link, and let it put the symbolic link in the default location.

11. Now, you're asked how much VRAM (Video RAM) you have. SuperProbe would have told you this information. In my case, it's 1024K (1M).

12. Now, just like you did with the monitor, you need to enter an Identification, Vendor, and Model information. Once again, this is used for display, not by any software.

13. Next it asks you about programmable clock chips. If SuperProbe told you that you have one, you need to select the proper one. If it didn't (my card doesn't have one), then hit Enter to skip this option.

14. Now the setup server probes your monitor and video card (if it refers to clock probing, this is what it means). Let it run its probe program, and you can watch the monitor go through all sorts of graphics modes, with some clicking and static noises that can be a little frightening your first time around. Once it's done, it gives you a list of clock numbers, which are timing values for your monitor and video card. Having this information ahead of time lets you avoid having to go through this process every time you start X-Windows.

15. The next option you're given is to re-order the default graphic modes and order they're used in. In my case, I'm happy with the initial defaults, so I choose OK.

16. Finally, you're asked where to write the config file! Select No for the first option it gives you. Select Yes to write it to the default of /usr/ X11R6/lib/X11/XF86Config. Once finished, the configuration program exits.

Starting X-Windows

Now, to start X-Windows, you just type **startx**. It will start up in your first default graphics mode (see figure 7.2).

Fig. 7.2
Here's the initial
X-Windows
window.

> **Tip**
>
> You can use Alt-+ to switch between graphics modes.

> **Tip**
>
> To get a menu of options from X-Windows, click the left mouse button.

> **Note**
>
> In the upper left hand corner of your window is a box divided into nine parts. Each of these parts is a virtual console, where basically you're using one huge screen that's nine times bigger than your monitor. You can click each of the small parts to jump to a different part of the larger screen.

> **Tip**
>
> To exit X-Windows, click the mouse button for the menu and drag to Exit Fvwm, and then to Yes, really quit.

Installing Netscape

There are a few Web browsers out there you can choose from. There's lynx, which is already installed on your system and is text only. There's also Netscape for Linux, which you can find by FTP at **ftp1.netscape.com** in the file `/netscape/unix/netscape-v112-export.i486-unknown-linux.tar.Z` (the version number may be different than 112 when you go to fetch the file). If you can't get into the server I listed here, you'll be given a list of mirror sites you can use instead.

> **Tip**
>
> You don't have to leave X-Windows to do this process. You can open a shell window within X-Windows. To do this, click your left mouse button (while on the blue background) to get the menu, go to Shells, and choose one of the shells.

When you get the file, uncompress it, gunzip it, and follow the instructions in the README file. These instructions are:

1. Go to the directory /usr/X386/lib/X11. If there isn't an nls directory there, copy the nls directory and its contents that came with Netscape into this directory. The items in this directory are required for Netscape to run, and since you can only get Netscape as a binary instead of as a source, they've provided them just in case.

2. Copy the **netscape** binary to /usr/X11/bin. This is where all X-Windows binaries go. Also copy moz2_0.car (a JAVA applet program Netscape needs to have handy) to /usr/local/netscape/java/classes.

3. Now, let's add Netscape to our X-Windows menu. Go to the directory /usr/X11/lib/X11/fvwm.

4. Edit the file system.fvwmrc. Every Netscape menu is contained in this file, and it includes pointers to every program you'll use.

5. Go to the Applications section. Where in this section you put it is your choice. The items this section contains will show in the menu in the order they're listed in the file.

6. Add the following line:

```
Exec "Netscape" exec netscape &
```

This tells it that when you choose the Netscape menu option, X-Windows should run the program /usr/X11/bin/netscape. Without the &, Netscape would try to replace X-Windows instead of running within X-Windows.

Testing Your Web Server

Now that you have two Web browsers (lynx and Netscape) you can test your server! First, we'll create a very simple Web page, and then we'll use it to test the server out.

Creating a Test Page

Now, I'll show you how to create a simple Web page so you can use it to test out your server. To create this page, do the following:

1. Log in as **root**.

2. Change to the directory you set DocumentRoot to. The default was /usr/local/etc/httpd/htdocs.

3. Edit the file `index.html`.

4. Enter the following:

```
<HTML>

<Head><Title>My first test page</Title></Head>

<BODY>

This is my test page.

</BODY>

</HTML>
```

This is the format for your most basic possible Web page. Note that each item has `<ITEM>` and `</ITEM>`. The first statement opens, the second closes, and what's in the middle is defined by the items surrounding it. For example, everything within the document is within HTML. Everything within HTML is within BODY.

5. Save and exit the page.

Accessing the Page To Test Your Server

Now that you've created your test page, you can use Netscape to access it as your test. To test your server, do the following within X-Windows:

1. Click the left mouse button, and drag down to Netscape (see figure 7.3)

Fig. 7.3
Choosing Netscape from your X-Windows menu.

2. You'll get a license agreement. Read it and click Accept.

3. Netscape will open (see fig. 7.4)

Fig. 7.4
Netscape in Linux
X-Windows.

4. Click the Open button. A dialog box appears.

5. Enter the URL for your main page. For example, **http://www.renaissoft.com/index.html.** Since you're using Netscape, you can drop the index.html. The program assumes it as its default.

You should also test your Web pages from lynx, the text browser. To do so, you just need to get to a shell prompt and type **lynx <URL>** (for example, **lynx http://www.renaissoft.com/index.html**, and this time you would have to include the index.html). The reason you should also test in lynx is that errors you made in your HTML coding don't always show up in Netscape, which is somewhat forgiving. However, they will show up in lynx.

Tip

Help on creating Web pages using HTML can be found all over the Web. A helpful reference is **http://krypton.mankato.msus.edu/reference.html**.

Chapter 8

Installing Gopher Server Software

Some people today think that if you're going to provide information, the Web is the only way to go. This isn't entirely true. The Web is certainly flashy for those who have graphical browsers, but if you are trying to track down information on a specific subject, it's easy to get sidetracked following other interesting links, or to end up at a dead end and have to backtrack. When it comes down to it, the Web is a great general catch-all tool, but if you have specific tasks in mind often a more focused tool is more efficient (e.g., an FTP client instead of a Web client).

Gopher, instead, offers an interface that is just as simple to use as the Web, but with a menu-driven setup enabling you to narrow down your subjects without quite as much sidetracking. Also, because Gopher is text based, it's faster to use and available to those on the Net who don't have access to the fancier tools—so you can reach a wider audience.

If you don't intend to install a Gopher server, feel free to go on to the next chapter. Or, read the first section describing Gopher and then decide whether you want to use a Gopher server on your site.

In this chapter, you learn how to:

- Define a Gopher server
- Configure your Gopher server
- Compile your Gopher server
- Install your Gopher server
- Test your Gopher server

What Is a Gopher Server?

Gopher is somewhat obscure on today's Internet. Developed at the University of Minnesota, it is the predecessor of the World Wide Web and offers several types of documents in an easy-to-navigate format. The primary difference between Gopher and the WWW is that Gopher is strictly a text interface—though it has graphically based clients, Gopher itself is only text. To look at a picture through Gopher, for instance, you must download it first, then pull it up with your graphics viewer.

Gopher's name comes from its function, in that it gets files for you: go-for. Gopher servers are menu based, each server pointing to items on its own site and on other sites; you simply select which menu item you want and press Enter to follow it or get the appropriate file. The type of file the menu points to is unimportant. Like the Web, it can point to text, graphics, word processor, sound files, and so on. It can also, like the Web, use clients' pointers to other applications to follow telnet, FTP, and other such links using the appropriate application.

Configuring Your Gopher Server

As a system administrator, you will discover over time that you have to compile most of the applications that you use on your site. Because of all the assumptions that have to be made in preparing something as a precompiled binary, it's common to find that binaries don't work on many individual setups.

Gopher is one such instance of a program that you need to compile. However, this compilation should be fairly painless.

Finding and Decompressing the Server Source

The Gopher server you're going to use is the University of Minnesota's (the very same university that initially developed Gopher) Internet Gopher+ distribution for Linux version 2.1.3. This is a daemon that will run in the background and wait for Gopher requests to come in.

> **Tip**
>
> If you find that the instructions for unpacking files in this section are too sketchy, the process is covered in more detail in chapter 7, "Installing Web Server Software."

To unpack the file containing everything necessary to compile your Gopher server, do the following:

1. Locate the file `gopher2_1_3.tar.gz` on the CD-ROM.

2. Copy it to `/usr/src`.

3. Type **gunzip gopher2_1_3.tar.gz.**

4. Type **tar –xvf gopher2_1_3.tar.**

Editing Files

The source code for Gopher isn't set up specifically for Linux; instead it's set up for UNIX systems in general. There are special cases included for the more popular UNIX systems so you can choose which one you want to compile it for. Therefore, since you need to tell the source code which UNIX OS you intend to use the binary on, you have some files to edit. And, of course, there are the usual changes you can make before compilation to configure the binary for your particular setup.

There are two files you will need to edit before you begin your compiling: `Makefile.config` and `conf.h`.

Editing Makefile.config

Because this is a generic UNIX server, you need to go through `Makefile.config` and edit it to ensure that it will not only compile for Linux, but also for your needs. As this is not a book on programming or compiling, I am going to show you the quickest ways of getting such programs ported to Linux.

Each part of `Makefile.config` is clearly labeled with commented lines explaining what it's used for. Let's jump past the revision listings and walk through the changes step by step:

Step 1

```
#-----------------------
# Your favorite C compiler
#
# Note that sun international users should use /usr/5bin/cc instead of cc
#
# Sco's cc compiler gives lots of problems that gcc will fix, and gcc
# is now reasonably easy to get running under SCO. Using this removes
# the need for -UM_XENIX -DSCO_UNIX as used for Gopher1.1
# note that if you use gcc, you'll also need -lintl in SCOLIBS
#

CC = cc
```

Although you likely have a `symlink` from `cc` pointing to `gcc` (Gnu C Compiler), just for neatness' sake you may want to change this to `CC = gcc`.

Step 2

```
#------------------------
# System Selection, note that you won't have to edit
# unless you have compilation problems.
#
# Add -DUSG        for System V
#     -DBSD        for BSD
#     -DNO_WAITPID if you have wait3 instead of waitpid()
#     -DUSE_FLOCK  if you have flock instead of fcntl() locking

GSYSTYPE=
```

Linux and BSD are closely compatible versions of UNIX. When you don't have the option of telling a `Makefile` that you're using Linux specifically, BSD is a good choice. Therefore, I'll change this line to `GSYSTYPE=-DBSD`.

Step 3

```
#------------------------
# Compatibility defines
#
# Most of these are automatically defined via the built in compiler
# definitions.  Don't worry about them unless you have problems
#
# Add -DNOSTRSTR    if you don't have strstr()
#     -DNO_STRDUP   if you don't have strdup()
#     -DNO_STRCOLL  if you don't have strcoll()
#     -DNO_TEMPNAM  if you don't have tempnam()
#     -DNO_BZERO    if you have memset()/memcpy instead of bzero()/
#        ➥bcopy()
#     -DNO_GETWD    if you have getcwd() instead of getwd()
#     -DNO_TZSET    if you don't have tzset()
#     -DNO_STRCASECMP if you don't have strcasecmp()
#     -DNO_SETEUID if you have setresuid/setresgid, but not
#        ➥seteuid/setegid
#     -DNO_GETDTABLESIZE if you don't have getdtablesize()
#     -DNO_LINGER   if you can't use linger with setsockopt()
#     -DNO_VFORK    if you have fork() but not vfork()
#     -DNO_PID_T    if your headers don't define pid_t
#     -DNO_STRFTIME if you don't have strftime()
#     -DNO_MKTIME if you don't have mktime()
#     -DNO_WAITPID if you have wait3() instead of waitpid()
#     -DUSE_FLOCK   if you want to use flock() instead of fcntl()
#        ➥locking
#     -DNO_UNISTD_H if you don't have a <unistd.h> header
#     -DNO_LOCALE   if you don't have <locale.h>/setlocale()
#     -DNO_XPGCAT   if you don't have the X/Open catopen() &
#        ➥catgets()

COMPAT =
```

Although you could certainly search through your libraries to make sure you have all of these items, there is another way to take care of this item. Simply leave it, and if the compiler tells you later that you don't have a particular library or function, then you can come back to this portion of the file and set the particular routine as not being there. For example, if the compiler says you don't have strcasecmp(), then you'll come back to Makefile.conf and enter **COMPAT=–DNO_STRCASECMP**. The compiler will take it from there.

Step 4

```
#-----------------------
# Where shall we install stuff?
#
PREFIX            = /usr/local
CLIENTDIR         = $(PREFIX)/bin
CLIENTLIB         = $(PREFIX)/lib
SERVERDIR         = $(PREFIX)/etc
# On SCO manuals are in /usr/man but it's easiest to do a
# symbolic link from /usr/local/man to /usr/man for this and other
   ➥packages
MAN1DIR           = $(PREFIX)/man/man1
MAN5DIR           = $(PREFIX)/man/man5
MAN8DIR           = $(PREFIX)/man/man8
```

> **Tip**
>
> When possible, try to put the programs you install under one of the /usr/local directories. It will make it easier to locate them later!

What these items are set to depends on your preferences. If you keep all your system items in /usr rather than /usr/local, then you'll want to change the value of PREFIX to PREFIX=/usr. If you leave PREFIX as it is but keep your man pages in /usr, then you may want to change the man lines to the following:

```
MAN1DIR           = /usr/man/man1
MAN5DIR           = /usr/man/man5
MAN8DIR           = /usr/man/man8
```

Step 5

```
#-----------------------
# DEBUGGING control…
#
# Comment this to make a slimmer executable…

DEBUGGING = –DDEBUGGING
```

This item turns on the *debugging flag*. Some like to have this flag on at first, compile the file, and run the program (in this case the server). The program will then run with debugging options on to help you find any problems. If the program runs fine, you can then go back into `Makefile.config` and comment this line out by adding a pound sign (#) in front of it (e.g., #DEBUG-GING = –DDEBUGGING). Without the debugging code, a program will be smaller, so it's a good practice to exclude it if you don't need it. Also, if you don't know how to use the debugger and don't have a use for it, don't include it.

Step 6

```
#------------------------
# Uncomment out the following lines to use SOCKS

#SOCKSFLAGS=-Dconnect=Rconnect -Dgetsockname=Rgetsockname
-Dbind=Rbind -Daccept=Raccept -Dlisten=Rlisten -Dselect=Rselect
#SOCKSLIBS=-lsocks
```

If you are using a socks-compliant firewall (firewalls will be discussed in Chapter 13, "Maintaining Linux"), uncomment these lines out (not the header, but the actual variables) by removing the pound signs (#) at the beginning of each line, like so:

```
SOCKSFLAGS=-Dconnect=Rconnect -Dgetsockname=Rgetsockname
-Dbind=Rbind -Daccept=Raccept -Dlisten=Rlisten -Dselect=Rselect
SOCKSLIBS=-lsocks
```

Note

SOCKS is used to create a firewall for your system for maximum security. For more on SOCKS, see appendix E, "Setting Up a Firewall."

Step 7

```
#------------------------
# Optional server features.
#
```

There are a number of server features you can choose to use or not use. To use any one of these, add it to the line as follows:

```
SERVEROPTS= -DSETPROCTITLE -DCAPFILES #-DBIO -DDL -DLOADRESTRICT
```

Note that anything on this line after the # is commented out, so this line originally really reads as follows:

```
SERVEROPTS= -DSETPROCTITLE -DCAPFILES
```

The following are the options you may want to consider:

- # Add -DADD_DATE_AND_TIME to add dates and times to the Gopher titles

  If you want Gopher menu items to show the last time the file they refer to was modified, use this option. You may not want the date and time the file was last modified to be displayed (perhaps you don't want the extra traffic through your server created by the date and time transmissions, or don't want people to see that a file is a year old). To demonstrate what I meant by simply adding the command to the SERVEROPTS line, the following is what you would have if you added the command to the initial default:

  ```
  SERVEROPTS= -DSETPROCTITLE -DCAPFILES -DADD_DATE_AND_TIME
  ```

> **Note**
>
> A number of the options mentioned in this segment that I didn't discuss involve WAIS (Wide Area Information Server). Setting up a WAIS server is not covered in this book, but there is a lot of information available on the subject from the Internet. Check out the following URL for more on WAIS:
>
> **http://www.earn.net/gnrt/wais.html**

Step 8

```
#-----------------------
# Libraries for clients and servers
```

You won't want to touch this part. These are special case statements, and you don't fall into any of the cases listed.

Step 9

```
#-----------------------
# If your hostname command returns the Fully Qualified Domain Name
# (i.e. it looks like foo.bar.edu and not just foo) then make
# the domain name a null string.
```

Log into your system and type **hostname**. If it just gives you the machine name (for example, davinci), then change DOMAIN=.micro.umn.edu to DOMAIN=.your.domain (e.g., DOMAIN=.renaissoft.com). If it returns the full host name (i.e., davinci.renaissoft.com), then change the DOMAIN statement to DOMAIN= to make it a null statement.

III

Setting Up Your Site

Step 10

\# SERVERDIR is the default directory for gopherd.

If you don't want your default gopherd directory to be gopher-data, change the statement SERVERDATA= /gopher-data to reflect the directory you want to use.

Step 11

\# SERVERPORT is the default port for gopherd.

If you don't want your default Gopher port to be 70, change the statement SERVERPORT= 70 to reflect the port number you want to use. Keep in mind, however, that it's often a good idea to stick with the default port because it makes it easier for people to locate your services.

Tip

If you do change the port from the default, go into the /etc/services file and change the port the gopher server is defined to use in this file to match the new one you assigned to SERVERPORT.

Editing conf.h

Although Makefile.config mostly deals with server configuration, conf.h mostly deals with client configuration. You will compile your system's Gopher client from the same code as the server, so make sure you go through this file carefully as well.

Caution

In this file, commented sections begin with /*, and end with */. Any line that starts with a pound sign (#) is *not* commented out in conf.h.

Once again, let's walk through the changes you will want—or need—to make, step by step:

Step 1

* Defaults for the client program

These two items define the home Gopher that a user's Gopher client will first contact upon starting up. Right now, they're set to two different aliases for the Mother Gopher at UMN (University of Minnesota). If you would rather have them connect to another home Gopher, go ahead and change one of these items. The Gopher server is determined randomly between CLIENT1_HOST and CLIENT2_HOST.

The variables CLIENT1_PORT and CLIENT2_PORT go with these items. Make sure to set these values appropriately if you change the host settings above (if you're not sure, the default port is 70 so try that first).

> ### Tip
>
> If you don't want two different home Gopher possibilities, just set `CLIENT2_PORT=0`.

Step 2

```
* Default language for client when multiple language views are
➥available
```

The language that is preset is English (US). If you would rather use another language from the available listing (Danish, German, English (UK), Spanish, French, Italian, Japanese, Norwegian, or Swedish), add a /* at the beginning of the English (US) definition line and erase the /* at the beginning of the line for the language you would like to use.

Step 3

```
* Define this if you want a To: prompt containing the
➥administrator's
 * address included for the gripe command.
```

If you want people to be able to easily modify the userid in the To line when they go to send a comment regarding a Gopher item, set this item. To do so, uncomment it. For example, it is in the file originally as

```
/* #define MODIFIABLE_GRIPE_TO /* */
```

You will want to change it to

```
#define MODIFIABLE_GRIPE_TO
```

Step 4

```
/* Define LOCAL_GRIPE_ADMINISTRATOR and use your site's Gopher
➥Administrator
 * address if you want gripes sent there for Gopher0 servers (or
➥Gopher+
 * servers without Admin info for the link).
```

If you want people to be able to easily send comments to the admin of your Gopher server, set this item. It is in the file originally as

```
/* #define LOCAL_GRIPE_ADMINISTRATOR "<GopherAdmin@host.domain>" /**/
```

You will want to uncomment it out, and configure it to match with your system. For example, if I was going to be the Gopher admin, I would set this to be

```
#define LOCAL_GRIPE_ADMINISTRATOR "<dee@renaissoft.com>"
```

Tip

Or, you could leave it as GopherAdmin and add an alias to your /etc/aliases file. For example, I'd add GopherAdmin: dee

---

Yes, I didn't touch on a lot of this file. Keep in mind, though, that several pages of it deal with configuration items specific to VMS systems, and you are obviously not running a VMS system.

Compiling and Installing the Gopher Client and Server

Compared to configuring Makefile.config and conf.h, actually compiling and installing the server and client can be a piece of cake.

Compiling the Client and Server

Now that you've configured both Makefile.config and conf.h, you can compile your Gopher client and server. Take your time handling any compilation errors—though there shouldn't be many!

To compile your Gopher server and client, do the following:

1. Log in as **root**.

2. Enter the directory where the Gopher files are stored (such as **/tmp/gopher2_1_3**).

3. Copy Makefile.config to Makefile. When you go to the next step, your system won't recognize Makefile.config as the file to use. It wants Makefile.

4. Type **make**.

5. Watch the messages the compiler gives you.

6. Deal with any problems that come up, and return to step 3 if you have to fix something before it will compile.

Installing the Server and Client

Installing your server and client, once you've configured and compiled them, is as simple as typing **make install** in the same directory that you did the compilation.

Setting Up and Testing Your Gopher Service

Now that you've got your Gopher server and client installed, you can start setting up its menus and the files you want to offer. Then, you can use the Gopher client you installed at the same time as the server to test it.

> **Tip**
>
> The same structure discussion here can apply to arranging your Web site as well, covered in chapter 7, "Installing Web Server Software."

Putting Files in Place

To put your files in place so your Gopher server can offer them, start in your gopher-data directory. This directory acts as your Home (main) Gopher menu, and is the first menu people will see if they tell their client to go to your server. Take a moment to decide how you might want to present your files. Maybe sketch out on paper what you want your directories to look like, or at least far enough to give you a general feel for how you want to lay them out (see figure 8.1).

First, let's create the directory menu items. To do this, simply create the direc-

Fig. 8.1
An example
partial Gopher
menu tree.

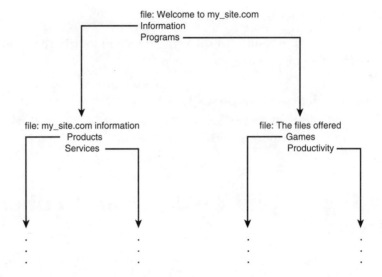

tories themselves. Following the example shown in figure 8.1—the first directories I would create inside the `gopher-data` directory are:

    Information

    Programs

Tip

You can have spaces in file names, so if you want to have a menu item with more
than one word, simply create the directory the way you want the menu item to look.

Note

If you put spaces in directory or file names, you may find that when you try to create
these directories and files they come out as a list of separate files and directories. Plus,
if you try to change into the directory or access the file you get the error `Too many`
`arguments`. If this is the case, you need to put quotes ("") around the file or directory
name so your system understands that it's all in one piece.

Now, to finish making the directory structure in my Gopher server look like
the one in the figure, I'll go inside the `Information` directory and create the
directories `Products` and `Services`. Then, I'll back up and go inside the `Pro-`
`grams` directory and create the directories `Games` and `Productivity`.

Next, all I need to to is put the files in place. I can quickly write up the three files referenced in figure 8.1 and put them in the proper directories. These should be text files if at all possible so people can easily read them. The following files go into the following directories:

- `Welcome to my_site.com` goes into the `gopher-data` directory

- `my_site.com Information` goes into the `gopher-data/Information` directory

- The `files offered` goes into the `gopher-data/Programs` directory

Testing Your Gopher Server

To test your Gopher server, you can use the client you installed at the same time you installed the server. However, first let's test the client itself and make sure it's working. All you need to do is log into an account and type **gopher** to start the client (see fig. 8.2). If you set CLIENT1_HOST and CLIENT2_HOST, the client will randomly choose between the two. If you only set CLIENT1_HOST, the client will go straight to that Gopher server.

```
      Internet Gopher Information Client v2.0.16
         Home Gopher server: gopher2.tc.umn.edu

-->  1.  Information About Gopher/
     2.  Computer Information/
     3.  Discussion Groups/
     4.  Fun & Games/
     5.  Internet file server (ftp) sites/
     6.  Libraries/
     7.  News/ ‘
     8.  Other Gopher and Information Servers/
     9.  Phone Books/
    10.  Search Gopher Titles at the University of Minnesota <?>
    11.  Search lots of places at the University of Minnesota  <?>
    12.  University of Minnesota Campus Information/



Press ? for Help, q to Quit                          Page: 1/1
```

Fig. 8.2
The main menu of the Mother Gopher, the Gopher at the University of Minnesota, itself.

Once you've verified the client is working, take it to your own server. If your server isn't defined as the home server, you can turn your client there by either starting it with gopher `<name of your Gopher server>` (e.g., gopher `gopher.renaissoft.com`), or if the client's already open choose o to open a new Gopher server (see fig. 8.3).

III

Setting Up Your Site

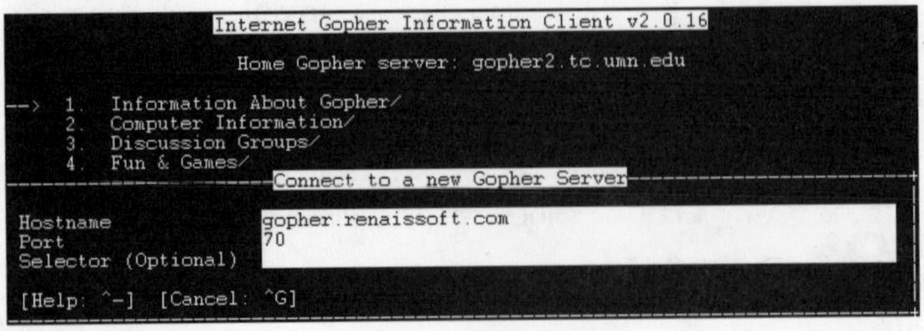

Fig. 8.3

Filled-in dialog box where you enter the machine and port of the Gopher server you want.

```
    ┌─────────────────────────────────────────────────────────┐
    │        Internet Gopher Information Client v2.0.16         │
    │         Home Gopher server: gopher2.tc.umn.edu            │
    │                                                           │
    │ --> 1.  Information About Gopher/                          │
    │     2.  Computer Information/                              │
    │     3.  Discussion Groups/                                │
    │     4.  Fun & Games/                                       │
    │ ─────────────────────Connect to a new Gopher Server────── │
    │                                                           │
    │  Hostname            gopher.renaissoft.com                │
    │  Port                70                                   │
    │  Selector (Optional)                                      │
    │                                                           │
    │  [Help: ^-]  [Cancel: ^G]                                 │
    └─────────────────────────────────────────────────────────┘
```

Enter the address of your Gopher server (once again, e.g., gopher.renaissoft.com). Enter the port if it's different from the default of 70. Press Enter to go to the main menu for the new server (see fig. 8.4).

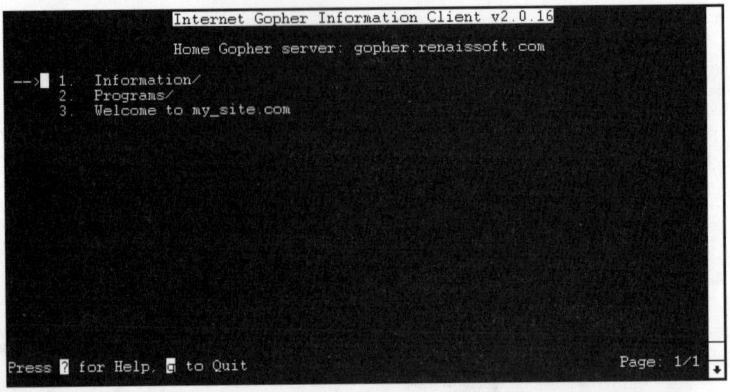

Fig. 8.4

The main menu for my example Gopher server.

```
    ┌─────────────────────────────────────────────────────────┐
    │        Internet Gopher Information Client v2.0.16         │
    │         Home Gopher server: gopher.renaissoft.com         │
    │                                                           │
    │ -->  1.  Information/                                      │
    │      2.  Programs/                                         │
    │      3.  Welcome to my_site.com                           │
    │                                                           │
    │                                                           │
    │                                                           │
    │                                                           │
    │                                                           │
    │                                                           │
    │                                                           │
    │ Press ? for Help, Q to Quit                   Page: 1/1   │
    └─────────────────────────────────────────────────────────┘
```

From here, wander through your server. Make sure you can enter all of the directories and download all the files. Try it from a non-root account, and ask someone to try it from outside your site as well. If you or someone else has problems accessing items, make sure the permissions are correct (the files are readable).

Chapter 9

Installing UseNet Server Software

Reading news and participating in UseNet and other news hierarchies is almost as popular an activity on the Internet as reading and writing e-mail. News is a way for people to participate in worldwide discussion forums or simply follow how various issues are viewed in other places.

Now is the time to decide whether you need to run a news server to handle news on your own site. If you do, it's time to install it!

In this chapter, you learn the following:

- How to decide whether you need a news server

- How to decide which kind of news server you want to run

- How to configure your news server

- How to verify your news server

Do You Need a News Server on Your Site?

Many sites don't need to run their own news servers. Instead, their news software is configured to access the news server of their own provider. While this process takes a bit longer on the user's end, it saves a lot of your system resources for other tasks.

The following are two different types of news service that your site can offer:

- Organizational news server, which occasionally downloads limited newsgroups for your users

- Full news server, which passes news onto other sites as well

Do You Want To Run an Organizational News Server?

Disk space, bandwidth, and your users' privacy are important considerations for you when deciding if you want to run an organizational news server.

Disk Space Considerations

Depending on the number of groups your users want access to and how much traffic each of these groups has, news can take up a small or huge amount of disk space. If you know which groups people on your site want access to, you can get an idea of the amount of material that comes through them on a regular basis by reading the file USENET_Readership_report for whichever month you are curious about. You can find this file via FTP at **rtfm.mit.edu** in the directory /pub/usenet-by-hierarchy/news/lists. The following is an example of what you will see in this file:

```
+-- Estimated total number of people who read the group, worldwide.
|       +-- Actual number of readers in sampled population
|       |       +-- Propagation: how many sites receive this group at all
|       |       |       +-- Recent traffic (messages per month)
|       |       |       |       +-- Recent traffic (megabytes per month)
|       |       |       |       |       +-- Crossposting percentage
|       |       |       |       |       |       +-- Cost ratio: $US/month/rdr
|       |       |       |       |       |       |       +-- Share: % of newsrders
|       |       |       |       |       |       |       |    who read this group.
|       |       |       |       |       |       |       |
V       V       V       V       V       V       V       V
 1 510000  3373  91%    39     0.6    22%  0.00  5.7%  news.announce.newusers
 2 260000  2759  57% 11408    11.5    46%  0.02  4.6%  alt.sex
 3 240000  1796  80%    78     0.3     0%  0.00  3.0%  rec.humor.funny
 4 220000  2508  51%  8307    58.7    34%  0.12  4.2%  alt.sex.stories
 5 200000  1348  88%  2451     0.5    99%  0.00  2.3%  news.answers
 6 180000  1205  87%     1     0.0     0%  0.00  2.0%  news.announce.important
 7 170000  2218  47% 18619   829.6    25%  2.00  3.7%  alt.binaries.pictures.erotica
 8 170000  1244  80% 34342    51.9    24%  0.22  2.1%  misc.jobs.offered
 9 160000  1119  87%  8296    14.0     2%  0.07  1.9%  news.newusers.questions
10 150000  1104  83%  5161     7.0    21%  0.03  1.8%  comp.lang.c
```

In the July 95 version of the USENET Readership Report, 3095 groups are listed, so it's fairly easy to get a feel for most of the groups your users might want to read.

When you have the raw numbers in front of you, it just takes a bit of math to figure out how much disk space a group might occupy. Take a look at the group **misc.jobs.offered.** The data passing through this group in a month totaled 51.9M. If you look at a 30 day month, that is 1.73M per day. If you want to be able to keep news on your site for a week (7 days) before it expires, then this group will consume around 12.11M of hard drive space as a general rule.

This is just one group, albeit one that takes up much more disk space than many pure text groups (such as **news.answers,** which only requires .5M in a month of traffic). However, as you can see with a quick glance at the top 10 groups listed above, if you are going to carry binary groups, you are going to have to be even more concerned about space!

If you don't think you'll have the hard drive space to handle the group load, consider using your uplink's news server—especially if you feel you aren't able to purchase the kind of hard drive space you really need to meet your site's needs. When everything is up and running, you can take a look at how much hard drive space you have available and determine whether you want to install a news server.

Tip

Traffic in newsgroups can fluctuate from month to month. If you're particularly concerned about disk space, you may want to average the traffic for the groups you're looking at over a few months' worth of samplings.

Tip

You can mount /var/spool/news from a hard drive dedicated to that directory just like you can do with /home. The process for mounting remote directories is discussed in chapter 5, "Setting Up Your Site for General Use."

Bandwidth Considerations

If you run your own news server, your site must periodically download the new news for every group you carry (e.g., once an hour). If you have a "slow" connection, such as one at 28.8 kbps, and unless you carry a minimal number of groups (high traffic binary groups count for more than one in this case), your news transfer can take a painful bite out of the bandwidth you have available every time your site downloads new news postings. Even with an ISDN connection at 64 kbps, a large amount of news traffic can take a chunk out of your bandwidth for every download.

To get a feel for the effect your news traffic will have on your bandwidth, use the calculations you made in the previous section. If you calculate that your news traffic will be around 750M per month, that's 25M per day (for a 30 day month). If you download new news posts once per hour, that's approximately 1M per hour.

If your connection is at 64 kbps, it will take approximately 2 minutes for 1M of data to pass through your connection if only news traffic is traveling at the time (time taken from experience). So, once an hour for an average of two minutes, your connection would be rather slow until the news transfer finishes.

This in itself can be annoying if you are trying to do something bandwidth-intensive when the news transfer hits. The more groups your users want, the more news traffic you will have. So if you find that you need to carry 2M or 3M worth of news, suddenly your bandwidth is slow for 4 or 6 minutes. That doesn't count anything else you and your users are doing that also eats up bandwidth, which will slow the news transfer down.

Note

Another solution to this problem is to download news from your feed site only at off times. The longer you wait between news downloads, the longer it will take. However, if you only update your newsgroups at 1 AM and 5 AM, for example, it won't matter too much to most folks if your bandwidth is slowed down for an hour or two. It simply depends on how often you want to have news updates available to yourself and your users.

However, if your provider has limited bandwidth, they may not appreciate the long drain on their resources.

User Privacy Considerations

Although it's easy to talk about asking your users for the newsgroups they want to read, or asking them to tell you if they want you to add anything, it can be an invasion of their privacy to do so. For example, a user may want to read or participate in a counseling newsgroup of some sort, and it's really none of the provider's business. After all, users can post anonymously, so there is no need for anyone to know who is reading and/or participating in a particular group.

Dealing with this issue is tricky. You may seriously want to consider using your provider's news server unless you have one of the following:

- A small personal site where the few users really don't mind telling you what groups they want

- A site where you have a reason to only offer a select list of groups, such as a business site that carries only groups in its field

Note

Privacy is an important issue for Internet users. No matter how many users you have, it is important to try to deal with them in a professional manner as a system administrator. Unless there is a serious reason to do so, you should not look into users' home directories.

If you offer paying accounts and require users to list the newsgroups they want to read, then people may decide against using your site.

An excellent place to start looking regarding legalities and privacy issues on the Internet is the Electronic Freedom Foundation's (EFF's) Web pages. This group, according to the first portion of their main Web page, is "A non-profit civil liberties organization working in the public interest to protect privacy, free expression, and access to online resources and information." The URL for the EFF is **http://www.eff.org/**.

Do You Want To Run a Full News Server?

If you have a large site with large bandwidth (e.g., T1), you may want to run your own full news server. By full news server, I mean a server just like your provider's: one that not only brings news in to your site, but passes news on to other sites, who may yet pass it on to other sites (see fig. 9.1).

A full news server always has a connection open to its feed site and the site it feeds, using a program called NNTPlink. Your provider has certain requirements that must be met by those who want to connect to their news server. Sometimes they may require a T1 or better, but there is no standard. This is something you will have to ask your provider about.

III

Setting Up Your Site

Fig. 9.1
Full news servers
take in news from
a feed and pass it
on to other sites,
who may pass it
along as well.

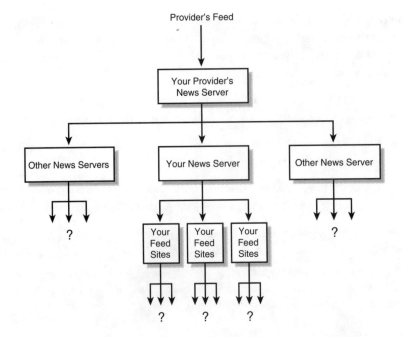

Of course, your newsfeed will also require an immense amount of disk space if you're going to carry a full feed. You'll need several gigabytes of disk space to store all of the news you'll be carrying. So, basically, unless you are running a large provider or company site, you probably won't have the necessary resources for a full feed.

Configuring Your News Server

The news server you are going to use (if you choose to run one) is INN. Fortunately, Slackware handles the actual installation for you, so this is one server you won't have to compile! There is quite a bit of configuration to do, however, so take it one step at a time.

Assigning Mail Aliases

You need two mail aliases on your site for INN: news and usenet. (In this example, you point them to root.) To add these, do the following:

1. Log in as **root**.

2. Change to the directory /usr/lib.

3. Edit the file aliases.

4. To add the news alias so that it points to root (to enable people to send e-mail to the user news and have that mail go to the system administrator), add the following line:

```
news: root
```

5. To add the usenet alias so that it points to root (because some programs and scripts want to send mail to usenet instead of news), add the following line:

```
usenet: root
```

6. Save and exit the file.

Now, to make sure your system has the new version of the aliases file in memory, type **newaliases** and press Enter.

Adding INN to System Startup

With most of the servers you'll deal with in this book, you add them to the file inetd. In this case, INN goes in the file rc.local. The reason for this is that the servers listed in inetd are started when they're needed; for example, when someone tries to get into your system via Gopher, the Gopher server starts up and handles the request. INN, on the other hand, sits quietly in the background all of the time, so it needs to be listed in rc.local among the other startup processes. The file rc.local is the last system startup script that's run when you're booting your machine. It's used to start up daemons and servers.

To add INN to the startup items for your system, do the following:

1. Log in as **root**.

2. Change to the /etc/rc.d directory.

3. Edit the file rc.local.

4. To add INN to the list of items to run at startup, add the following line:

```
/usr/lib/news/etc/rc.news
```

The program rc.news is your INN startup script.

5. Save and exit the file.

III

Setting Up Your Site

Adding INN to Your *crontab*

To automate a few of INN's duties so you don't have to make sure it does them, add some things to your system's crontab. A sample containing some recommendations is included with INN in the file crontab-news, as follows:

```
SHELL=/bin/sh
#
MAILTO=root
#
#==============================================================================
#
# INN-1.4 (Inter Net News)
#
#       Sample crontab file by andreas@knobel.knirsch.de (Andreas Klemm)
#
#       copy it to /usr/spool/cron/crontabs/news
#
#       Reboot your system or
#       kill and restart the crond job, to activate this file
#
#==============================================================================
#
#------------------------------------------------------------------------------
# send news batches to your news feed
#------------------------------------------------------------------------------
#
0,15,30,45 * * * *      /usr/lib/news/bin/sendbatch -c manlobbi > /dev/null
#
#------------------------------------------------------------------------------
# Daily housekeeping … expires news and other things …
#------------------------------------------------------------------------------
#
0 22 * * *              /usr/lib/news/bin/news.daily < /dev/null
#
#------------------------------------------------------------------------------
# offer spooled news - that was spooled into the incoming directory when the
# INNd server wasn't available - again to the INNd server.
#------------------------------------------------------------------------------
#
15 * * * *              /usr/lib/news/rnews -U
```

Take the following quick walk through this file to see what it does (note that there's one change you'll definitely want to make):

1. SHELL=/bin/sh

This line tells your system to start up an sh shell and use that shell to interpret the rest of the file.

2. `MAILTO=root`

This tells your system to send any mail regarding error messages to root.

3. `0,15,30,45 * * * * /usr/lib/news/bin/sendbatch -c manlobbi > /dev/null`

This tells your system to send any outgoing news batches to your news feed every hour on the hour, and at 15, 30, and 45 minutes past the hour.

Change `manlobbi` to an alias you'd like to use for your provider's news server. You'll soon add this alias to your newsfeeds file.

4. `0 22 * * */usr/lib/news/bin/news.daily < /dev/null`

This tells your system to do its daily housekeeping chores (i.e., expiring news) every day at exactly 22:00 (10 PM). The exact tasks covered under "daily housekeeping" are listed in the file `news.daily` shown above.

5. `15 * * * */usr/lib/news/rnews -U`

This tells your system to hand any spooled news to INNd that, for some reason, couldn't be dealt with in the previous attempt. This is done every hour at 15 minutes after.

If you don't like the intervals assigned to any of the processes above, feel free to change them to match your preferences and needs. (`cron` files are covered in more detail in Chapter 5, "Setting Up Your Site for General Use").

Making Sure Newsreaders Can Find the Necessary Configuration Files

A lot of newsreaders are hardcoded to look for news configuration files in `/usr/local/lib/news`. However, your configuration files are in `/usr/lib/news`.

An easy way to ensure that people won't have problems when they use a particular newsreader is by using a *symbolic (soft) link*. A soft link creates a pointer to a file such that if someone tries to access the pointer, they are redirected to the file it references.

Create a soft link from the location some clients expect to find your news configuration files, to where yours actually are. The syntax is:

```
ln -s /original_path /non-existant_path_to_point_from
```

III

Setting Up Your Site

Therefore, type:

```
ln -s /usr/lib/news /usr/local/lib/news
```

> **Caution**
>
> Be sure to enter the paths for symbolic links in the correct order! Otherwise, you will
> erase the original file you want to link to.

Modifying Your News Configuration Files

There are a number of configuration files found in /usr/lib/news that need to
be set up to meet your system's requirements. Let's go through them one by
one and see what needs to be changed.

The expire.ctl File

The expire.ctl file is used to tell INN how article expiration is to be handled
(i.e., how long to keep an old article around before removing it from the hard
drive). Take a look at the example file first, and then I'll discuss the modifications you may want to make:

```
##  $Revision: 1.8 $
##  expire.ctl - expire control file
##  Format:
##      /remember/:<keep>
##      <patterns>:<modflag>:<keep>:<default>:<purge>
##  First line gives history retention; other lines specify expiration
##  for newsgroups. Must have a "*:A:…" line which is the default.
##      <patterns>      wildmat-style patterns for the newsgroups
##      <modflag>       Pick one of M U A -- modifies pattern to be only
##                  moderated, unmoderated, or all groups
##      <keep>          Mininum number of days to keep article
##      <default>      Default number of days to keep the article
##      <purge>         Flush article after this many days
##  <keep>, <default>, and <purge> can be floating-point numbers or the
##  word "never."  Times are based on when received unless -p is used;
##  see expire.8

##  If article expires before 14 days, we still remember it for 14 days in
##  case we get offered it again. Depending on what you use for the INNd
##  -c flag and how paranoid you are about old news, you might want to
##  make this 28, 30, etc.
/remember/:14

##  Keep for 1-10 days, allow Expires headers to work.
*:A:1:8:never

##  Some particular groups stay forever.
dc.dining*:A:never:never:never
uunet*:A:never:never:never
```

Now it's time to configure your expiration times for news articles. Common choices are anywhere from three days to a week, depending mostly on how much hard drive space there is available to store the files. You can even set some hierarchies to expire differently than others, which is useful for large binaries groups that may threaten to overrun your drive space in only a matter of two days.

The following is an example of setting up an `expire.ctl` file and the decision process that goes into it:

1. `/remember/:25`

News articles aren't sent to a sight just once. As they circulate, they'll often pass through your site a number of times. The `remember` function retains the history of the article (the official article number and other identifying features) after the article has expired.

The line above tells your news server to remember a particular article for 25 days from the time it arrived at your site. This ensures that within those 25 days, you won't be storing another copy of the article.

2. `*:A:1:5:25`

This is a line defining what the server should do with articles for particular groups. You *must* have one line of this structure, starting with an asterisk (*:A), which refers to all groups, moderated and unmoderated. It's the only way the server will know how to handle groups to which you don't assign specific expiration procedures.

The line reads as follows, from left to right:

- `*`: All groups. You can use wild cards in this statement to refer to group hierarchies instead of complete group names.

- `A`: All groups once again, but this time choose among A (All), U (Unmoderated), or M (Moderated).

- `1`: All articles should be kept a minimum of one day. You could also put `never` here if you don't ever want articles expired (a quick way to run out of hard drive space).

- `5`: Sets the default to five days for the period that articles are kept. You could also put `never` here if you don't ever want articles expired (once again, a quick way to run out of hard drive space).

- `25`: Sets the maximum amount of time an article is kept to 25 days (you can also use `never` here if you'd like).

III

Setting Up Your Site

3. `alt.binaries.pictures.*:A:1:3:5`

Here, I've set everything in the `alt.binaries.pictures` hierarchy (instead of all groups), both moderated and unmoderated groups, to have a minimum stay of one day, default stay of three days, and a maximum stay of five days. I made this choice because the posts that go through pictures groups are huge, and I can't afford to have too many days' worth filling up my hard drive.

I could continue with the list, assigning varying expiration rules to different hierarchies or specific groups. You can go as far as assigning different times to each group you carry.

The hosts.nntp File

The `hosts.nntp` file tells your server what sites it gets news from. An example of this file is:

```
##   $Revision: 1.4 $
##   hosts.nntp - names and addresses that feed us news
##   Format
##       <host>:
##       <host>:<password>
##   <host> can be a name or IP address; no wildcards. Any hosts not
##   listed here are handed off to nnrpd.
# news.foo.com:
```

All you need to have in this file is the site that feeds you news. If it doesn't require a password, you just need the site name followed by a colon, as follows:

```
machine.site.com:
```

If it does require a password, you need to include it after the colon, as follows:

```
machine.site.com:Password
```

The INN.conf File

The `INN.conf` file tells your site the important data it needs to know about itself, such as its domain and host. The example file is as follows:

```
##   $Revision: 1.5 $
##   INN.conf -- INN configuration data
##   Format:
##       <parameter>:<whitespace><value>
```

```
##   Used by various programs and libINN. The following parameters are defined:
##      domain          Local domain, without leading period.
##      fromhost        What to put in the From line; default is FQDN
##                      of the local host.
##      moderatormailer Where to mail moderated postings, if not found
##                      in the moderators file; see moderators(5).
##      pathhost        What to put in the Path and Xref headers; default
##                      is FQDN of the local host.
##      organization    If $ORGANIZATION doesn't exist. What to put in
##                      the Organization header if blank.
##      server          If $NNTPSERVER doesn't exist. Local NNTP server
##                      host to connect to.
##
# organization:     A poorly-installed InterNetNews site
# server:           news
#
organization:     Andreas Klemm, 41469 Neuss, Germany
server:           knobel.knirsch.de
domain:           knirsch.de
```

For example, I would fill the values of this file in as follows:

1. `domain: renaissoft.com`

Don't include a host name here. It just wants the domain name you're registered with InterNIC.

2. `fromhost: renaissoft.com`

The default here is the FQDN (Fully Qualified Domain Name) of the host. For example, if I didn't fill a `fromhost` in, and I posted from the machine `catherine`, then the `From line` of articles coming out from your site would show as `catherine.renaissoft.com`. Because I set it to just `renaissoft.com`, the machine name will not be included in postings.

3. `moderatormailer: dee`

Generally, you'll use the moderators file instead of this feature. However, if you only have one moderator on your site, then all posts to moderated groups will go to that one person, so you can bypass the moderators file by setting it here.

4. `pathhost: renaissoft.com`

As with `fromhost`, the default for `pathhost` is the FQDN (Fully Qualified Domain Name) of the host. `Pathhost` sets what machine shows in the path and Xref headers of articles that go out from your site.

5. `organization: Renaissoft Enterprises`

If the user doesn't set an organization in his own news configuration files, then the organization header contains what's set here. Often the default is the name of the provider, or if it's a business site, the name of the business.

6. server: news.renaissoft.com

If the user doesn't set a local news server to connect to in his news configuration files, then his server is whatever is set here. The host name, news, is an alias I set to my server machine so the user doesn't have to know the exact machine or the port number that the news server is on.

Tip

You'll at least want to include definitions for the variables domain, server, and organization. The rest only if you want or need them.

The moderators File

The moderators file tells your system where to mail posts for moderated groups to their moderators instead of trying to post them directly to the group. The example moderators file is as follows:

```
## $Revision: 1.4 $
## Mailing addresses for moderators.
## Format:
##      <newsgroup>:<pathname>
## First match found is used.
##      <newsgroup>
Shell-style newsgroup pattern or specific newsgroup
##      <pathname>      Mail address, "%s" becomes newgroup name with dots
## changed to dashes.
gnu.*:%s@tut.cis.ohio-state.edu
*:%s@uunet.uu.net
```

The line assigning the reroute address, from left to right (using the first one listed as an example), is a follows:

- gnu.* is the newsgroup's name, or a hierarchy with asterisk (*) wild card.

- %s represents the newsgroup's name, but with hyphens (-) instead of periods (.) to break up the hierarchy. This value is used as the username in the e-mail address the post is rerouted to.

- @tut.cis.ohio-state.edu represents the host e-mail address to which the post is rerouted.

If you look at the last line in the moderators file, you will see it covers all newsgroups because of the asterisk in the first field. Therefore, the only lines you need to add are those for any local moderated groups you have at your site.

The newsfeeds File

The newsfeeds file defines how you distribute incoming news to the sites you feed. The basic structure for feed definition is:

```
site[/exclude,exclude…]\

:pattern,pattern…[/distrib,distrib…]\

:flag,flag…\

:param
```

The terms used above each have a particular function, as follows:

- site

    The full name of one of your feed sites (the name it uses to identify itself in the path lines of articles it passes through or posts), or an alias if you're referring to special local items, such as archivers and gateways. This item is used by your server to decide whether each article that comes in should be forwarded to the sites you feed. If it doesn't see this name in the article's path header, it is forwarded.

    To avoid confusion, if you use an alias for a local item (e.g., if you have an archiver program that you use to archive posts from certain groups, so use the alias archive for it), be sure to put an exclamation point (!) at the end of it. If I just used archive, and there's actually a news site out there with the word archive in its name (e.g., **news.archive.com**), any post that came through **news.archive.com** won't be resent to your archive because INNd will think it has already been there. If you use archive! instead, there's no risk of having your alias mistaken for an actual host name.

- exclude

    You can use this item to tell your server not to forward articles to a particular site if they've already passed through other specific sites listed in the paths.

- `pattern`

  Use this item to define what newsgroups you pass along to the sites you feed news to. The default is to just pass everything, which is fine if that's what the site you're feeding wants. If they don't want specific groups or hierarchies, put an exclamation point (!) in front of it (e.g., if they don't want anything in the alt.binaries.pictures hierarchy, you would add `!alt.binaries.pictures.*`). If they don't want all of the groups your site takes in, then you can specify what groups or hierarchies to pass on by listing them as usual (e.g., if they want everything in the comp, news, and rec.arts hierarchies, you would use `comp.*`, `news.*`, `rec.arts.*`).

  If they want nothing in a specific hierarchy except one particular group, you can assign this as well. For example, if they wanted everything in rec, but nothing in rec.pets except rec.pets.cats, you would use the line `rec.*`, `!rec.pets.*`, `rec.pets.cats`.

- `distrib`

  If used, checks the Distribution header of an article for the following items, in order:

  1. If the Distribution header matches anything you list here in the `distrib` section, the article is forwarded to the news server the `distrib` section relates to.

  2. If the Distribution header matches anything you list in the `distrib` section with an exclamation point in front of it, the article is not forwarded to the news server the `distrib` section relates to.

  3. If the Distribution header doesn't match anything you listed in the `distrib` section, and you don't have anything in the `distrib` section with an explanation point in front of it, the article is not forwarded to the news server the `distrib` section relates to.

  4. If the Distribution header doesn't match anything you listed in the `distrib` section, but there are items listed that start with an exclamation point, the article is forwarded to the news server the `distrib` section relates to.

  The default, if you don't include any `distrib`s, is to send all articles in the groups to which they subscribe to all of your sites.

  - `flag`

This item contains the miscellaneous other parameters available to you in a newsfeed definition. The flags (listed in table 9.1) you list can be in any order, and if you need to include a number with one, include it directly after the flag as part of the flag (no space between the flag and the number).

Table 9.1 Flags You Can Use in the Newsfeeds File

Flag	Parameters	What It Does	Example
<	size	Defines the maximum size (in bytes) of an article you can forward to the site whose feed you are defining. If you don't list a value here, the default is forward articles of any size.	<size1000 Forward all articles smaller than 1000 bytes
Ad		Only forwards an article if it contains a distribution.	Ad header
Ap		Tells the server to not check the path header of articles before passing them on.	Ap
B	high/low	Sets the size of a buffer for use when large posts come through. Eliminates waiting for files to be written completely before they can be dealt with. Has two parameters, the first being the number of bytes the server should have waiting before it starts draining its buffer. The second is the number of bytes it should get down to before it stops writing and returns to buffering. The default value is no buffering.	B5000/2000
F	name	Use this to assign the name of the file your server will use if it needs to spool news for the site whose feed you're defining. The default path is /usr/spool/news. The default file is togo.	Fspooled

(continues)

Setting Up Your Site

III

Table 9.1 Continued			
Flag	**Parameters**	**What It Does**	**Example**
G	count	Defines a maximum number of groups a post can be cross posted to and still be passed on to the site you're defining the feed for.	G10
H	count	Defines a maximum number of sites a post can have in its path line and still be passed on to the site you're defining the feed for. The default for count is 1.	H20
I	size	Defines the size (in bytes) of the internal file feed buffer. This buffer is used when there are more files trying to feed in than your system allows. Once the buffer reaches the size you set, the system starts writing the data out to files.	I1000
Nm		Use this item if you only want moderated groups for the section you're defining.	Nm
Nu		Use this item if you only want unmoderated groups for the section you're defining.	Nu
S	size	Tells the server when to switch over to spooling data queued up to go to this particular feed site. If the data queued reaches the number of bytes specified, it's appended to the file used for the F flag if you set it. Otherwise, the spool is in `/usr/spool/news/out.going/sitename`.	S1000
T	type	Defines the type of feed (discussed in more detail later in this chapter) you're using for the site you're defining. The options are:	
	c	Channel feed	Tc
	f	File feed (most common)	Tf
	l	Log entry only	Tl

Flag	Parameters	What It Does	Example
	m	Funnel	Tm
	p	Program	Tp
	x	Exploder	Tx
W	items	Used to control what information is written in the files used for file, channel, and exploder feeds. You can use more than one item, and each item is written to file in the order you refer to them after the W. The items you can write to file are:	
	b	Size of the article in bytes	Wb
	f	The article's full path	Wf
	g	The newsgroup the article was posted to (or the first one if it's crossposted).	Wg
	m	Article's Message-ID	Wm
	n	The article's path relative to your spool directory	Wn
	s	The site that fed the article to your server, taken from the path header.	Ws
	t	Time the article arrived as seconds from the epoch	Wt
	*	Names of all of the sites that get this article (funnel entries)	W*
	D	The value of the article's distribution header, or ? if empty.	WD
	H	Tells the server to go ahead and write all of the article headers to the file. The Xref and Bytes header are included. If you use this item, it should be the only one you use. Otherwise, it will create a new line and then list all of the headers, probably duplicating information that was already written.	WH
	N	The value of the News-groups header.	WN
	O	The file's overview data. This data is used for the program overchan. If you use this item, it should be the only one in the list.	WO
	R	The information needed for article replication.	WR

> **Note**
>
> If the site is fed by a program feed, only the asterisk (*) item is of use.

Param

This field is specific to which type of feed (see table 9.2) you're using to provide news to the site in question.

Table 9.2 Types of News Feeds Available

Feed Type	Distinctive Features
Log	Simplest of the feed types. The only data written when using this kind of feed is a mention in the news logfile.
File	Another simple feed, and also the default if you don't specify one. When a site is supposed to get a particular article, a line is written to the file that tracks what articles need to be sent.
Program	Each time an article comes in that goes to the site being defined, a process starts up to handle this article.
Channel	Each time an article comes in that goes to the site being defined, a line is sent to a process telling it about the article. If this process exits, it's restarted or the data is written to a file if it can't be restarted for the moment, and handled later when the process starts back up. This differs from the program feed in that there's only one process handling the articles.

What you need for the `param` statement differs for each feed type, as follows:

- Log: No param statement is necessary.

- File: This is the full path name telling the server where to save the article data. If you only include a file name, the file is saved to `/usr/spool/news/out.going`. The default value if you don't use the `param` statement *is* `/usr/spool/news/out.going/`*sitename* where *sitename* is the name assigned to the site you're feeding.

- Program: This is the path name to the article. Use a simple %s to insert the path name relative to the spool directory.

- Channel: This is the full path name for the process to start.

ME Definitions

You must have one and only one ME definition in this file. It also needs to be the very first server entry in the file. The ME item also serves as the base subscription for the sites you feed. It's added onto the beginning of each site's subscription list.

An example ME line is as follows:

```
ME\

:*,!junk,!foo.*,!control.*
```

This example breaks down as follows:

- ME: This is the name of the site being defined—in this case, your own site.

- *,!junk,!foo.*,!control: This is the patterns used for your newsgroup subscriptions. Here, you're subscribing to *all* newsgroups (the first item in the list is a *) and then telling it to not get the junk groups from your feed site, the foo hierarchy, or the control group.

> **Note**
>
> The control group carries control messages, which are used to make changes in your newsgroups on your site. If you run a large news server with a large group list, it's a good idea to use control because otherwise, you'll have to maintain it by hand. However, if you run a small site, you'll have problems with the month posting to control of the checkgroups file. This file resets the newsgroup listings of the server it goes to, so suddenly your partial listing would become a full listing! If you don't have the space to hold this, you definitely don't want the control group.
>
> Also, the control group is used to carry control messages, such as article cancellations.

Other Site Definitions

Here are some examples of setting up site definitions for various purposes.

You can set a site definition to handle archiving the posts for specific groups by sending the appropriate articles to an archiving program. Let's say you want to archive the posts to all of the **comp.os.linux** groups. The definition would look something like the following:

```
source-archive!\
:!*,comp.os.linux.*\
:Tp:/news/bin/archive %s
```

One method of feeding news to a site is by sending news batch files to the site downstream. Here I'll set the definition to send everything but local administration traffic to the site **news.downstream.net.**

```
downstream\
:!junk/!foo\
:Tf,Wnm:news.downstream.net
```

Another method of providing newsfeeds is through UUCP. Here's an example of sending all of the comp groups to the UUCP site buddy.

```
buddy\
:!*,comp.*\
:Tf,Wfb
```

The nnrp.access File

The nnrp.access file defines what hosts clients can access your news server from, and what they're allowed to do (read and/or post). The example file is as follows:

```
##  $Revision: 1.4 $
##  nnrp.access - access file for on-campus NNTP sites
##  Format:
##      <host>:<perm>:<user>:<pass>:<groups>
##  Connecting host must be found in this file; the last match found is
##  used, so put defaults first.
##      <host>          Wildcard name or IP address
##      <perm>          R to read; P to post
##      <user>          Username for authentication before posting
##      <pass>          Password, for same reason
##      <groups>        Newsgroup patterns that can be read or not read
##  To disable posting put a space in the <user> and <pass> fields, since
##  there is no way for client to enter one.
##
## Default is no access, no way to authentication, and no groups.
# *:: -no- : -no- :!*
##  Foo, Incorporated, hosts have no password, can read anything.
# *.foo.com:Read Post:::*

*:: -no- : -no- :!*
*:Read Post:::*
```

An example access definition is as follows:

```
catherine.renaissoft.com:Read Post:::
```

This definition breaks down as follows:

- The host being defined is **catherine.renaissoft.com.**

- People from this host can both read and post articles.

- The client doesn't need a user id to connect to the server.

- The client doesn't need a password to connect to the server.

- The client has access to all of the groups the server carries.

The nntpsend.ctl File

The `nntpsend.ctl` file defines the list of sites `nntpsend` transfers news to. The example file is as follows:

```
##   $Revision: 1.2 $
##   Control file for nntpsend.
## Format:
##      site:fqdn:max_size:[<args…>]
##      <site>              The name used in the newsfeeds file for this site;
##                          this determines the name of the batchfile, etc.
##      <fqdn>              The fully-qualified domain name of the site,
##                          passed as the parameter to INNxmit.
##      <size>              Size to truncate batchfile if it gets too big;
##                          see trunc(1).
##      <args>              Other args to pass to INNxmit
##   Everything after the pound sign is ignored.
# nsavax:erehwon.nsavax.gov::-S -t60
# walldrug:walldrug.com:1m:-T1800 -t300
```

This is the file where you assign the aliases you referred to in the other news configuration files. A breakdown of the second example above (`walldrug:walldrug.com:1m:-T1800 -t300`) is as follows:

- `walldrug` is the alias for the site being defined.

- `walldrug.com` is the actual site being defined.

- `1m` tells it to send batches in files no larger than one megabyte. You can also use k for kilobyte (e.g., `500k`) or g for gigabyte (e.g., `1g`).

- `-T1800 -t300` are arguments passed to the program `INNxmit` (available arguments are shown in table 9.3).

Table 9.3   Arguments Passed from *nntpsend.ctl* to *INNxmit*

Argument	Use	Example
–A	Assign an alternate spool directory to use if it can't find an article.	–A/usr/spool/news/outgoing
–a	Always rewrite batch file.	–a

(continues)

III

Setting Up Your Site

Table 9.3   Continued

Argument	Use	Example
–d	Print debugging information.	–d
–M	Changes MIME articles that are not in seven-bit format to quoted-printable.	–M
–r	Don't requeue an article if the remote server sends an unexpected reply code.	–r
–t	How long to wait for the connection to be made.	–t180
–T	Total amount of time an article transfer should be allowed to take.	–T2000
–p	Purge the batch file of entries that no longer exist	–p

The passwd.nntp File

The passwd.nntp file contains the passwords you'll need to connect to the news server that provides your feed. You won't need to use this feature often; ask your provider.

The example file is as follows:

```
##   $Revision: 1.4 $
##   passwd.nntp - passwords for connecting to remote NNTP servers
##   Format:
##       <host>:<name>:<pass>[:<style>]
##   Clients need only one entry, for where INNd is running. The
##   server will have more entries for connecting to peers to feed them
##   articles.
##       <host>          Host this line is for.
##       <name>          Name to use to authenticate with
##       <pass>          Password to send, after sending name
##       <style>         Optional authentication style, defaults to "authinfo"
##   <name> and <pass> can be empty string; a peer INNd doesn't need a
##   <name>, for example.
# news.foo.com:rsalz:martha
```

The example above breaks down as follows:

- `news.foo.com` is the name of the host you get your feed from.

- `rsalz` is the user name for connecting to the server, if required. If not, just leave this blank.

- `martha` is the password for connecting to the server, if required. If not, just leave this blank.

There's a fourth optional item that is not listed that defines the type of authentication to use. Ask your provider if this item is necessary to connect to the news server.

History and Log File Creation

There are now a few empty files you need to create for your news server's use. Do the following:

1. Log in as **root**.

2. Change to the directory `/usr/lib/news`.

3. Type **touch history.**

4. Type **touch history.dir.**

5. Type **touch history.pag.**

6. Type **touch errlog.**

7. Type **touch log.**

8. Type **chmod 664 history** to change the permissions: the owner can read and write and everyone else to read only.

9. Repeat the `chmod` for each of the files you just created.

10. Type **chown news.news history** to set the file's owner and group to news.

11. Repeat the `chown` for each of the files you just created.

Making the Final Necessary Directories

Fortunately, this last part is taken care of for you! There is a script that will set up all of the remaining directories on its own. To run it, do the following:

1. Log in as **root**.

2. Type **sh** to start an sh shell.

3. Type **makekdirs.sh** to run the script.

Verifying Your News Server

Now that you have your news server installed, it's time to test the following:

- Connecting to your feed site

- Connecting to the sites you feed

- Connecting to clients

> **Tip**
>
> The FAQs that come with INN are an excellent source for more information on all aspects of INN. Also, there are man pages available for almost all of the files you installed in this chapter, so be sure to check them out.

> **Tip**
>
> If you haven't started INNd yet (do a ps aux to see if it's in your process list), just type **/usr/lib/news/etc/rc.news**.

Connecting to Your Feed Site

Before you can connect to your feed site, your provider has to properly have you in their files. You may need to get on the phone with them if you run into problems that don't make any sense to make sure you're properly entered. Especially make sure you're properly entered as a news *server* and have posting permissions.

Let's take a look at some of the problems you'll run into at this stage.

innd Won't Run

If you try to start up innd and it exits without doing anything, there are a few things that can cause this. Look in the /usr/local/news directory and make sure the file history exists. If the file doesn't exist, run the BUILD script that comes with the INN source.

Can't Send Out Posts

If you can't send posts out from your site, make sure you have a newsfeeds entry listing the site the posts are supposed to go to! If you do, try to telnet into the machine that's your provider's news server to the nntp port (e.g., **telnet news.server.com nntp**). You'll get messages back from the news server telling you what permissions you have. Type **help** for help on what you can do at this stage, and **quit** to leave. If it doesn't tell you that you have posting permissions, contact your provider.

Connecting to the Sites You Feed

Make sure you have the sites that you feed news to set as feeders, which means that you include them in hosts.nntp. Also, if you require passwords and userids, make sure the news admin on the other end knows exactly what they need to use!

To figure out what's wrong with feeder connections, configure one of the machines on your site as a feeder, and try to log into your server. Take a look for the error messages you get from the server when you try.

> **Tip**
>
> If you have to edit your host.nntp file, don't forget to run ctlinnd reload afterwards. This command takes a fresh look at the hosts.nntp file.

Clients Connecting to Your Server

When you set up shell accounts, include default configuration files for the newsreaders (in the skeleton file). This will cut down on a lot of problems from shell users!

Individual Host Can't Connect

Make sure the host having problems connecting to your news server via news clients is listed in your nnrp.access file.

Posting Problems

To make sure people can post both on your site and locally, try from a few machines to post to a local group, and also to the group misc.test on the Internet, which is where all test posts should go. If you can't post locally and/ or on the Internet, it's a problem with the server, not the client.

III

Setting Up Your Site

Check the following two things if your posts aren't getting out:

■ Is the device that's supposed to store the posts full?

■ Is your `newsfeeds` file configured correctly?

Chapter 10

Installing FTP Server Software

Having an FTP server is an excellent way to make information available to people, regardless of what kind of Internet software they're using. You can also use it to allow people to upload files to your system, either anonymously or through an account with a password. So, whether you want to make information on your company's services available, or allow the people with whom you're working on an important project to upload their work to your system so you can take a look at it, setting up your FTP server is worth the time and effort.

In this chapter, you learn how to:

- Compile your FTP server
- Install your FTP server
- Make sure your FTP server is secure
- Verify that your FTP server works

How To Compile Your FTP Server

Slackware comes with an FTP server that you can install automatically, but I've chosen a more feature-rich server for you to install. If you would rather use the simple FTP server that comes with Slackware for now, you can access the man pages for it by typing **man tftpd**. However, this is a very basic server. Installing the one included in this chapter will give you better site security. It will also give you more features, since the FTP server installed in this chapter supports a number of nonstandard FTP services, including the capability to:

- Log file transfers

- Compress and archive files in the middle of tasks

- Classify users

- Define what each class of users can do

- Set upload permissions for individual directories

- Create restricted guest accounts, so unknown users can only get to a limited number of files

Finding and Uncompressing the Server Source

The FTP server you're going to use is wu-ftpd-2.4, from Washington University (the site of WUArchive). The features it has to offer in addition to the standard FTP protocols make it a worthwhile addition to your site's servers.

To locate and uncompress wuftpd:

1. Locate the file `wu-ftpd-2.4.tar.Z` on the CD-ROM.

2. Copy it to `/usr/src`.

3. Type **gunzip wu-ftpd-2.4-fixed.tar.gz** (you may see this file as `wu.ftpd-.000`).

4. Type **tar -xvf wu-ftpd-2.4-fixed.tar**.

Editing pathnames.h

Before compiling your FTP server, you need to look at the file that defines where wuftpd's configuration and data files go. To do this, you will edit the file `pathnames.h` (located in the directory where you have stored your `wuftpd` files in the `src` subdirectory) and determine whether the defaults set there fit your needs. If they don't, change them to where you want the files listed to be stored.

> **Note**
>
> You can either choose to have the various configuration files used for wuftpd in various locations, or within one directory. I generally prefer to keep the configuration files for an individual program all in one place. This makes my life easier when I try to locate problems with the server, or make configuration changes later.

Other sysadmins have other ways of handling such configuration files, of course. If you have another structure in mind, or prefer to go with the defaults given, go ahead and use it. There is no one true way to structure your files.

For example, perhaps you prefer to keep all path configuration files for the programs you compile together in one directory. Or maybe you prefer to keep your program configuration files together, but grouped according to program type (e.g., all server configuration files in a single directory, all configuration files for programs for the sysadmin in one place, and so on).

To change a statement to what you want for your own system, just change the path within the quotes. The various path statements stand for:

- **_PATH_FTPUSERS**

  Points to the file that lists the userids that are not allowed to FTP in. For example, most services don't allow access by anyone using root or "services" accounts (nobody, ftp, etc.) If you prefer to keep such files centralized in one particular directory to make them easier to locate later, change this item. The default location is /etc/ftpusers.

- **_PATH_FTPACCESS**

  Points to the server's configuration file. If you prefer to keep your server configuration files together or all of your FTP server files together, change this item to the same as _PATH_FTPUSERS. The default location is /etc/ftpaccess.

- **_PATH_EXECPATH**

  Points to the directory that contains the binary files used with the SITE EXEC command. This directory is relative to the FTP home directory (~ftp). If you prefer to keep all of your FTP files together, change this item to the same location as the others. The default location is /bin/ftp-exec.

- **_PATH_PIDNAMES**

  Points to the file template that handles which classes get which PIDs (process id's). The percent sign (%) in the file name refers to a specific class. The server will automatically choose the proper pid file for each class (as long as that file exists). If you prefer to keep all of your FTP files in one place, change this item to match the others. The default location is /usr/adm/ftpd/ftp.pids-%s.

III

Setting Up Your Site

- **_PATH_CVT**

  Points to the file that contains the configuration for converting a file to a UNIX compressed (.Z) file. If you would rather keep this file somewhere else or want to keep it with your other FTP files, change this item. The default location is `/etc/ftpconversions`.

- **_PATH_XFERLOG**

  Points to the file where your FTP logs will be kept. If you prefer to keep all of your FTP or log files in one place, change this item. The default location is `/usr/adm/ftpd/xferlog`.

- **_PATH_PRIVATE**

  Points to the file that contains the group password file for the SITE GROUP and SITE GPASS commands. If you prefer to keep your FTP files together, change this item. The default location is `/etc/ftpgroups`.

- **_PATH_UTMP**

  Points to your `utmp` file, one of the files used to record the details of access to your services. If you keep your `utmp` file somewhere other than the default, change the appropriate pointer. There should be only one `utmp` file on your system. The default location is `/etc/utmp`.

- **_PATH_WTMP**

  Points to your `wtmp` file, one of the files used to record the details of access to your services. If you keep your `wtmp` file somewhere other than the default, change the appropriate pointer. There should be only one `wtmp` file on your system. The default location is `/usr/adm/wtmp`.

- **_PATH_LASTLOG**

  Points to your `lastlog` file, which is used to show the last X logins by various people. There should be only one `lastlog` file on your system, so if the default does not point to your `lastlog` file, change it to the appropriate path. The default location is `/usr/adm/lastlog`.

- **_PATH_BSHELL**

  Points to where your bourne shell (sh) is. If this item is not accurate, change it to the appropriate path. The default location is `/bin/sh`.

- **_PATH_DEVNULL**

  Points to where to send things that are trashed instead of stored. This one is pretty standard. If you use something other than `/dev/null` to mean "dump it," change this to the appropriate path. The default location is /dev/null.

- _PATH_FTPHOSTS

    Points to the configuration file that handles individual user access. If you would rather keep this file in a central place with your other FTP files, change this item appropriately. The default location is /etc/ftphosts.

Compiling wuftpd

To compile wuftpd, do the following:

1. Log in as **root**.

2. Change to the directory in which your wuftpd precompilation files are stored.

3. Type **build lnx** to build the Linux version of the daemon. This is a script that comes with wuftpd that handles compiling (which you would otherwise do with make) and installation (which you would otherwise usually do with make install).

4. Watch the compilation progress. Keep in mind that just because it looks like it finished, it didn't necessarily compile correctly. So, if you find that you try to move on to the installation and nothing is happening, check over your compilation and make sure it completed properly.

    > **Note**
    >
    > If you aren't sure the compilation finished correctly, and want to make sure that you didn't miss any error messages, use the following syntax when telling it to compile:
    >
    > ```
    > build lnx > blort 2>&1
    > ```
    >
    > The first > *redirects* the output from the command build lnx to the file blort. The second instance, using 2>&1 tells your system to send any error messages to the file blort as well. Therefore, when you're done compiling, you'll have a file containing all the messages the compiler gave, both standard and error.
    >
    > You won't see any of the compiler messages on your screen because of this. The redirecting tells your system to send them to the file blort instead of to your screen.

III

Setting Up Your Site

5. Fix any problems that surface. Return to step 3.

> **Note**
>
> If the compile ends before it should, listing as its problems strunames, typenames, modenames, or other such items being undefined, go to the directory /usr/in-clude/arpa and make a backup of the file ftp.h. Then, go back to the directory in which you have your FTP files for compilation, change to the support directory, and copy the file ftp.h from there to /usr/include/arpa. That should fix the problem.
>
> If the compiler ends before it should listing problems with pid_t, go to the directory in which you have your FTP files for compilation, go to the src directory, and edit the config.h file. Add the line:
>
> ```
> typedef int pid_t;
> ```

Installing and Starting Your FTP Server

Installing your FTP server will take a while because you need to make sure there are no tricky little security holes! So, just take your time and follow along carefully.

Basic wuftpd Installation

To complete the basic wuftpd installation, do the following:

1. Log in as **root**.

2. Change to the directory in which your wuftpd files are stored.

3. Type **build install** to install your server.

4. Go to the directory in which your precompilation FTP server files are stored.

5. Copy /bin/compress to ˜ftp/bin/compress. When I refer to any directory with a tilde (˜) at the beginning, I'm talking about /home/directory_name (e.g ˜ftp is the same as saying /home/ftp). Just like ˜fred would be the same as /home/fred.

> **Note**
>
> Often, you would use a soft link to handle this instead of copying the program. However, when wuftpd starts up, it changes its definition of "root directory" to ˜ftp.

Once it does this, it can't see outside of ˜ftp, and so a soft link pointing to /bin/ compress would be pointing to somewhere that wouldn't exist to wuftpd. Wuftpd would try to find it in ˜ftp/bin/compress, which is where you're putting it, not where it's coming from.

Some Initial Security Measures

Now, you're going to set up some necessary directories and files, according to smart security precautions. To accomplish this, do the following:

1. Change to the ˜ftp directory.

2. Make sure this new directory has the following ownerships and permissions to ensure that it's secure:

```
chmod 111 bin
```

Using 111 sets the permissions so that everyone can execute what's in this directory, but no one can read or write to it. This makes it hard for people to snoop around in this directory.

3. Change to the bin directory.

4. Copy /bin/ls into ˜/ftp/bin. For the same reasons as with compress, you can't use a soft link for this.

5. Change the ownerships and permissions of ls, once again, to root.wheel and 111.

6. Change to ˜ftp/etc.

7. Create the files passwd and group, just as you find in /etc.

8. Make these files mode 444. Using 444 sets the files as readable by everyone. This might seem to be lax security, but keep in mind that even your standard /etc/passwd and /etc/group files have these permissions—though the passwords in these files are encrypted. For some, this is a good enough reason to use *shadow passwords* (discussed in chapter 12).

9. If you want user and group names to show when doing an ls ˗l while someone is in your FTP server, do the following:

- Edit ˜ftp/etc/passwd. You want the following users in this file: root, daemon, uucp, and ftp. You can also add users for people who you want to show as owning various files. An example of an entry is:

```
ftpadmin:*:350:4:FTP Administrator::
```

This entry tells your FTP server that you want user number 350 to show in an ls -l as username ftpadmin. Group number 4, as a general rule, would be the group ftp.

- Edit ˜ftp/etc/group. You only want one group in this file, ftp. In the case of the example above, the entry would be:

```
ftp:*:4:root,daemon,uucp,ftpadmin
```

No one can actually log in using the items you have set in the ˜ftp/etc passwd and group files. This is simply a way of mapping user and group numbers to words within the FTP server.

You do not need to create these files if you don't want to do so. If you don't do this, all the users and groups will show as UID and GID numbers instead of being mapped to names.

10. Return to the ˜ftp directory.

11. Create the directory pub. This is where the files you want to offer to the public are stored. Now, set its ownership to the account that will be used to maintain the FTP server and root (i.e., ftpadmin.root). Set the permissions to 2555. Mode 555 sets the item so that everyone can read and execute it. The 2 in the front (set-group-id) sets the directory so that every file created inside it will also be of the group assigned to the directory (in this case, group ftp).

Some additional simple things you can do to ensure that no one can take advantage of the user ftp existing on your system are the following:

1. Log in as **root**.

2. Change to the directory ˜ftp.

3. Create the file .rhosts, but leave it empty.

> **Tip**
>
> If you want to create an empty file, you can use the command touch.

4. Create the empty file .forward.

5. Change the permissions of the two new empty files to 400. This makes the files readable by their owners (root, in this case), and not accessible at all by anyone else. This precaution makes sure that if someone does get logged in as FTP somehow, he can't change the .rhosts file to allow himself to log in to FTP again remotely later. It also makes sure that he can't change the forward file to sneak mail through your system.

Creating Data Files

There are a few files you need to create now for server security. The examples shown in this section can be found by going to the directory where you stored your precompilation FTP server files, and then changing to the doc/ examples directory.

The ftpconversions File

You might not need to change the ftpconversions file, as its purpose is to handle file compression and uncompression. The contents are as follows:

```
:.Z:  :  :/bin/compress -d -c %s:T_REG¦T_ASCII:O_UNCOMPRESS:
➥UNCOMPRESS
  :   : :.Z:/bin/compress -c %s:T_REG:O_COMPRESS:COMPRESS
:.gz:  :  :/bin/gzip -cd %s:T_REG¦T_ASCII:O_UNCOMPRESS:GUNZIP
  :   : :.gz:/bin/gzip -9 -c %s:T_REG:O_COMPRESS:GZIP
  :   : :.tar:/bin/tar -c -f - %s:T_REG¦T_DIR:O_TAR:TAR
  :   : :.tar.Z:/bin/tar -c -Z -f - %s:T_REG¦T_DIR:O_COMPRESS¦
➥O_TAR:TAR+COMPRESS
  :   : :.tar.gz:/bin/tar -c -z -f - %s:T_REG¦T_DIR:O_COMPRESS¦
➥O_TAR:TAR+GZIP
```

If the paths above are not correct, you need to change them to the appropriate value.

Now, copy this file to the location you assigned in pathnames.h.

The ftpusers File

First, take a look at the example file for ftpusers:

```
root
bin
boot
daemon
digital
field
gateway
guest
nobody
operator
ris
sccs
sys
uucp
```

These are usernames that cannot log into your FTP server. You can remove or add to this list as you wish, but keep in mind that the defaults were chosen because of the possible security holes they cause.

When finished with this file, copy it to the location you assigned in `pathnames.h`.

The ftpgroups File

The `ftpgroups` file is meant to allow you to create a group of predefined people who are allowed to FTP into your system. The contents of the example of the ftpgroups file is as follows:

```
test:ENCRYPTED PASSWORD HERE:archive
```

The items in the example above stand for:

`test`	This is the access group name. You can make this name up out of letters, numbers, and punctuation.
`ENCRYPTED PASSWORD HERE`	This is the password for the group, encrypted via `crypt` (which is also the program that encrypts the passwords for `/etc/passwd`).
`archive`	This is the group name from the `/etc/group` file with which this entry is associated.

> **Tip**
>
> One way to create this password is to create a dummy user, give that user a password, and then copy that password straight from `/etc/passwd` to where you need it. Then, just delete the dummy user.

For a user to take advantage of this feature, he would log in to your FTP server through the standard anon procedure. Then, he would execute the commands SITE GROUP and SITE GPASS to gain the additional group privileges assigned to the `/etc/group` item to which he assigned himself.

Once you finish editing this file (if you want to use it at all; I didn't), copy it to the directory to which it's assigned in your `pathnames.h` file.

The ftphosts File

If you want some control over where various users can FTP in from (allowing and disallowing certain hosts), you can use the ftphosts file to allow or deny access. This is useful if you only want people to be able to FTP in from particular locations, or if you find someone is using your site in a way you want to prevent from particular locations (e.g., uploading files you don't allow, such as copyrighted material). The contents of the ftphosts file are:

```
# Example host access file
#
# Everything after a '#' is treated as comment,
# empty lines are ignored

     allow    bartm    somehost.domain
     deny     fred     otherhost.domain 131.211.32.*
```

Note that the syntax is in three columns:

- allow or deny

- Username of the account whose access you want to allow or restrict

- List of full domain names or IP address(es) from which the person is allowed or forbidden to log in, including the name of the specific host (or an * if you are referring to all hosts at that site). Only a space is required between names/IPs.

> **Caution**
>
> If you use allows, only people coming from the hosts you explicitly listed can FTP in as the specified username.

Setting Up SITE EXEC Programs

If you want to allow anonymous users to run executables on your FTP server, put these programs into the directory assigned in pathnames.h.

> **Caution**
>
> Be extra careful what you put in this directory; you do not want to create a security hole for yourself!

III

Setting Up Your Site

Final Installation Steps

There are just a few more things you need to do to install your FTP server:

1. Log in as **root**.

2. Go to the directory in which you stored your FTP precompilation files.

3. Change to the `bin` directory.

4. Run the file `ckconfig` to double-check that you've installed the extra files properly. This program will tell you if all of the extra configuration files were put where they need to be. You may want to redirect the output to a file (I'll use `blort` again here) so you can catch any mistakes, by typing instead:

   ```
   ckconfig > blort
   ```

Starting Your FTP Server

Starting your FTP server now is easy! Just do the following:

1. Find the process ID for `inetd`.

2. Type **kill -HUP** *process ID* **#** (i.e., `kill -HUP 345`) to kill and restart your server.

Verifying That Your FTP Server Works

After all of this work, it will feel good to be able to use your FTP server! Let's put a file into your FTP site to look at, install a better FTP client, and test the server to make sure it works.

Storing Files in Your FTP Server

If you want to know what people will see when they log in to your FTP server, take a look in the directory `˜ftp`. This is the directory in which they start. From there, you can structure your server's filesystem as you wish. As a general rule, the `˜ftp/pub` directory you already created is where the files you want to make available to the public are placed.

Another standard is the `˜ftp/incoming` directory, from which people can upload materials to your site. If you do create this directory, be sure the permissions are set so that people can write to it!

> **Caution**
>
> Only create an incoming directory if you're certain you want to allow people to FTP materials onto your site. You may find that you have problems with people using this directory to upload any number of illegal items so their friends can pick them up before you see and remove them, such as pirated software and child pornography.
>
> If you do use an incoming directory, be sure to check it on a regular basis and look over the files it contains beyond just looking at the file name.
>
> If you are seriously concerned with determining what kinds of files are illegal, you'll need to contact a local lawyer. You can also contact the EFF (Electronic Freedom Foundation). The URL for its home page is given in chapter 9, "Installing UseNet Server Software."
>
> Also, check all MS-DOS and Macintosh System files that appear in your incoming directory for viruses, especially if you're not sure who uploaded them!

If you have any files you want to make available, go ahead and start arranging them in your FTP server! Be sure that the permissions on your directories and files are as you want them.

Alternative FTP Client

Even though you already have an FTP client, another alternative is NcFTP. This is a more flexible and "fancy" client that allows you to do extra things, such as view files without downloading them and resumes file transfers that died for one reason or another.

Finding and Uncompressing the Client

The FTP client you're going to install here is `ncftp-2.1.0`.

To locate and uncompress NcFTP:

1. Locate the file `/slackware/n4/tcpip.tgz`

2. Copy it to `/user/src` or `/incoming`.

3. Type **gunzip tcpip.tgz**.

4. Type **tar -xvf wu tcpip.tar**.

5. Inside this package is the binary file for NcFTP. See the README file for where this package belongs.

Testing Your FTP Server

Now let's see if everything works! There are a number of access avenues and features that need to be tested.

FTPing into Your Site

Test both the ability to FTP in anonymously, and FTP into a user account.

For example, I'll FTP anonymously into ftp.renaissoft.com. From my personal account, I'll just type **ftp ftp.renaissoft.com**. NcFTP is smart enough to figure out your e-mail address for itself, so you don't have to type it in as your anon password. Then, I get the welcome message to the machine and am given a prompt (see fig. 10.1).

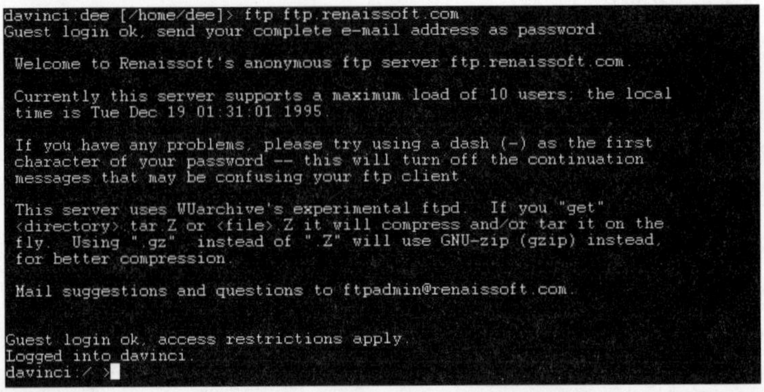

Fig. 10.1
FTPing anony-
mously into
ftp.renaissoft.com.

```
davinci:dee [/home/dee]> ftp ftp.renaissoft.com
Guest login ok, send your complete e-mail address as password.

Welcome to Renaissoft's anonymous ftp server ftp.renaissoft.com.

Currently this server supports a maximum load of 10 users; the local
time is Tue Dec 19 01:31:01 1995.

If you have any problems, please try using a dash (-) as the first
character of your password -- this will turn off the continuation
messages that may be confusing your ftp client.

This server uses WUarchive's experimental ftpd.  If you "get"
<directory>.tar.Z or <file>.Z it will compress and/or tar it on the
fly.  Using ".gz" instead of ".Z" will use GNU-zip (gzip) instead,
for better compression.

Mail suggestions and questions to ftpadmin@renaissoft.com.

Guest login ok, access restrictions apply.
Logged into davinci.
davinci:/ >
```

> **Tip**
>
> A handy feature of NcFTP is that it remembers site names. Next time I wanted to go to ftp.renaissoft.com anonymously, I could just type **ftp renaissoft**.

As you noticed, you didn't even have to type in **anonymous** as a userid. This is because NcFTP assumes you want to do an anon FTP by default. I'll do another example here of a non-anonymous FTP. This time, I want to go to the same machine, but to my own account. I'll type **ftp -u ftp.renaissoft.com**. Then, I'll enter my userid at the prompt (**dee**), and my password at the password prompt. From there, I go straight to a prompt in my own home directory (see fig. 10.2).

Fig. 10.2
FTPing into a
machine as a non-
anonymous user.

Access

Test the following directory and file access concerns:

- Getting into directories people should be able to access. Following from
  the anonymous login example, I'll get a directory listing using the command dir (see fig. 10.3).

Fig. 10.3
Getting a directory
listing in an FTP
server.

Now, I'll choose a directory to enter. Generally, the /pub directory will
be your first step, so I'll go there using cd pub (see fig. 10.4).

Fig. 10.4
Changing into a
directory on an
FTP server, and
looking to see
what's there.

- Fetching files people should be able to access. Backing up to
  ftp.renaissoft.com's main directory (using cd ..), I'll get the site's
  welcome.msg. Such files tend to give information about the FTP site and
  its policies. I'll get the file with the command get welcome.msg. I'm
  given both a progress bar and a countdown of the projected time left in
  the transfer. When the file transfer is complete, I'm told how many
  bytes were received how quickly (see fig. 10.5).

III

Setting Up Your Site

Fig. 10.5

Getting a file from an FTP server.

> **Tip**
>
> With some servers, if you want to get a number of files, you can use the command mget. For example, if you wanted to get file1 and file2, you could type **mget file1 file2**. However, this command doesn't work with all servers.

> **Tip**
>
> NcFTP remembers the directory you were in the last time you left a particular server and takes you back to it when you return.

■ Putting files into the incoming directory. Log into the FTP site (I'm going in as anon), then change to the incoming directory. Now, set the directory you want to be in on the machine you FTP'd in from by using the lcd (local change directory) command. For example, I want to take a file from /home/dee, so I'll type in **lcd /home/dee**. The lcd is confirmed. Then, I can put the file into the directory if I have permission to do so. To put the file example.txt into /incoming, I need to type **put example.txt** (see figure 10.6).

Fig. 10.6

Putting a file into /incoming on an FTP site.

> **Tip**
>
> Just as some servers support mget, some also support mput for putting multiple files.

- Making sure people cannot put files into directories other than incoming. As a simple example of the difference in permissions between an /incoming directory and another directory, take a look at the two file listings in figure 10.7.

```
d--x--x--x   2 root    wheel    1024 Apr 22  1995 etc/
drwxrwxrwx   6 root    wheel    1024 Dec 19 02:03 incoming/
```

Fig. 10.7
The difference between the permissions for an /incoming directory and any other FTP directory.

If you have problems with one or more of these items, check the permissions and ownerships carefully.

Special Configuration Options

If you used any of the special items from the pathnames.h file, such as user groups, test these as well. If you're having problems with these and cannot figure them out, keep in mind that because you installed the server, you have access to the manual pages.

> **Tip**
>
> There is an X-Windows FTP client called *xftp*. You can find it through a Web search using Netscape. It should be available at **sunsite.unc.edu** and its mirrors.

III

Setting Up Your Site

## Chapter 11

Installing Finger Server Software

If you want people to be able to get particular types of information about your users, such as when they were last online, or when they last checked mail (which information is offered is configurable), you will want to install a Finger server. Instead of installing the default Finger server, you are going to install a more configurable one that will give you and your users more control of the information going out to the world.

Offering Finger is a simple way to let people set up something to tell the world a little bit about themselves. In a way, Finger offers the chance to make a simple, personal Web page! Also, outside users can use Finger to find out someone's e-mail address.

In this chapter, you learn how to:

- Configure your Finger server

- Compile your Finger server

- Install your Finger server

- Configure Finger output

- Verify that your Finger server works properly

Configuring Your Finger Server

Once again, this is a server that you have to compile. However, code just doesn't get much simpler than a Finger server, so this compilation should be

III

Setting Up Your Site

pretty headache-free. Just take your time and make sure not to make any typos during what little file editing you may do.

Finding and Decompressing the Server Source

The Finger server you're going to use is Kfingerd-0.04. This is a daemon, which runs in the background and waits for Finger requests to come in.

To locate and decompress Kfingerd, perform the following procedure:

1. Locate the file `kfingerd-0.04.tar.gz` on the CD-ROM.

2. Copy it to `/usr/src`.

3. Make a directory for your Finger work, e.g., `md finger`.

4. Move `kfingerd-0.04.tar.gz` into the directory you just made.

5. Type **gunzip kfingerd-0.04.tar.gz.**

6. Type **tar –xvf kfingerd–0.04.tar.gz.**

Now, there is a little file editing you need to do before compiling your Finger server. In fact, you don't need to edit anything if you don't plan to create *dummy accounts* (fake accounts created just so people can Finger them and get information from your site, for example info).

If you don't plan to create dummy accounts, skip to the next section. If you're not sure, then go ahead and follow along and make the few necessary changes.

To make the changes you want, do the following:

> **Note**
>
> The comment lines in this program begin with /* and end with */.

1. `/* #define NO_DUMMY_PROGRAMS */`

   You will probably want to uncomment this line. It will plug a potential security hole some intruders may know how to use. I will uncomment this line as follows:

   ```
   #define NO_DUMMY_PROGRAMS
   ```

2. `/* Define NOSUCHUSERPATH and NOSUCHUSERFNM to enable custom handling */`
`/* of Fingers of unknown users.`

If you want to set how Finger handles incoming requests for accounts that don't exist, then uncomment the items in this portion of `dummy.c`. The first item, `NOSUCHUSERPATH`, defines the path where Finger should look to see what to do with a request for information on an unknown user. The second `NOSUCHUSERFNM` defines the file name Finger should look for in the defined path. I will stick with the default file names and uncomment the lines as follows:

```
#define NOSUCHUSERPATH "/etc/"

#define NOSUCHUSERFNM "badfinger"
```

Take a look at the default `badfinger.c` file to see if you want to stick with it; many sysadmins will not. The default file's response to a request for an invalid user gives a list of valid users, which may not be acceptable to you. You may want to change `badfinger.c` so that it gives a customized text response because if you don't use this file, the response to a request for an invalid user will be `finger: username: no such user`.

Compiling and Installing Your Finger Server

Finger is a simple program, so it takes little time to compile and requires only a bit of file shuffling and security consideration to install.

Compiling Kfingerd

To compile Kfingerd, do the following:

1. Log in as **root**.

2. Enter the directory where the Finger files are stored (e.g., `/tmp/kfingerd`).

3. Type **make.**

4. Watch the messages the compiler gives you.

5. Deal with any problems that come up, and return to step 3 if you have to fix something before it will compile.

Installing Kfingerd

There are a number of fairly small and simple steps involved in installing your Finger server.

Creating Finger's Home Directory

First, create a home directory for Finger itself. This is where you will put your dummy accounts later. To create this directory, do the following:

1. Log in as **root**.

2. Change to the directory home.

3. Create the directory finger.

4. Change the permissions of the Finger directory so only trusted persons (owners) are allowed to write to it (type **chmod 755 finger**). This will permit other people to read in this directory, but considering that they can get the same information by just fingering accounts, this isn't generally a problem.

Moving Kfingerd

Move the compiled file, Kfingerd, to somewhere like /usr/sbin, where most daemons and other items that only root should be running go.

Adding Kfingerd to the Startup Daemons

To run Kfingerd at startup with the other inetd items, do the following:

1. Log in as **root**.

2. Go to the /etc directory.

3. Edit the file inetd.conf.

4. Make sure the following line exists as you see it here:

```
finger     stream     tcp     nowait     root     /usr/sbin/tcp
➥/usr/sbin/kfingerd
```

> **Tip**
>
> You will find this line already in your inetd.conf file, but the user is incorrect. All you need to do is change the user daemon to root in this line.

5. Save and exit the file /etc/inetd.conf.

Tip

You can either reboot your system to get Kfingerd running, or type **kill -HUP #** where # is inetd's process ID number, and then type **/etc/inetd** to get it running again.

Configuring Finger Output for Users

One reason I chose Kfingerd instead of the standard, normal, everyday Finger is because it is a more configurable program. The standard Finger hands out a list of information that not everyone wants people to have access to. Kfingerd allows each user to choose what information is available to outsiders fingering their accounts, and what information is not available.

The file used to individually configure Finger output is called .fingerrc.

.fingerrc Commands

There are a number of commands available to users who want to configure their Finger output (see table 11.1).

Table 11.1 Commands Available in a .fingerrc File	
Command	**Function**
[no]mail	[doesn't] provide information on new mail, or if all mail has been read
[no]remote	[doesn't] provide information on where people are logged in from if it's an outside site
[no]ttys	[doesn't] provide information on what tty someone is logged in from
[no]idle	[doesn't] provide information on how long someone has been idle
[no]log	[doesn't] log the Finger request in ~/.fingerlog
[no]plan	[don't] show the user's plan file
[no]proj	[don't] show the user's project file
[no]auth	[don't] use ident to get a username for the person making the Finger request
projfnm	Define the name of the project file

(continues)

III

Setting Up Your Site

Table 11.1 Continued	
Command	**Function**
planfnm	Define the name of the plan file
progfnm	Define a program Finger should call
subdfnm	Define a subdirectory where plan files are kept

Note

Items in brackets ([ ]) are optional.

For the last four items (those that define files to call or use), if you don't include the name of the file, the item is disabled. For example, if you just enter **projfnm** without a file name, project files are disabled.

You can also add the parameters in table 11.2 in front of any of the commands listed in table 11.1.

Table 11.2 Additional Command Parameters	
Parameter	**Function**
IP[!]	[Don't] execute the command following this parameter unless it comes from the IP address listed
HN[!]	[Don't] execute the command following this parameter unless it comes from the host name listed
HNR	Remap host names somewhere else

Example .fingerrc File

Now, to get a feel for how all of these commands work together, create a sample .fingerrc file. Let's say that I would like to have the following information available and not available:

■ Let outsiders see what my mail status is.

■ Don't provide my login locations.

■ Don't provide my idle time.

- Log Finger requests.

- Show my plan file (`[td]/.plan`).

My `.fingerrc` file would contain the following:

```
#Enable mail information
mail
#Don't show login locations, whether tty or remote machine
noremote
nottys
#Don't show idle time
noidle
#Remap my local host names to one local host name
HNR     davinci.renaissoft.com     local
HNR     catherine.renaissoft.com     local
HNR     magellan.renaissoft.com     local
HNR     vivaldi.renaissoft.com     local
#Log Finger requests except from my own site
!HN= local     log
#Show plan file and assign location to ~/.plan
plan
planfnm ~/.plan
```

> **Tip**
>
> You may want to create a default `.fingerrc` file to put in all user home directories, with comments, so your users can modify them to fit their preferences.

Verifying That Finger Works

Now, test Finger to make sure that you've installed it properly! Fortunately, verifying Finger is pretty quick and easy. There are four procedures you should test:

- Fingering an unknown user

- Fingering an account without a `.fingerrc` file to check out the defaults

- Fingering an account with a `.fingerrc`

- Fingering a dummy account you have set up

> ### Note
>
> Kfingerd only affects remote Fingers (Fingers from an outside host). It doesn't affect local Fingers, meaning that if you just type **finger dee**, for example, you will get the default Finger response instead of the custom response I set up for myself. This difference in response is caused by the fact that if you don't include the name of the host, the Finger client doesn't bother asking the server about the settings that would point it to the `/home/dee/.fingerrc` file.
>
> If you want to change this, you will need to locate the source for your Finger client and edit it to ensure that it *always* checks with the Finger server instead of assuming that check is not necessary with local Fingers.
>
> You can find an up-to-date version of the Finger client source by FTPing to **sunsite.unc.edu**, going to the directory `/pub/Linux/system/Network/finger`, and getting the file `finger.atbug.tgz`.

Unknown User

Make up a userid that doesn't exist on your system, and Finger it at one of the host computers (for example, in my case, **finger blort@davinci** would be a good test, see fig. 11.1).

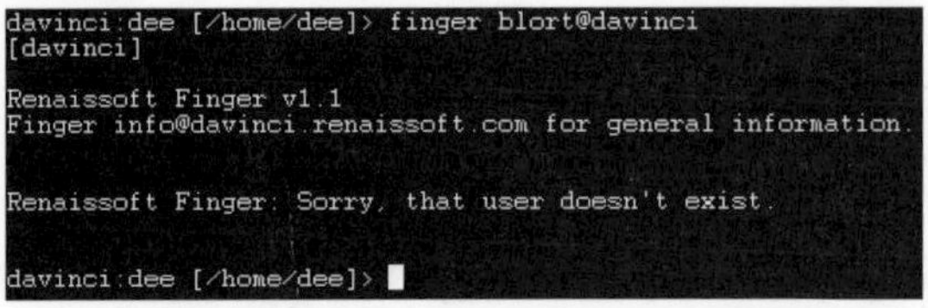

Fig. 11.1
Fingering an account that doesn't exist on my site, and getting the response I set in my badfinger.c instead of a list of accounts on my site.

```
davinci:dee [/home/dee]> finger blort@davinci
[davinci]

Renaissoft Finger v1.1
Finger info@davinci.renaissoft.com for general information.

Renaissoft Finger: Sorry, that user doesn't exist.

davinci:dee [/home/dee]>
```

Confirm that what you included in your `badfinger.c` file works properly by fingering an account that you know doesn't exist on your site, and making sure it gives the output you wanted. If not, you may need to change `badfinger.c` and recompile `Kfingerd`.

Fingering a Known Account without a .fingerrc

Finger an account you know exists (your own will certainly do, an example for me would be **dee@catharine**, or just **dee** since I'm not fingering from outside). Take note of what kind of information shows in the Finger response (see fig. 11.2).

Fig. 11.2
Fingering my
account and seeing
that it works.

Fingering a Known Account with a .fingerrc

Write up a simple `.fingerrc` file and place it in, say, your home account.
Then, Finger your `account@host` (e.g., **dee@catharine**) and see if it looks
different from the default. If not, make sure you didn't comment out any
important lines (using # at the beginning of the line), or that you didn't
mistype **.fingerrc**.

Fingering a Dummy Account You Created

First, before you can Finger a dummy account, you have to create one. Create
a quick dummy account by doing the following:

1. Log in as **root**.

2. Go to the directory `/home/finger`.

3. Create a file with the name of the dummy account you want, for
   example, `info`.

4. Put the Finger response in the text of the file.

5. Save and exit your dummy account file.

6. Change the ownerships of the dummy account file to `root.nobody`.

For an example, I fingered **info** on my site (see fig. 11.3).

Fig. 11.3
The output from
the dummy
account info on
my site, contain-
ing contact and
server information.

III

Setting Up Your Site

Chapter 12

Security

Being on the Internet full time leaves your site open to potential problems with hackers and mischief. I don't want to blow this out of proportion; many sites will have no problems with such things. However, as the saying goes, "Better safe than sorry."

When it comes to security, it's best to decide what kinds of security measures you're going to take before you start setting up any more of your site. Your security route will determine how each of your servers contacts the Internet.

In this chapter, you learn:

- The security options open to you
- How to set up security for your site
- About the infamous SATAN program

Security Options

There are two basic routes you can take with Internet site security. You can use some basic Internet smarts and other tricks to make your site as secure as possible, or you can set up a firewall to cut off access to most of your site from the outside world.

Basic Internet Smarts and Tricks

You can make a fairly secure site on the Internet without doing anything spectacular. The things you should consider doing are discussed in detail in the section "Setting Up Your Security." A brief list of what you'll want to consider includes:

- Disable services you don't want to offer to the outside

- Limit access to logging in as root to make it more difficult for attackers outside your site to get root access

- Address Linux and Internet security issues

- Test your security

You can run a fairly secure site this way (and many sites of all sizes do), but this method isn't sufficient for people who have the need to *ensure* that no one can get into their systems. If you absolutely, positively have a need to keep people out, and have an extra computer to devote to it, see the next section on firewalls (instructions on installing firewalls are in appendix E).

Firewalls

A *firewall* is like a one-way mirror. It lets your users see out of your site, but doesn't let anyone (even your users) see in from outside. The firewall acts as a central server, somewhat like directing traffic. It knows where the packets for your services and your users all need to go, and routes them to the proper machines and ports accordingly. However, it looks to the rest of the Internet as if all your servers are on that machine.

Running a site with a firewall is a lot of extra work for the system administrator (you), but worthwhile if you think a firewall is necessary. You have to implement many extra security measures on each computer on your network, and you can't allow users to install their own software.

You might want to use a firewall for one of the following reasons:

- If you have data on your site that you absolutely need to make sure people can't get to. The type of data you might want to protect with a firewall is data you think people might actively try to get. Moreover, it's data that you can't *afford* for people to get. For example, vital data that can make it or break it for your business may not be a good thing to keep on a computer that's accessible to the Internet without it being protected by a firewall. However, keep in mind that to get that information someone has to first get into your site, then either know it's there or find it accidentally, then know what to do with it. If you don't want to have a firewall but also are concerned about some files you have on your system, consider keeping them on floppies or on a computer that isn't connected to your network, and only having them on your network when you're working on them.

■ If you feel that your site in particular will be a target for intruders because of its nature. For example, if you are in a highly competitive field and there have been problems with people stealing information from one another, you may want to consider a firewall.

■ If you want experience in setting up and maintaining a firewall

You also may *not* want to run a firewall for the following reasons:

■ Firewalls make a lot of extra work for the system administrator. If a user wants to run a program that reaches out to the Internet, you have to compile that client/program yourself and add it to what the server knows how to route properly. So, you have the choice between restricting what your users can do from your site, or spending a good amount of time recompiling programs to be able to use the firewall, and setting up the firewall to know what they are. If you prefer a fairly low maintenance site, you may not want to use a firewall.

■ If you have a small network (2-3 machines) where you can physically keep an eye on what's happening on each of them on a regular basis, you probably don't need a firewall. As long as you can check on the processes running on your site and the devices being mounted, you have a good feeling for what's going on and what looks a little funny. As you get more machines (10 and up), it's easier for things to slip past.

If you intend to run a firewall, first go through the basic Internet smarts security setup in this chapter, and then see appendix E for how to set up the firewall itself. After all, you'll still want some security on the machines behind the firewall! The next section covers how to set up your basic security.

Setting Up Your Security

Now that we've talked a bit about the kinds of security options you have, and why you might or might not want to go as far as using a firewall, we can get started on setting up everything. If you're not sure whether you want to use a firewall, you can see how happy you are with the security on your site as it stands after the basic setup, and then make the decision.

You can take a number of simple precautions to increase your site's security. The idea is to deadbolt as many doors as you can and to make sure the rest are securely locked and the keys are properly protected.

User Passwords

Onehuge security hole most system administrators have to deal with is that of user passwords. Of course, it's imperative that intruders not be able to guess a user's password.

Initially, you need to ask the user for a password to use for the first login. Be sure to emphasize that this password should be changed as soon as possible to prevent anyone breaking into the user's account.

> **Tip**
>
> If you offer SLIP accounts without shell account access, you'll have to handle changing their passwords for them! Or, you can let them telnet in and use their limited shell account and use the `passwd` command from there.

One of the initial pieces of e-mail you send to your users should be a guide to selecting passwords. Remember, the more informed your users are, the better choices they will make and the better off your site will be! Many passwords are poor because they can be readily obtained by someone who takes the effort to learn about your users (see table 12.1).

Table 12.1 Passwords That Make for Poor System Security

Type	Examples
Family Names	Your name, your spouse or significant other's name, any of your parents', pets', or childrens' names.
Other Names	Your friends' names, coworkers' and boss' names, names of favorite fictional or historical characters. Names in general are a bad idea.
System Related	The name of your computer, operating system, site, user name.
Personal Information	Your phone number, social security number, birthday, or other easily found personal info.
Dates	Any birthday of your friends or family. Your wedding anniversary or favorite holiday.
Ego Trips	Don't choose anything like God, Wizard, famous wizard's names, famous leaders' names or titles.

Type	Examples
General	Because so many system break-ins happen due to people having access to programs that simply try passwords one by one until they get into an account, it's really best to avoid any of the following: words from the English dictionary, words from any foreign dictionary supported by your system, place names, or proper nouns. Also, avoid any of the words listed in any of these dictionaries spelled backwards or with a number at the front.
Garbage	Passwords of all one letter, or simple junk keyboard patterns like **asdt**.

The best choices for a password are acronyms or two unrelated words placed together. You can also intersperse numbers and any other keyboard characters. An example is TMY^stacc (This Is My first account), where you've got acronyms, a non-letter character, a number, and abbreviations. Of course, now that I used this here, it's a bad password, so choose another one!

Shadow Passwords

Pretty much anyone breaking into your system knows to do whatever they can to try to get the /etc/passwd file. If they do that, they've got every password for every user and process on your site. Of course, the passwords in this file are encrypted, but people have access to the encryption program and can just compare items they encrypt themselves to the ones in your file. This is one reason why it's so important not to choose a password that's easy to guess!

> **Note**
>
> Remember, your /etc/passwd file has to be world-readable! That's not really the best security, because anyone can read the file. If everyone can read the file, they can also copy the contents. Then, they can try to decode the passwords contained in this file; the encryption used in /etc/passwd isn't as secure as most of us would like.

To better protect the passwords for your site, you can replace the standard password system with Shadow passwords. This program keeps your password file in a separate file that doesn't have to be world readable, and that has better encryption.

Of course, there are down sides to using Shadow passwords. You need to compile a few of your servers so that they don't look in the /etc/passwd file for your user passwords. You can't use the adduser command to add a new user to your system because the standard adduser utility looks straight at the /etc/passwd file. I will walk you through how to deal with these things once you have Shadow passwords installed.

> **Tip**
>
> The first part of installing Shadow passwords is to save things out so you can easily uninstall Shadow password's changes, so it's not that risky of a change to your system.

I highly recommend that you install Shadow passwords to make your system more secure. It's worth the extra work.

Installing Shadow Passwords

If you want to use or try Shadow passwords, you need to install the Shadow passwords package. First, to prepare for the installation, do the following:

1. Login as **root**.

2. On the CD-ROM, go to the directory /extras.

3. Copy the file shadow.tgz to the directory where you unzip your source file for compilation (e.g., incoming).

4. Uncompress the file using gunzip.

5. Untar the file by using tar -xvf shadow.tar.

6. Change into the new directory shadow-mk.

7. Type **make save** to save all the old binaries that will be replaced by Shadow password's binaries. This makes it easy to backtrack if you decide to go back to not using Shadow passwords. The binaries are all saved into the shadow-mk/save directory.

> **Tip**
>
> You can restore the old nonshadow binaries by typing **make restore** in this directory.

Now, to compile and install shadow passwords on your system, do the following (you are logged in as root, in the shadow-mk directory):

1. To compile the shadow passwords group of programs, type **make all**. This compilation can take a while.

2. To install the shadow passwords group of programs, type **make install**. This puts all the compiled binaries where they should go, sets permissions, and so on.

Finally, you need to perform a few housekeeping tasks to complete your shadow passwords initial setup (you are logged in as root, in the shadow-mk directory):

1. Type **/usr/sbin/pwconv** to run the binary that converts your system to shadow passwords.

2. Type **mv ./npasswd /etc/passwd** to move the file shadow-mk/npasswd to /etc/passwd. Now you've replaced your old password file with one that contains no passwords. All the passwords are in the next file.

3. Type **mv ./nshadow /etc/shadow** to move the new password file into place.

4. Change the modes of the password file back to world readable, but only owner writable, by typing **chmod 644 /etc/passwd**.

5. Change the modes of the shadow file (your new password file) to owner writable, group readable, and world nothing (anyone who's not the owner or group has absolutely no access to the file) by typing **chmod 640 /etc/shadow**.

6. Change the ownership of the shadow file by typing **chown root.shadow /etc/shadow**. The shadow file is much more secure than was /etc/passwd.

7. Create the following log files with the touch command:

```
/var/adm/lastlog

/var/adm/ftmp

/var/adm/faillog

/var/adm/sulog
```

Changing Your Binaries for Shadow Passwords

Some of the programs you run on your system will no longer work with
Shadow passwords. Basically, any server that needs to handle logins—and,
hence, passwords—needs to be recompiled to handle Shadow passwords (e.g.,
FTP). All the source for the binaries on the CD-ROM is also included there.
Often there's an option in the Makefile itself to set to compile for Shadow
passwords.

Adding Users While Using Shadow Passwords

The adduser script automatically uses the /etc/password file, so you need to
replace it with something that will use the /etc/shadow file. Fortunately, the
Shadow passwords package comes with a program you can use! From now on,
while adding users, use the program useradd instead of the program adduser.
The program useradd understands how to handle Shadow passwords.

> **Tip**
>
> For more on the /etc/shadow file see the man page for shadow (**man shadow**) and
> the man 4 page for shadow (**man 4 shadow**).

Disabling Outside Access to Root

Now is the time to decide what you want people to have access to from outside your site and individual machines. Be careful not to cut yourself off completely because you might want to telnet into your site to maintain it if
you're away.

In the file /etc/securetty is the list of all the *ttys* (the specific terminal addresses each login session uses) that are considered secure enough that people
can log in as root from them. It is important not to allow root logins from
just anywhere, because it becomes too easy for people to have a chance at
trying to get your root password. The terminals you want to allow access to
are the straight tty ones (e.g. tty1, tty2, and so on). Even there, you may not
want to limit how many of those people can log into root. In a typical Linux
setup, tty1 through tty12 are your function keys. Therefore, if you only allow
tty1 through tty6 to log in as root, you can only log in as root with function
keys F1 through F6.

Note

You cannot log in as root from terminals not listed in the securetty file, but you can su (superuser) into root. By typing **su** you can temporarily act as though you're in another account. Typing **su** by itself means you're trying to superuser into root. To su into another account you'd use **su userid** (e.g. **su joe**). You'll be asked for the account's password, then you're in.

While this fact may seem to make the security measure useless, keep in mind that someone trying to break into your system would first have to get a password into another account before they could try for the root password. This slows them down a bit, which gives you more time to catch onto the problem.

Tip

To see what ttys you have available, go to the /dev directory and type **ls tty*** (see table 12.2 for an explanation of tty naming). All the files listed refer to a single terminal.

Table 12.2 Terminal Naming Conventions and Types

tty Type	Purpose
tty	Console login, directly from the keyboard. The numbering for ttys is in hexadecimal, so ttya, ttyb, and ttyc are actually tty10, tty11, and tty12.
ttyS	Serial login (e.g., modem)
ttyp	Telnet login

Note

To add a tty, use the mknod command. Type **ls -l tty*** in /dev and look at the file listing. Notice that instead of a file size, there are two numbers listed separated by commas. The first number is the major number, and the second is the minor.

(continues)

(continued)

The major number is the same for every tty definition. For the minor number use the next one in the sequence for the particular tty type unless it is already being used for another tty definition.

For example, if I wanted to add another modem dial-in terminal, and the last one available was ttys3, at 4, 67, I would type in **mknod -m 660 /dev/ttyS4 c 4 68**. This line breaks down as follows:

- mknod: The command being run.

- -m 660: Sets the mode of the file to 660 (owner can read and write, group can read and write, all others have no access).

- /dev/ttyS4: The device name for this terminal.

- c: Creates a device that handles characters (e.g., on a terminal, you're typing in one letter at a time, but on a disk—a block device—sends data in blocks/chunks).

- 4: Major number for the device. All devices of the same type will have the same major number. For example, all tty definitions are the same type of device, so every tty entry will have the same major number (4 in this example).

- 68: Minor number for the device. This number is specific to this definition. Follow the sequence of numbers that already exist for the type of tty.

If you occasionally find the need to be able to log in directly as root remotely, you can choose one terminal to allow this from and then disable it again once the need has passed.

Disabling Services You Don't Want To Offer to the Outside

If you don't want outside users to have access to a specific service (for example, FTP), be sure to disable this access. See the chapter covering the service you want to limit for your options on limiting access to services (e.g., chapter 7 for your Web server).

If you decide that you don't want to offer a service at all, don't install the server or disable it. To make sure the daemon isn't running, go to the appropriate file (e.g., /etc/inetd) and comment out or remove the line that refers to the server, and then be sure the process is killed:

- If the item was in inetd, kill and restart inetd.

- If the item was not in inetd, kill the process itself.

> **Caution**
>
> Be sure to remove the item from the file that starts it up in the first place. Otherwise, it will restart the next time you reboot your system.

Keeping Up with Linux Security Issues

It is important to keep up with Linux security issues. When a security hole is found, information is broadcast along a few channels to let sysadmins know about it. Unfortunately, in explaining how to correct the problem, the problem itself must be revealed. So, if you don't fix the problem at your site, suddenly you become vulnerable to attack along the lines of the correctable problem.

You can join two mailing lists to keep track of security issues:

1. *linux-alert* This moderated mailing list publishes Linux-specific security problems. To join the list, send e-mail with the message subscribe linux-alert youremailaddress@your.site (e.g., subscribe linux-alert dee@renaissoft.com) to **majordomo@linux.nrao.edu**. You can also access list archives by FTPing to **linux.nrao.edu**, going to the directory /pub/linux/security/list-archive and getting the file linux-alert.

2. *linux-security* This mailing list is for the discussion of linux security issues. To join the list, send e-mail with the message subscribe linux-security youremailaddress@your.site (e.g., subscribe linux-security dee@renaissoft.com) to **majordomo@linux.nrao.edu**. You can also access list archives by FTPing to **linux.nrao.edu**, going to the directory /pub/linux/security/list-archive and getting the file linux-security.

If you want to subscribe to only one of these lists, subscribe to linux-alert. You may still want to take a look at the archives for the linux-security list on occasion to keep up-to-date on current happenings.

Testing Your Security

Testing your site's security is a good way to make sure to catch any holes. One excellent method of testing security is the SATAN program (see the section on SATAN later in this chapter for information on installing and using this program).

The reason SATAN is such a useful tool is that it finds your security holes and tells you how to fix them! It's also important to use SATAN to test your system because people outside your site can also use it on your system. It's better to catch the problems yourself and fix them than to have an intruder find the problems first and exploit them.

Tip

One interesting security avenue to follow is to locate hacker FAQs on the Internet. Search the Web for **hack** and ask around.

Tip

There is a program on **sunsite.unc.edu** in /pub/linux/system/admin called **Crack**. You can use it to check the passwords on your site and see how many of them it can figure out (how many it can crack). Then, notify the users whose passwords you found that they need to change them, and give them suggestions on how to choose a secure password.

Using SATAN on Your System

You can use SATAN to test your system security. It attacks a good number of entry points to see if it can get anywhere, and then reports back to you to let you know how far it got, and how to seal up the holes. This is definitely worth doing!

Getting the Source

The source for SATAN is on the CD-ROM in /estras/satan.tgz. Copy it to /usp/src, un-gzip it, and un-tar it. It will create the directory satan-1.1.1.

Applying the Patch from the CD-ROM

You first need to apply a patch file to the source. This file is available at Sunsite in /pub/Linux/system/network/admin/satan-linux.1.1.1.diff.gz, and there is a README file. Copy it into the directory where your satan-1.1.1 directory is.

> **Caution**
>
> To use SATAN you need to have Perl installed. It's on Slackware's disk d10.

> **Tip**
>
> Keep a clean, compressed copy of SATAN around in case something goes wrong as you're patching it.

Now, do the following (as root) to apply the patch:

1. First, move your satan-1.1.1 directory to satan-1.1.1.linux. This patch needs two copies of the files to do its work.

2. Now, untar satan-1.1.1.tar again to get your second copy of the files.

3. Move satan-1.1.1 to satan-1.1.1.clean. Now you have the two copies you need.

4. Type **zcat satan-linux.1.1.1.diff.gz | patch** to actually patch the SATAN source. Text will fly across your screen as the patches are applied.

Compiling SATAN

Now it's time to compile SATAN. Fortunately, it's got compiling rules for Linux, so we don't have to port it from a generic UNIX version!

> **Caution**
>
> You must compile SATAN on a machine that has a Web browser.

Do the following:

1. Change to the directory `satan-1.1.1.clean`. This is the patched version of the source.

2. Type **reconfig** to apply patches that let the source know where to find a number of your files.

3. Type **make linux** to compile SATAN.

Running SATAN

Now, let's test out SATAN! First, to configure it, do the following:

1. Start up X-Windows (covered in chapter 7, "Installing Web Server Software").

2. Open a shell and enter the directory where you have SATAN.

3. Type **satan**. A Netscape session will start up with the SATAN Control Panel (see fig. 12.1).

Fig. 12.1
The SATAN
Control Panel in
Netscape.

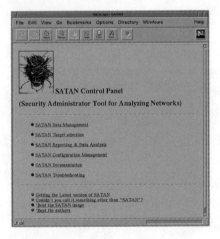

4. First, let's configure SATAN. Click SATAN Configuration Management. This takes you to the Configuration options (see fig. 12.2).

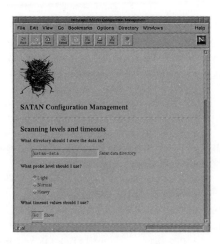

Fig. 12.2
The SATAN
Configuration
Management page.

5. In the Satan data directory, if you want to save your scan data some-where else change the value from the default of satan-data.

6. Click the probe level you want: Light, Normal, or Heavy. I'll click Normal.

7. If you want the timeout values to be different, change them from the defaults, which are a good first choice.

8. Leave the kill signal at 9 (for kill -9).

9. Leave maximal proximity and proximity descent where they are for now.

10. Leave Stop selected for when I go below 0 probe level.

11. If you don't have any subnets, leave it on Just the Target under subnet expansion. If you do have a subnet and want it probed as well, click The Entire Subnet.

12. If the machine you're running SATAN on is trusted by the machines you're testing (did you include it in their rhosts file?), leave the default checked. Otherwise, click the untrusted host option.

13. If you want to limit your search to specific things to be probed, do so. I'll limit it to our server, **davinci.renaissoft.com**. I could search all of renaissoft.com, however, by entering **renaissoft.com**.

III

Setting Up Your Site

14. If you want to limit your search to specific things not to be probed, do so. I've only entered one item, so there's nothing for me to enter here. If I was searching all of renaissoft.com but didn't want to search the machine vivaldi, I would enter **vivaldi.renaissoft.com**.

15. If you're running nameservice, leave the next default selected. If you aren't (you only have a hosts file), then tell it not to use nslookup.

16. If you can ping, leave the next default selected. If ping on your system is broken for some reason, select not to use ping.

17. Click Change the Configuration File. You will get a screen warning you that SATAN may give away information on you to any Web servers you use it to connect to. Since we're only using it on our site, this isn't a problem. Click the Reload button and click OK to "Repost Form Data?"

18. Click Back to Satan Control Panel.

Now, to actually test out SATAN:

1. Click SATAN Target Selection (see fig. 12.3).

Fig. 12.3

The SATAN Target Selection page.

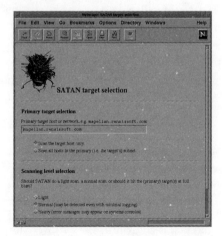

2. Double-check the information on the page to be sure it's accurate. If it's not, change it to what you'd rather use.

3. Click Start the Scan.

4. Watch all the system information appear on the new page (see fig. 12.4).

Fig. 12.4
The items SATAN scanned on my server.

5. Click Continue with Report and Analysis. This takes you to the page SATAN Reporting and Analysis (see fig. 12.5).

Fig. 12.5
The menu page for the reports SATAN generated.

6. Now, just click the options on the menu page and see where your vulnerabilities are. For each vulnerability, SATAN will offer a recommendation on how to fix it.

III

Setting Up Your Site

Part IV

Maintaining Your Internet Site

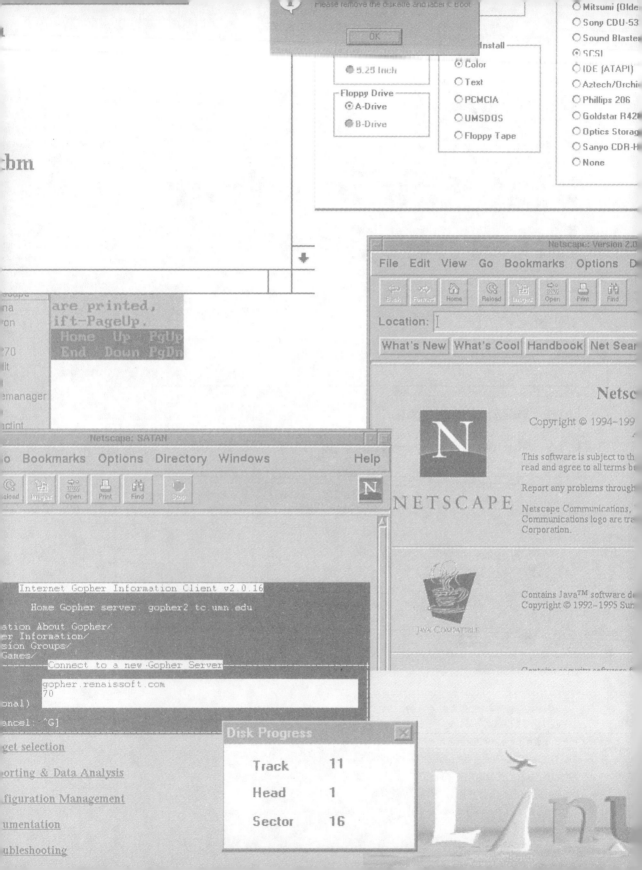

Chapter 13

Maintaining Linux

Now that you've set your system up the way you want it, you've crossed into the next phase of being a system administrator. Instead of focusing on setting everything up, you'll now focus on maintaining and improving your site (improving is covered in Part V, "Upgrading and Adding to Your Site"). After all, an Internet site is somewhat like a car or a house—you need to constantly attend to it, rather than wait for things to get so out of hand that major repairs are necessary.

In this chapter, you learn how to manage:

- Users

- Disk space

- Network resources

Managing Your Users

The majority of what happens on most Internet sites is done by users. Therefore, the majority of what you'll need to attend to management-wise deals with users. This is especially true if you run a site that has a user base that changes on a regular basis (e.g., a commercial site with people signing on and then leaving, or an educational site with people coming in and out each semester).

Interacting with Your Users

Part of being a system administrator is dealing with people. These people are the others responsible for your site (if you don't run it alone), occasionally the administrators of other sites, and the users who utilize your site. Users can be the most difficult of the three to deal with because most of your communications with them involve complaints and requests. You may want to save any compliments or thank-you's that come along for your own morale!

There are a few things to keep in mind when dealing with user calls or requests.

Be professional. Being a site administrator may be a labor of love for you, but it's also a job. If you find you dislike a user, or find one difficult to deal with, sometimes it's best to just smile and be friendly and efficient. The sooner the problem is solved, the sooner you can go on to other things.

Be patient. You will run into users who are technophobes, unsure of their abilities, or simply computer illiterate. Often with these kinds of users you have to drag the information you need out of them in order to solve their problem. You may find that a simple e-mail form that includes some of the basic questions you need answers to (e.g., what platform they're running on, what software the problem occurs with, error messages they see). After all, most of the complaints you get are through e-mail or local newsgroup postings. If you tell the user you're sending the form while you're on the phone with him, do it as you're talking to him so you won't forget.

Be as prompt as possible. There is little more frustrating to a user with a serious problem than having to wait weeks or months for a solution. If you're swamped with system problems, try to organize yourself so you don't lose individual people's problems under piles of paper—perhaps set aside a special e-mail box, and/or a special In box.

Be firm. Many system administrators work themselves to death trying to make their users happy, which includes fulfilling special requests. Remember, you're only human, and there are times the line needs to be drawn between a legitimate request and a request that goes against an important and necessary policy. Keep a copy of your Acceptable Use agreement to refer to.

Be authoritative when necessary. You will run into the occasional problem user. This person is someone who either is a problem on the Internet itself (e.g., spamming newsgroups, stalking, and so on) or is a problem on your site (e.g., is a resource hog or uses your system for illegal purposes). Be sure your Acceptable Use policy gives you the power to deal with such people.

Tip

Spamming newsgroups means sending the same post to many unrelated groups. For example, sending out an advertisement for a computer you're selling to every single newsgroup in the comp hierarchy.

> **Note**
>
> For some fiction involving the exploits of a ruthless and frightening system operator, see the BOFH articles by Simon Travaglia by FTP at **sunsite.unc.edu**, in /pub/ docs/humor/bastard-operator. You can also see these articles on the Web in HTML at **http://www.renaissoft.com/bofh/bofh-index.html**.

Dealing with Problem Users

Dealing with problem users on your site is likely one of your more difficult jobs. It requires a mix of patience, fairness, tact, and determination. There are a number of reasons such users are challenging to deal with.

You have to be sure the user is a problem. After all, the account may have been hacked, or the person complaining may not be entirely honest about the situation. It's helpful to require some sort of proof that there is a problem. This proof could consist of forwarded news posts, e-mail, IRC logs, and so on. Keep in mind however that this proof may be altered or false. State in your Acceptable Use policy (making this policy is discussed in more detail in chapter 5, "Setting Up Your Site For General Use") what measures you will take to verify a complaint against a user.

The user may threaten legal action. If you make sure to have a solid Acceptable Use policy stating the things you won't allow or put up with on your site, and how offenders will be dealt with, you are generally covered. If you run a large site and are concerned, you may want to have a lawyer look over your Acceptable Use policy and help you fine tune it.

Some problem users are both spiteful and computer-knowledgeable. These users are actually capable of damaging your system. It is important if you tell a user you intend to remove his account to do so right away (more on removing users in the next section)! State in your Acceptable Use policy the number of days, hours, or minutes it will be between when you say you will remove an account, and when you will remove it. You can give a flexible time or a time range.

Removing and Suspending Users

There are times you will need to remove users, whether they're simply leaving your provider or are in violation of your Acceptable Use policy. There are a few scenarios you may want to handle differently:

- If a user informs you that he wants his account canceled at the end of the month, inform him that all the data in his home directory will be erased on a particular date. Once that date is reached, you can expect that the user has copied all the files he wanted to keep. You can then proceed to completely remove the account by erasing the appropriate home directory, and the account's mention in the /etc/passwd file and the /etc/shadow file (if you use it).

■ Suspending access to a user's account (be sure your Acceptable Use policy covers reasons for account suspension) is simple. Go into the /etc/passwd file or /etc/shadow file and simply add an asterisk (*) to the beginning of the person's password. Be *sure* to deal promptly with problem users, especially disgruntled and computer-knowledgeable ones. You don't want to risk damage to your site. If you decide to re-move the account eventually, follow the same procedure detailed above.

Managing Your Disk Space

A precious resource for any Internet site is hard disk space. After all, you need to be able to store all that news, mail, and general stuff that users like to collect.

It's important to keep up with your disk space management. If you let it go too long, you'll find that your site suddenly starts kicking back mail or news saying that there's no more room!

Disk Quotas

You may find at some point that a number of users on your site are using a large amount of disk space for personal file storage. You can deal with this problem, of course, by simply asking them to cut their disk usage down to a level you find more appropriate. However, this may not always help.

There are two solutions to this problem. You can either add more hard drive space to your site or implement disk quotas. Adding more space, while a nice solution for the users, won't solve the problem if resource hogs continue to eat up your disk space. You can set up disk quotas; give your users a bit of fair warning so that they have time to clean up their directories. Installing disk quotas is covered in detail in chapter 5, "Setting Up Your Site for General Use."

To set a quota for only one person:

1. Log in as **root**.

2. Type **edquota user**. You can also set quotas for multiple users by simply listing the users, such as typing **edquota user1 user2**.

IV

Maintenance

> **Caution**
>
> Remember to turn your quotas on as discussed in chapter 5!

You can also use flags to specify various options with edquota:

g   Edit the group quota file.

p   Copy the settings for the first user to any other users listed on the command line.

t   Edit the soft time limits assigned to each filesystem's quota.

u   Edit the user quota file. This is the default option if you don't specify one.

3. A temporary file opens for you to edit. If you have any quotas set for the users you listed on the command line, these quotas show in the file. An example entry for this file is:

```
fs /home/joe blocks (soft=15000, hard=25000) inodes (soft=0,
➥hard=0)
```

In this case, you're setting the filesystem to contain the quota to /home/joe, you're setting the quotas in blocks to a soft quota of 15000, and a hard quota of 25000. We're not using an inode quota in this one.

4. Save and exit the file. The edquota program now makes sure the proper quota files are altered to contain the updated information.

Trimming Log Files

If you don't trim some of your log files from time to time, they will eventually overrun your hard drive. You can simply do this by hand whenever you're wandering through the drive to regain some lost space, or you can add items to your cron jobs (discussed in the next section) to take care of it on a regular basis.

Take a look at each log file on your system over a short period of time. See how large it gets within, say, a day and a full week. Look at the information stored there to see how helpful it is to you on a short term and a long term basis.

An example of this process (done as **root**) is:

1. I'll select one log file to study. The major system logs are, as a standard, in /var/adm. However, you may have set up your system so that all your log files show up in a central place (a helpful idea if you want to be able to check through all your logs at once). Adjust this example to fit your particular setup.

The log file I'll look at is /var/adm/syslog.

2. The syslog file is where most of your system logging takes place. Therefore, if you have it in one piece (see the note after this procedure list for how to break your syslog into service-focused files), it gets huge pretty fast. For example, a small site that runs a large and active mailing list and has a small user pool that logs on frequently can find its syslog file reaching 500,000 bytes in a single day. That's a meg every two days! This file definitely needs to be trimmed on occasion.

3. At this point I have to decide how many days' worth of information I want to be able to get from the syslog file at one time. Some of the information here is particularly important in helping to track things down (e.g., every piece of mail that goes through the site is logged here), so in this case I'm going to keep a week's worth of syslog around, and then delete it. However, I'm also going to gzip the file before I delete the originals so I have access to it if required.

4. I'll create a directory to put my compressed log files in called /var/ admin/stored_logs. I'll give it permissions 600 so only root has access, and ownerships root.root. I can do this because the processes run by a crontab file are owned by the user the crontab belongs to.

5. Now to add to root's crontab file. Use the command crontab rather than directly editing the file by hand, since this command will ensure permissions stay set the way they need to be. The flags for this command are:

u   Copy the file inputted on the command line (crontab filename -u user) to also be the crontab file for the user listed.

l   List the crontab file for the user

e   Edit the crontab file

d   Delete the crontab file

c   Specify the crontab directory to use (crontab -c directory) for the user

As root, type **crontab -e** to edit the crontab file.

> **Tip**
>
> To edit the crontab file for an account you're not logged into, you must be logged into root. No one else can edit a crontab for an account other than the one they're using.

6. Before I erase the syslog file, I want to compress and save it. There are the three commands I'll use, in order:

   ```
   gzip /var/admin/syslog
   ```

   This compresses the log file.

   ```
   mv /var/admin/syslog.gz /var/admin/stored_logs
   ```

   This moves the compressed log into the directory I created earlier to keep my old log files in.

   ```
   rm /var/admin/syslog
   ```

   If /var/admin/syslog still exists, delete it with this command. It's likely that gzip already deleted it for you.

7. Now, I need to decide when I want to do this. I already decided that I'll do it once a week because it takes that long for the file to get large enough for me to want to compress it to save disk space, now I just have to determine the particular times. I'll take a look through the current crontab file and see when the machine doesn't have any other tasks to do—not that this is a very process-intensive task, but it's a good habit to get into. I'll choose every Wednesday at 3 am, since my system looks to be fairly idle at that point when it comes to cron jobs. The crontab entry for this choice looks like:

   ```
   L0 3 * * Wed
   For
   Minute Hour Day Month Day-of-Week
   ```

8. Now, to put this all together, I have two choices. I can string all the commands onto one line, or I can write a small script. I'll demonstrate here how to include them all in one line:

   ```
   0 3 * * Wed gzip /var/admin/syslog; mv /var/admin/syslog.gz /
   ➥var/admin/stored_logs; rm /var/admin/syslog
   ```

9. Save and exit the file. Every minute the cron daemon checks all the cron files to see what it needs to do; you don't need to kill and restart any processes to assure that your new cron file is used.

Partitioning Syslog

You can partition your syslog file according to the items kept in it. To do this, edit the file /etc/syslog.conf. You can tell this file to save out the log data for any type of system process. The following minitable shows examples of the processes for which you can make separate log files.

Process Type	Description
auth	Login authorization processes
daemon	Server processes
kern	Kernel processes
lpr	Printing processes
mail	Mail processes
user	User processes
uucp	UUCP processes

When you assign a log file to a particular type of process (e.g., daemon), you also can assign what kinds of messages you want written to the file. The levels of messages are shown in the following minitable, from most to least serious (not all these levels are used by all the process types).

Message Type	Description
emerg	A kernel panic (mostly used with kern)
alert	A serious error that your system needs you to deal with immediately
crit	A critical error such as hardware failure
err	All errors
warn	All warnings
notice	General, noncritical messages
info	General information messages

Two special levels are *debug* (include all debugging information) and *none* (don't include anything).

Now, you just put these items together. For example, let's say I want my mail and daemon processes plus all error messages in general to each have their own log files. Also, I need to choose the levels for each of them. The entries I might use are:

```
mail.info       /var/admin/mail.log
```

Send all information produced by mail to the specified log file.

```
daemon.notice       /var/admin/daemon.log
```

Send all notices produced by my daemons to the specified log.

```
*.err      /var/admin/err.log
```

Send all error messages to the specified log.

Backups

It's important to keep backups of data from your site. The extent of the back-ups depends on your own needs. Today, a tape drive for backups isn't all that expensive, so most people shouldn't have to resort to floppy disks. In fact, unless you're doing the most minor of backups involving only one more file, you want to avoid floppy disks for backing up. They're simply not feasible for most sites' backup needs!

To use a tape drive for your backups, you'll need two programs. First, you need a driver to actually run the tape drive: ftape. Second, you'd need a program to actually do the backups. You can use tar, or AFIO.

> **Tip**
>
> Another form of backup is to keep an extra hard drive and to compress your entire primary drive onto it.

> **Tip**
>
> See the Hardware How-To for the other backup technologies supported by Linux.

Ftape

Ftape is one of the packages included with Slackware. It's the actual driver that runs your tape drive. Once you install it from the Slackware disks, that's it! No setup is required.

> **Tip**
>
> See the Hardware How-To to find out which brands of tape backup systems are supported by Linux.

Installing AFIO for Backups

You have two main choices when it comes to actually making your backups. You can use tar itself. However, if a small portion of any file among the data gets damaged, you won't be able to recover even a part of the file. If you don't want to worry about damaged files, the better choice is AFIO. It's designed for archiving purposes, and so has more error-handling capabilities.

To install the program, do the following:

1. Locate it on Sunsite under `/pub/Linux/system/Backup/afio. 2.4.1.tgz`.

2. Move it to your favorite unzipping location.

3. Unzip and untar the file. You'll see a file called PORTING, but rejoice, this program was written specifically for Linux!

4. Enter the file's directory.

5. Type **make** to compile the program.

6. Type **make install** to install it properly on your site.

Now, if you intend to back up to tape, you'll want to look at the `tob` script. To install this script, do the following:

1. Locate it on the CD-ROM in `/pub/Linux/system/Backup/tob-0.13.tar`.

2. Move it to your favorite unzipping location.

3. Unzip and untar the file.

4. Enter the file's directory.

5. Copy the script `tob` into one of the directories in your path, like `/sbin`. This installs it.

6. Take a look in the sample rc (resource) files in the `tob/sample-rc` directory. The two files that exist for AIFO are:

   - `tob.rc.afioz`: Uses compressed AIFO backups.

   - `tob.rc.remote-afioz`: Uses compressed AIFO backups, but backs up to a tape drive on another machine.

> **Tip**
>
> If you have only one tape backup, you can use the first resource file on the machine with the drive and the second file on the machines connected to it.

Choose the file you want for this machine (I'll choose the first).

7. Edit the rc file so that it suits your needs. The default file listing is as follows:

```
# Resource file for tob (version 0.01 and higher), using
# afio'd compressed archives. I use "ftape.o" as loadable
# module, hence the PRECMD and POSTCMD. See the docs for a
# full explanation.

VERBOSE='yes'

TOBHOME="/usr/etc/tob"
BACKUPDEV="/dev/ftape"
PRECMD="insmod /sbin/ftape.o"
POSTCMD="rmmod ftape"

# Let's see what we're up to.
if [ "$TYPE" = "full" ] ; then
 echo "About to make a FULL backup of volume $VOLUMENAME."
elif [ "$TYPE" = "diff" ] ; then
 echo "About to make a DIFFERENTIAL backup of volume
$VOLUMENAME."
elif [ "$TYPE" = "inc" ] ; then
 echo "About to make INCREMENTAL backup of volume
$VOLUMENAME."
fi
```

The variables in this script are as follows:

- VERBOSE='yes'

  Tells all the messages displayed during backup to be displayed. If you set this to 'no' some of them will be suppressed.

- TOBHOME="/usr/etc/tob"

  Tells your system where to find tob. If you put the tob script somewhere other than /usr/etc/tob, be sure to change this here. For example, I put it in /sbin, so I'll use:

  ```
  TOBHOME="/sbin/tob"
  ```

- BACKUPDEV="/dev/ftape"

  Defines the device used in the backup. Be sure this matches where your ftape is installed.

- ```
  PRECMD="insmod /sbin/ftape.o"
  ```

  Executed before ftape starts the backup. Be sure this matches where your ftape.o is located.

- ```
  POSTCMD="rmmod ftape"
  ```

  Executed after ftape is finished with the backup.

- ```
  if [ "$TYPE" = "full" ] ; then
  ```

  ```
  echo "About to make a FULL backup of volume $VOLUMENAME."
  ```

  If it's set to make a full backup, it states this on the screen.

- ```
  elif [ "$TYPE" = "diff" ] ; then
  ```

  ```
  echo "About to make a DIFFERENTIAL backup of volume
  $VOLUMENAME."
  ```

  Otherwise, if set to make a differential backup (comparing what's been backed up before with what's on the drive), the program states that on-screen.

- ```
  elif [ "$TYPE" = "inc" ] ; then
  ```

  ```
  echo "About to make INCREMENTAL backup of volume
  $VOLUMENAME."
  ```

  ```
  fi
  ```

  Otherwise, if the program's set to make an incremental backup, it states that here. The if loop also ends.

8. Move the file to one of the following directories: /etc, /usr/etc, or /usr/local/etc.

9. Create the directory TOBHOME/volumes. For example, I used /sbin/tob for my TOBHOME directory, so I'd create /sbin/tob/volumes.

10. Now we'll set up the .startdir file in the directory we assigned to TOBHOME/volumes earlier, which defines the top-level directory the backup starts in. If I name the backup "everything," and want all the files on the my only drive backed up, my everything.startdir file will contain one line:

    ```
    /
    ```
    ```

That one line refers to everything on that drive. If I had two drives, and that second drive was only home directories, the file would have two lines:

```
/
/home
```

11. If you want to exclude a directory or files from a backup you can do this as well. For example, my `everything.exclude` file (also in the `TOBHOME/volumes` directory) would look like this if I didn't want to have any `tmp` directories included:

```
.*/tmp/.*
```

> **Caution**
>
> The first part of the filename must match with the item in Step 10 that it refers to.

12. Create the directory `TOBHOME/listings`. In my case, it would be `/usr/sbin/listings`.

Making Backups

Now you need to come up with the line to add to `root`'s crontab file to handle your backups. You can invoke tob without any arguments, but all that does is list usage information. The available arguments are listed in the following table.

Table 13.1 Available Arguments

Argument	Description
rc rcfilename	Use this if you want to select an rc file that isn't tob.rc. Make sure to use the full path since this file isn't necessarily in one of the directories that tob will expect it in otherwise. If you use this switch, it must be the first one on the command line.
backups	Displays which backups were made and when, finding the data in TOBHOME/lists directory.
check	Tells tob to check its settings and report any errors. Tob checks the environment settings and its resource file to determine this information.
full volumename	Start a full backup of the volume listed (e.g., everything).

(continues)

Table 13.1 Continued	
fullcount volumename	Tells tob to report the size a full backup of the volume (e.g., everything) listed will be.
diff volumename	Start a differential backup of the volume listed. At least one full backup must be done prior to a differential backup.
diffcount volumename	Tells tob to report the size a differential backup of the volume listed will be.
restore item	Restores everything that matches up with item (e.g., /home/ralph/*).
find item	Tells tob to scan its files and list anything that matches the item. Item in this case can contain regular expressions.
verbose	Lists the contents of the backup device.

If you want your standard backup to be a differential backup, you'll want to do the following:

1. Put a tape in your tape drive.

2. Type **tob -full volumename** (e.g., **tob -full everything**). This command will do a full backup of your hard drive, and likely take a while. It's best to do this at a time when things are very slow or not being used at all.

3. Now, use crontab -e to enter a cron job for your differential backups.

4. Save and exit the crontab file.

Make sure to keep a tape in for the differential backups! Do them fairly frequently, at least every couple of days, if not every day.

Note

A way to ensure you have a good backup system going is to follow the son, father, grandfather tape backup method (which requires 10 tapes). The son tapes you use every day of the week except for one, maybe Sunday, one per day. On the seventh day (the day you use the other tape, Sunday in this case) you use the father tape, one per each Sunday. Then, you go back to using the son tapes. Then, once a month, you use the grandfather tape instead of the father tape.

So, your schedule may look like this:

Monday every week	Put in Monday son tape
Tuesday every week	Put in Tuesday son tape
Wednesday every week	Put in Wednesday son tape
Thursday every week	Put in Thursday son tape
Friday every week	Put in Friday son tape
Saturday every week	Put in Saturday son tape
First Sunday of the month	Put in first father tape
Second Sunday of the month	Put in second father tape
Third Sunday of the month	Put in third father tape
Last Sunday of the month	Put in grandfather tape

Tip

You may occasionally want to backup a file listing for your site with all of the permissions intact (type **ls -lR** | **listing** to save this to a file called listing). Then, if something happens that messes up your permissions you have something to look back to!

Managing Your Network Resources

The major site resource you'll need to watch over is your network resources. Without close management, you'll find that your system will get annoyingly bogged down at times. By *network resources*, I mean your actual CPU and bandwidth.

Managing Processes

One thing that can slow your system down is the processes people are running on it. There are, however, ways for the system administrator to adjust the load so that the system runs most processes at a speed that's comfortable for both yourself and your users.

Determining Process Intensity

If you feel the response time of your system is slow, it's good to find the culprit process. First, take a look at how badly bogged down your system is by using the uptime command. This program lists what time it is, how long the system's been up, how many users are on, and the load average from three quick samples. Generally, you want to keep the load average below 3 or so.

If you feel your load average is too high, you can get a listing of the top processes running to see what's happening. To get a listing of, say, the top 10 processes, type **ps aux | head -10**.

> **Tip**
>
> Typing **ps aux** by itself lists all processes.

Take a look at the process listing and see how much of your system's effort the top ones are taking up (percent CPU). Any process taking more than 50 percent of your CPU time for 30 seconds or longer is a problem.

> **Tip**
>
> If you find that your system is constantly having load problems, it may be time to add more RAM to the CPU.

Slowing Some Processes Down

You can start a CPU-intensive process with the nice command to make sure it takes up less of the processor. You can also change the nice value of a process that's already running.

In Linux, the nice range is from -20 to 19, with -20 being highest priority and 19 being lowest. The default nice value is zero, and if you type it without an argument the process's nice value goes up by 10. For example, if you wanted to start the calculate process and really weren't in much of a hurry, you could give it a nice of 15 to slow it down: nice 15 calculate. Or, if you were starting the rush process and wanted to make sure it got done quickly, you might nice it to -20: nice -20 rush.

If you see a process running that is taking up too much of your CPU time, you can use the renice command as root to change its nice value. Get the process number from the ps listing, and decide on the new nice value for it. For example, if rush was process 235 and you realized it was just bogging things down too much, you could use: renice -15 235.

> **Tip**
>
> All users can `nice` their own processes. If you have users who are constantly running CPU-intensive processes, they may be willing to `nice` them for you.

Getting Rid of Useless Processes

Sometimes a process just plain dies, or hangs. In this case, you may need to kill it so it's not wasting your CPU's time. Once again, you'll need a process's id (PID) number to do this.

> **Caution**
>
> Killing a process kills its child processes. If you kill one of your shells, you will also kill the processes you were running in that shell.

You'll want to try killing a process in the following order (for example, process number 345):

1. `kill 345`

   This is the most gentle and clean kill from your system's point of view. If the process you're trying to kill is too much of a mess, this version won't work. Try a `ps 345` to see if it's still running.

2. `kill -9 345`

This is a harsher kill, but probably the one you'll use most often. Since the process its killing doesn't get to clean up after itself, the files involved may be in a bit of a mess.

Managing Bandwidth

Managing bandwidth isn't as simple as managing other features of your site. A few tips are:

- *If you have dial-in users, don't allow more on your site than it can handle.* Also, make sure the dial-in connection is slower than your connection to the Internet. This way, even if they max out their own bandwidth, they don't max out yours as well.

- *Don't overreach your resources.* If you want to run a news server, get it set up, and discover that it sucks down way too much of your bandwidth, seriously consider taking down your news server and setting up your site to use your uplink's instead.

■ *Watch the number and size of mailing lists you run.* They're not only CPU intensive while being processed, but all those posts have to be sent back out as well.

■ *Watch your logs.* Perhaps someone is offering something like a Web page that's getting so many hits that your bandwidth is suffering. If so, you may need to ask them to move it elsewhere.

Maintaining Your System

An important aspect of site maintenance is maintaining your servers. Because these programs perform all of the services your site offers to both your own users and other people on the Internet, you've got to keep them running smoothly.

In this chapter, you learn how to:

- Maintain each server you installed
- Maintain the file areas associated with each server

Maintaining Your E-mail Servers

It's important to keep your e-mail running smoothly, as it's in many ways the most essential service on your site. If you lose access to e-mail, you lose communication with your users and the rest of the Internet.

You have one server to maintain in this case, Sendmail. It's not the server software itself you're maintaining here. You'll be keeping track of the log files, mail spool space, and other mail-related features.

Maintaining Sendmail

There are only a few things you need to do to maintain your Sendmail server. The rest is taken care of by the software itself. Things to take care of include the following:

- Sometimes your mail spool will get jammed, and mail will sit in the queue without being delivered. You may want to add a cron job (a section to your root **cron** file) to run the command sendmail - q once a day. This will flush any mail that's still sitting in the queue (sometimes mail doesn't go out immediately because of technical problems, and so it will sit in the queue until it's flushed).

The mail queue will get especially jammed if a lot of mail is sent while your connection is down. You may want to make it a habit to flush the mail queue whenever your connection goes down and comes back up.

■ Be sure to keep an eye on your mail logs (the default path would be /var/adm/messages, if you aren't using the default, look in your /etc/ syslog.conf file to see what file you assigned your mail files to go to) so they don't take over your hard drive space. They often aren't worth archiving unless you're having problems with mail forgery. If people are forging mail from users on your site, you may want to start keeping mail logs for a while so you can determine if mail really came from the user or not. Otherwise, you may just want to delete (with the rm command) them once a day.

Maintaining Mailing Lists

Most mailing list maintenance involves adding and removing users by hand. While the software does handle this aspect itself, there are times you'll need to do the following:

■ If an account subscribed to your mailing list ceases to exist, you'll get e-mail to the listmaster for that specific mailing list after every single post that goes out to the list, telling you that particular account no longer exists. You'll definitely want to remove this user from the list.

To remove a user from a list in Majordomo, go to the directory where you keep your list user files (likely /usr/local/majordomo/lists) and locate the list of users for the mailing list you're working on, which will be the same filename as the list's name. Edit the user list and find the e-mail address you want to remove. Delete the e-mail address, then save and exit the file.

■ Sometimes people move between sites or parts of sites, and the list no longer recognizes them. They'll likely contact you and complain that they're no longer on the list. You'll need to get the address they subscribed from and go in by hand and adjust their subscription if they can't return to the old account, unsubscribe, then resubscribe from the new account.

To do this, e-mail them and ask what address they originally subscribed from. Then, locate and edit the user list for the mailing list. Find the old e-mail address—if they weren't sure, look for the same userid and the same site as the person making the complaint, it's just the host that may be different. Delete the old e-mail address and replace it, or edit it to match the new one. Then, save and exit the file.

- Keep in mind that sometimes it's easier for you to simply remove a troublesome user from a mailing list. If you're doing it at their request, there's no problem. You'll want to be sure your list rules (contained in the info file you send out to all new list members) contain a clear picture of what's acceptable and what's not, and what actions you'll take if someone insists on breaking the rules. This way, if you're having to remove a user because they're a problem, you can point them to the rules if and when they complain.

The rest of mailing list maintenance involves wading through e-mail that comes back to the list owner for various reasons. A lot of this mail is:

- Warnings about e-mail that was held on its way, but will still be delivered. This e-mail will be taken care of by the site holding it, so no further action is necessary.

- If a user's e-mailbox is full, their mail will bounce back. Hopefully, the user will take care of this problem soon and you can just deal with it by deleting the error messages. If it goes on for too long you may want to eventually delete the user to save yourself from having to constantly delete bounced posts.

- If a host on a site has been renamed or the site is temporarily unreachable, mail will bounce back. Just delete the errors for a few days and see if the problem is fixed. If after a week or so there's still a problem with mail bouncing, you may want to remove the user.

For the above examples, if you don't have a need to save the error messages you'll get in your mailbox (if you run the list), just delete them.

Maintaining Your Web Server

Maintaining a Web server is a little more involved than maintaining your e-mail servers, but not by much. Most of the work simply involves keeping things up-to-date.

Checking Links

If you have Web pages set up for your site in general (e.g., a Web page with a list of frequently asked user tech support questions), and it has any links to outside sources, it's important to check it regularly for accuracy. Things on the Internet change constantly, so you may find that the links you point to go up and down or move to another URL. The sooner you find out, the more likely you are to get a page letting you know where the new resource is.

To check out a link, just click it and see if it takes you where it's supposed to.

Basic HTML

All HTML formatting commands have an opening code, and a closing code. The difference between them is that the closing code ends with a slash (/). For example, the code that begins every document should be <HTML>. The entire Web page goes after this, and at the end of the page, the last code should be </HTML>.

As shown in chapter 7, "Installing Web Server Software," this is the most basic Web page you can have:

```
<HTML>
<HEAD><TITLE>My first test page</TITLE></HEAD>
<BODY>
This is my test page.
</BODY>
</HTML>
```

Note that the page begins and ends with an HTML code. The second code you always need to have is the HEAD code, which marks off the header for the page, which is displayed at the top of the browser window if you're using Netscape. The next one is the TITLE code, which defines the page's title, which is displayed within the page itself. Finally, the last necessary code is the BODY code, which defines marks off the main portion of the page.

Tip

You don't have to capitalize the codes. A lot of people do it as a way to make sure they stand out from the rest of the text.

HTML has a number of word-processor-like codes as well. Some of them are:

Code	Meaning
<H1>...</H1>	Main header
<H2>...</H2>	Secondary header. There are 6 headers, each one less prominent than the one before it.
<B>...</B>	Bold
<I>...</I>	Italics
<U>...</U>	Underline
<UL>...</UL>	Bulleted list. Each bulleted item should begin with <LI>. There is no ending </LI>.

This is a very basic guide to HTML code. For a more in-depth guide, check out QUE's *Special Edition Using HTML*.

Keeping Track of Usage

You can keep track of accesses to your Web pages by simply looking through your server's log files. However, you can also get a program off the Internet that tracks all sorts of usage statistics, makes graphs, and so on. This program is *wusage*, and you can get it one of the two following ways:

- FTP to **isis.cshl.org**, fetch the file pub/wusage

- Go to the URL **http://siva.cshl.org/wusage.html** and click the link *How do I get wusage?* You can click a link at this point that allows you to download it.

Compiling wusage

To compile wusage, complete the following steps:

1. Move it to your favorite unpacking and compiling location.

2. Decompress and untar the file.

3. Change into the wusage directory.

4. Edit the Makefile and change the compiler from CC=cc to CC=gcc.

5. Save and exit the Makefile.

6. Type **make all** to compile the program.

Configuring wusage

To configure wusage, do the following (the configuration file is huge, so I'll only discuss the changes you need to make here):

Step 1

Edit the sample file `wusage.conf`.

Step 2

```
#Type of server log:
#If your server CAN use COMMON format, then DO, in all cases.
```

The server you installed does work with the COMMON format (COMMON is a format used by the httpd you installed to format log files), so insert the line:

```
COMMON
```

Step 3

```
#Name of your server as it should be presented:
Quest
```

Change Quest to the name of your server. For example, my server is simply **Renaissoft**.

Step 4

```
#File to use as a prefix; MUST BE A COMPLETE FILE SYSTEM PATH.
➥REALLY:
#NOT A URL.
/home/www/prefix.html
```

If you don't want it to store its prefix file in this path, change it to one appropriate for your needs.

Step 5

```
#File to use as a suffix; MUST BE A COMPLETE FILE SYSTEM PATH.
➥REALLY:
#NOT A URL.
/home/www/suffix.html
```

If you don't want it to store its suffix file in this path, change it to one appropriate for your needs.

Step 6

```
#Directory where HTML pages generated by usage program should be
➥located:
/home/www/web/usage
```

If you don't want it to save the pages it creates to display your usage statistics in the path above, change it to suit your own needs.

Step 7

```
#URL to which locations of HTML pages should be appended for
➥usage reports:
#(the same as the first line, but in web space, not filesystem
➥space)
/usage
```

The directory above is relative to your Web server's file system. For example, /usage above would be /public_html/usage. This item should match the item from step 6.

Step 8

```
#Path of httpd log file:
/home/www/ncsa/logs/access_log
```

If your httpd log file isn't in the location shown above, change this item to point to the location of your file.

Step 9

```
#Top-level domain only (i.e., org not cshl.org):
org
```

Change this item to match your top level domain. For example, I'm **renaissoft.com**, so I would enter com instead of org here.

Step 10

```
#Directories/items that should never register in the top ten:
#To inhibit everything on a path, use /path*
{
}
```

If you have pages on your site that you don't want mentioned in the statistics even if they're in the top ten, list their full paths here between the brackets.

Step 11

```
#items that should never register at *all*, even:
#for the total access count
{
}
```

If you have pages you don't even want counted when determining the total number of accesses, put their full paths between the brackets.

Step 12

```
#Sites that should never register in the usage statistics:
{
}
```

If you don't want to see particular sites listed in your usage statistics (e.g., your own site), enter the domain name between the brackets. I included my own site here, because I don't want any of my page testing to count as real accesses, for example, {*.renaissoft.com}.

Step 13

Save and exit the file.

Step 14

Move wusage into your main Web directory (or really wherever you prefer to have it).

Step 15

Move wusage.conf to your main Web conf directory (or elsewhere if you prefer), which is inside the same directory as cgi-bin one.

Running wusage

To actually use wusage, just use crontab -e to make a cron job to tabulate your site statistics (calling wusage itself) once a week or however often you want. When you refer to the file in the crontab, call it as /fullpath/wusage ms]c /fullpath/wusage.conf. If you want to go ahead and see how it comes out, enter this same syntax on the command line now.

All you have to do now is edit your home page and add a link to the files wusage generates!

Cleaning Out the Access Log File

If your site gets a lot of Web page hits, occasionally clean out the httpd access log file (not regularly, simply whenever it starts to look excessively large to you). To keep the access log down to a reasonable size without interfering with wusage, first take a look at your wusage page, and jot down the dates of the week it did its last report for.

> **Tip**
>
> You may want to back up the directory wusage keeps its HTML files in before proceeding, and compress and save a backup of the httpd access log (from the next step) first.

Now, edit the httpd access_log and find the entries from the last day of the week for which the last report was finished. Look through these entries and find the last entry from that particular date. Then, delete everything from the oldest items to the above last entry you just found. Don't touch anything dated after the last week that was already reported. Finally, save and exit the file.

> **Note**
>
> The folks at Quest Protein Database Center (the programmers of this great utility) sincerely want to know that you're using their software. Feel free to send the author, Thomas Boutell, e-mail at **boutell@boutell.com**. If you don't mind, include the URL for your usage page. If you'd rather not have it known because, for example, it's for a private site, then just drop him a note saying you use the software.

Maintaining Your Gopher Server

Maintaining a Gopher server is a fairly straightforward process. After all, it's mainly a simpler version of a Web server.

The main way to maintain your Gopher servers is to check your Gopher menu pointers on occasion to make sure they're accurate.

To make a pointer to a menu item outside your own gopher server, you need to create a file containing the necessary information. I'll walk you through an example that points to something that's actually back at my own site. The entry would be as follows:

```
Name=Renaissoft's Programs
Type=1
Port=70
Path=/Programs
Host=gopher.renaissoft.com
```

This breaks down as follows:

1. Name is the name of the menu choice you want to offer. The menu choice someone would select to go to this option is **Renaissoft's Programs**.

2. Type refers to the data type of the file. The data types available are as follows:

   0   Text file

   1   Directory

   2   CSO name server

   7   Full text index

   8   Telnet session

   s   Sound

   The type I entered in the example is type **1**, a directory.

3. Port is the port the gopher client needs to connect to in order to reach the gopher server you're pointing them to. The port I entered was **70**.

4. Path is the file path the gopher client needs to go to in order to find the item you're pointing to. The directory this menu item points to is in gopher-data/Programs.

5. Host is the machine the gopher client needs to connect to in order to get the item you're pointing to. The host I pointed to was **gopher.renaissoft.com**.

Maintaining Your News Server

Keeping your news server in good working order is mainly taken care of by the news.daily script. The issue you'll want to keep an eye on is your hard drive usage.

To ensure that news doesn't overrun your hard drive, do the following:

- If you find that some groups are building up too large for you to handle, go into the expire.ctl file to change their expiration times. This can help considerably with binary groups.

- You may find that you have the resources to access more groups than you originally planned for, or that you don't have room for the groups you originally thought your site could carry. If the latter proves true, trim down the newsgroups that you set your site to get.

> **Tip**
>
> Every day INN runs a script called news.daily, which sends you information on your site. This includes statistics for your site, including hard drive usage of your news spool, and errors that occurred during the day.

Maintaining Your FTP Server

Once again, FTP server maintenance is fairly simple—server maintenance is fortunately easier and less time-consuming than server installation! It's important to keep an eye on your FTP files, especially if you have a server with an incoming directory where outside users are dropping files off.

Keep the following in mind while maintaining your FTP server:

- Keep your files up-to-date. If you offer particular software packages, stay current with new releases so you aren't offering ones that are three versions old.

- Watch incoming directories carefully. You don't want your site used for illegal traffic (e.g., copyrighted material).

- Check all new MS-DOS and Macintosh files for viruses. You will need to do this on the appropriate machine (e.g., a Mac or an MS-DOS machine).

- If the load on your site is too high on a consistent basis because of your FTP server, and getting higher bandwidth isn't an option, you may want to find an FTP site to mirror yours. There is mirroring software available on **sunsite.unc.edu** under /pub/Linux/system/Network/ file-transfer/pmirror-1.6.tar.gz, and you would need to locate a site that's willing to mirror yours.

- Keep any special user permissions up-to-date.

Maintaining Your Finger Server

Finger servers, due to their simple nature, don't have much to maintain. All you need to do to keep an eye on them is keep track of your dummy users. Keep their info up-to-date, and be sure not to leave old unnecessary ones laying around.

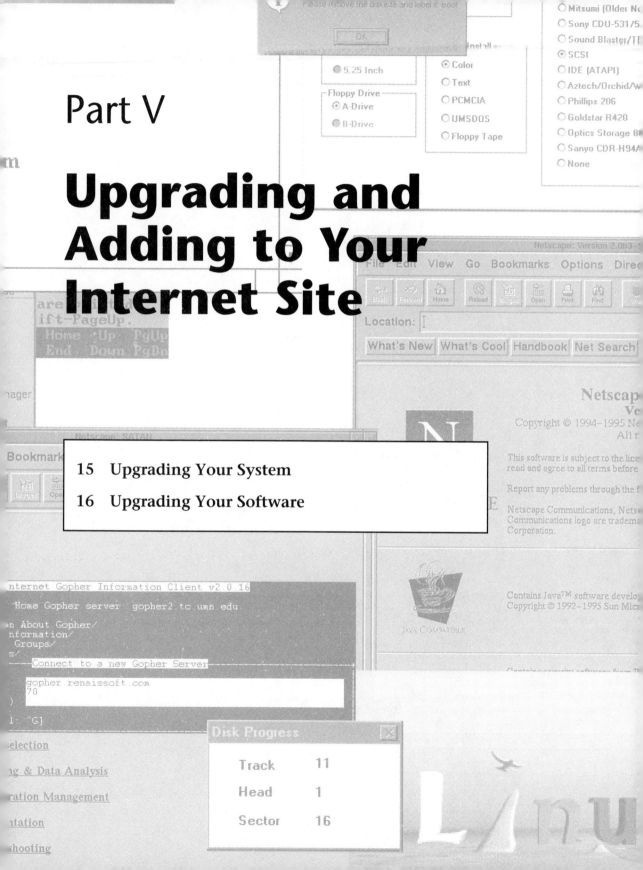

Part V

Upgrading and Adding to Your Internet Site

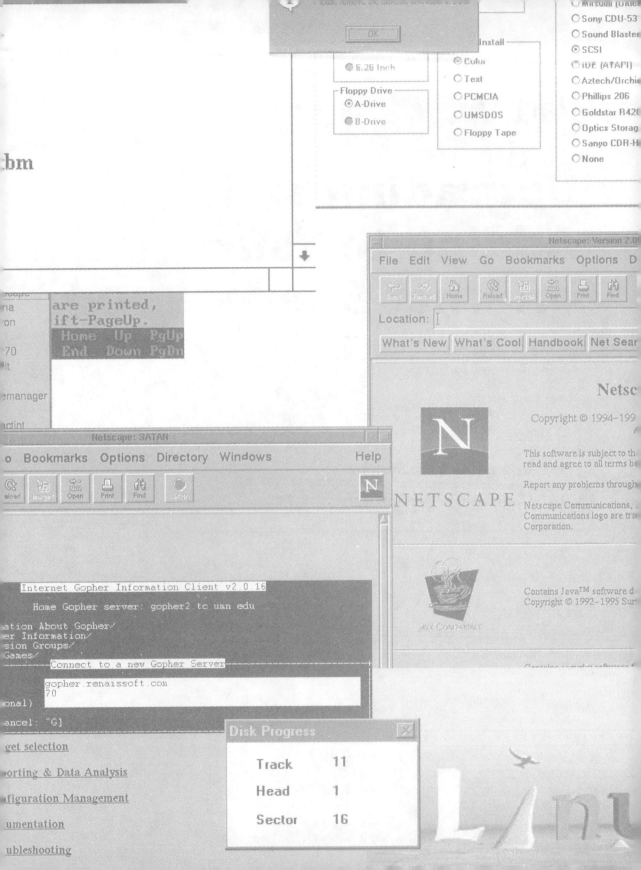

Chapter 15

Upgrading Your System

There are times when you'll want or need to upgrade your equipment. As your site grows, it will require better hardware to perform routine tasks. Standards change over time, and hardware you couldn't afford when you started suddenly comes into your price range. Or you simply decide to offer more services that require hardware you don't have yet.

The primary issues sites have to contend with when it comes to hardware are bandwidth and hard drive space. Sites eventually require greater bandwidth as the number of users increases, and the options on the Internet include more and more bandwidth-intensive services, such as the World Wide Web and various voice and voice/video transmission protocols. Hard drive space easily gets eaten up in time as you and your users take up all of the space you can, as your services get larger, and you get more users on your site.

In this chapter, you learn:

- Considerations when upgrading your hardware
- Considerations when upgrading your connection

Upgrading Your Hardware

Hardware upgrading refers to anything from adding RAM to adding printers or even purchasing a whole new server. There are a number of important factors to keep in mind when choosing brands and models of equipment for your site. For advice on how much memory, hard drive space, etc., that your site will require, read Chapter 2, "What Kind of Hardware and Connection You'll Need."

> **Note**
>
> The following is a quick review of which aspects of a computer's hardware affect which aspects of performance:
>
> - *CPU speed* is the base processing speed, and is the most difficult aspect of a computer to upgrade.
>
> - *RAM* effects how many processes your computer can handle at once. It is simple to upgrade unless you run into compatibility problems, then you just get a replacement chip.
>
> - The *hard drive* is storage space. Although not something that you actually upgrade, you can either replace a hard drive completely or add another one to your system.
>
> The *monitor* and *video card* effect your ability to view graphics of any form except plain ASCII. If you plan to use X-Windows, it is especially important to review Appendix F, "The Linux Hardware How-To."

Driver Availability

When purchasing equipment for a Linux system, don't choose a brand entirely by the features that are listed on the packaging. The programs that come with most hardware (e.g., tape backup systems) are written for MS-DOS or MS-Windows systems, so you can't always count on using some of their special features.

> **Caution**
>
> Be *sure* that you look at appendix F before purchasing any hardware for your system. There is nothing worse than getting a component and then discovering you can't find any drivers for it!

As new versions of the kernel come out, more and more hardware is supported. Check the most recent version of the Hardware How-To in the Linux Documentation Project files if you want to see if something in particular has been added. Then, just get the necessary patches from Sunsite to upgrade your kernel to that level.

> **Tip**
>
> You may find that if you're willing to go to an experimental kernel, you can find drivers available for a particular piece of hardware that weren't available before. See chapter 16, "Upgrading Your Software," for more on experimental kernels and the pros and cons.

Working Efficiently

You probably remember being impatient as a user with every second of downtime your own provider had. Your users will be the same with you. I'll go over some methods here of making sure that you minimize your downtime as much as possible. By keeping your downtime minimal, you not only make your users happy, but your life gets easier because you don't have as many complaints coming in.

Hardware Compatibility

Be sure the hardware you purchase is compatible with your system. Check out new versions of the Linux Hardware How-To (available at Sunsite and on the Linux Documentation Project Web pages) and be sure to get something on that list. Look at the drivers required to support this hardware, and see which kernel these drivers were introduced in. Be fully aware of the work you'll have to do to install one brand which may only work with a brand new, experimental driver, over another which may have a driver in your current kernel that's perfectly stable.

Warn Your Users

Give your users as much warning as possible, including an estimation of how long the system will be down. You may be tempted to give a nice short guess, but keep in mind that you may run into unforeseen problems. Keep in mind also that most experienced users will add a few hours to whatever estimates you give them, so don't overestimate either.

Remember, if it's going to take eight hours or more to get something repaired, you're going to have to arrange to feed the people doing the work!

V

Upgrading and Adding

Tip

If you run a large site, you may want to pay someone to stay until later at night (e.g., 10 pm), or even keep technical staff in 24 hours a day, seven days a week. People who use the Internet for work and fun tend to do it at all sorts of hours, and appreciate being able to get at least bigger problems solved when they come up.

Be Prepared To Get It Done Quickly

Have a distinct plan ready when you take the system down. Know all of the steps you will need to take, and try to know some of the more common problems. The more informed you are, the more quickly the operation will be finished.

This means that you should read all the instructions for all the software and hardware you're dealing with. If there are FAQs available on the Net, read those, too.

Another part of being prepared is making sure all of your cables will connect up properly to one another! There's little worse than having all of the equipment on hand but finding out you're trying to connect a female cable to a female port and don't have a converter on hand.

Making Backups

If you're dealing in any way with your file systems, make backups! If you're even just concerned that something *might happen* to your file systems during the upgrade, make backups. When it comes to backups, it's better to have spent the time making them and not need them than to need them and not have them.

Also, it's highly useful to make a backup of your file listings with the permissions intact. On occasion most system administrators slip up and type the wrong thing in the wrong place, and half of your file permissions are suddenly completely wrong. If you've kept a backup of how things should be set, you can refer back to it rather than just having to see what won't work to track the problems down!

Keep Track of Your Cabling

If you're simply pulling one computer out from your Ethernet network, don't forget that you need to keep the cabling plugged into the card if you're keeping the rest of the site up and running. If an Ethernet connector is so much as jiggled out of place on one machine, all of your machines will lose their networking.

Another way to handle it if you're working on the machine at the end of your network, is to move your Ethernet terminator up by one machine. This way, you have a new end of network defined for a while, so everything stays up and running.

Basically, there has to be a terminator at both ends of your network. If one of your connections comes loose, you suddenly have an end of network without a terminator, because the network can't pass the point where the connection isn't there. Moving your terminator and cutting off part of the network if you're going to work on a machine in the middle may be the only way to work on it without shutting the whole network down.

Be Ready for Things not To Work

Try to have a backup plan in case the new setup doesn't function properly. For example, don't write off the old hardware immediately (unless the whole reason for the change is that something was broken). Keep things around for a week or so in case something malfunctions.

Plus, you may want the old items one day to install on a new machine for a transitional period before you go out to buy nicer equipment. I've even run into occasions when an old dial-in modem needed to be put into a slot where a new modem had been because the user assigned to that line had a modem that wasn't compatible with the newer one. So, as long as you have the room to store it, you may as well keep the majority of the old hardware around that was only removed because it was obsolete.

Handling RAM Upgrades

When it comes to memory chips, you may want to actually call your computer's motherboard manufacturer. Some SIMMs just don't work with some motherboards, even though they should according to their specs. (There should be a listing in the manual of what kind of SIMMs your motherboard requires.) Of course, it's easy enough to remove the offending SIMM and get it replaced if it doesn't work. It just means that you suddenly don't have that extra RAM you thought you'd have at that point.

> **Tip**
>
> See chapter 2, "What Kind of Hardware and Connection You'll Need," for more on specific hardware considerations and types.

V

Upgrading and Adding

Upgrading Your Connection

Connection upgrades require a lot of forethought. This is especially important when major changes are required, such as new kinds of modems or new lines. After all, technology changes rapidly, and you don't want to find that your expensive connection upgrade wasn't the way to go!

It's a good idea to keep in touch with both your phone company and your provider concerning connection options. Keep up-to-date on their plans involving their own technology upgrades, short and long term. You may find that you can afford a sensible upgrade earlier than you thought, or that it's not the right time to move to the next level because something better is coming around the corner.

Tip

For more on the various types of connections available, see Chapter 2, "What Kind of Hardware and Connection You'll Need."

Let's do a quick review of the connection types that are available and some of the considerations you need to make, in order of connection speed.

Upgrading to Paired 28.8 Modems

Upgrading from a single 28.8 to a paired 28.8 modem setup requires a few things. First, check with your provider to see if they support load balancing. Then, find out how much they charge. It may be that they charge you for two full Internet connections. If they do this, find out how much an ISDN connection costs, it may be close to the total cost of the load balancing.

If the connection is cost feasible, then you'll first need to make sure that your server has enough serial ports to handle the extra modem. If not, you may need to get a new multiport serial card to handle it. Also, of course, you'll need to get the second modem. I personally prefer external modems because you can monitor the data lights and know your connection's status at a glance. You will also need an extra standard phone line to carry the second modem's data.

See chapter 2, "What Kind of Hardware and Connection You'll Need" to learn how to set up your load balancing connection.

Upgrading to ISDN (One or Multiple Channels)

If you are moving from a 28.8-based connection to an ISDN connection, you once again first need to make sure your provider can offer you an ISDN connection on their end. You also need to make sure the local phone company can offer you an ISDN connection to your home.

If this is possible, then you can cancel the phone line that you use for your modem connection to the Internet unless you have another use for it. You can also remove the 28.8 modem handling it from your machine.

> **Tip**
>
> You can always use that extra line and modem for an incoming dial-in connection.

From this point, you'll need to obtain the equipment discussed in chapter 2. You may find it helpful to talk to your service provider and phone company about what kind of equipment is best to work well with theirs.

Upgrading to FT1 (Partial T1) or T1

As usual, you need to first contact your service provider to see if they can offer you an FT1 or a T1 connection. You may find that they can't, as they may not have the bandwidth to feed that fast of a connection through. If you do find you have to switch providers, remember that you have to go through InterNIC and file a routing change. Your old provider or the new one will likely be willing to handle this for you since they'll want the transition to go smoothly.

You also need to check with your phone company. They will have to lay a T1 line to your site, and this can get costly if the area you're in doesn't have a digital line structure already. If it's going to be a costly installation, put some serious thought into how long you plan to be at that site.

As with upgrading to ISDN, your 28.8 modem (if that's what you're upgrading from) and the standard phone line you used it with is no longer necessary for connecting your site to the Internet.

From here, see chapter 2 for more on selecting your equipment. Your provider, phone company, and even local computer consultants would be good people to talk to about equipment. You can also research brands and options on the Internet via the World Wide Web, and get information at computer shows.

Upgrading to FT3 (Partial T3) and T3

The considerations for a T3 are mostly the same as for a T1. Keep in mind that you can use multiple T1 connections before you need to upgrade to a whole new connection type. The phone company will once again have to wire a new line to your site, as T3 doesn't use the same exact wiring as a T1 (that's how it gets more bandwidth). This also means you will have to get a new interface between the line and your system, because it will be a different size wire you're plugging in. See chapter 2, and talk to your phone company, provider, and local computer consultants for more on choosing equipment for this type of connection.

Upgrading to "other"

You may want to contact your local cable company and find out how soon it will be before they're offering Internet connectivity through their coaxial cables. You'll likely have to get the specialized equipment straight from the cable company. There is more on this in chapter 2.

Chapter 16

Upgrading Your Software

You'll upgrade your site's software much more often than you'll upgrade its hardware. By *software,* I'm referring to everything from the kernel itself to your server programs, including new applications that you add for yourself or your users. Kernels change especially often with updates sometimes coming out every few days.

In this chapter, you learn how to:

- Upgrade your kernel

- Upgrade your servers

- Add new applications

Upgrading Your Kernel

With some software, an upgrade means completely replacing what you have, including getting a whole new version of the source. As discussed in chapter 1, "Why Create Your Own Site with Linux," the Linux kernel advances in small steps involving patches. Each time a fix or improvement is added, a patch is released. You then apply this patch to the source code.

> **Caution**
>
> All of the backup warnings apply heavily when you upgrade your kernel. Do backups before doing any major system changes!

Deciding Whether To Apply Patches

You won't always want to apply patches to bring your kernel up to the version you want. This is especially true if you haven't patched it in a while and are a number of patches behind. Sometimes it's easier to grab a whole new version of the kernel source than to have to apply ten small patches in a row.

It's not necessary to apply patches immediately when they come out. In fact, it's not always wise to do so. Unless you absolutely need to upgrade in order to get a driver for a piece of hardware, you probably don't want to do so more often than every six months or so. This is simply because you will likely run into problems you need to diagnose and fix with most patches, and if you have paying customers you don't want to risk having to take your site down for a major kernel problem from a new patch.

Also, if you need three or more patches to be able to move to the new kernel version you want, you may as well download the whole kernel source for that version. Using a large number of patches can get messy.

When a new patch comes out, an announcement is posted to the newsgroup **comp.os.linux.announce** (and often most of the other Linux groups as well).

> **Tip**
>
> If you're not sure of exactly what kernel version number you're using, type **uname –r** at the prompt to display it.

Take note of what the patch announced is declared to fix, what drivers it adds and, in some cases, what it's known to break (shown in the changes directory listed below if you didn't see the announcement on a newsgroup). In fact, if you don't need any of the new items, it's good to wait and see if anyone complains that something you need is now broken. If so, you'll want to wait for a new patch to fix that item and then apply both of them, or wait awhile through a number of patches until a feature you want is offered.

All of the kernel and patch items are available via FTP at **sunsite.unc.edu**—or one of its mirror sites—in a subdirectory of /pub/Linux/kernel. The kernel directory contains (according to the INDEX file) the following:

Table 16.1   The Contents of /pub/Linux/kernel on Sunsite

Item	Description
COPYING	The Linux kernel copyright notice
INSTALL	Installation instructions for the kernel
changes/	List of what's changed with each kernel release
changes-new/	Changes to recent kernels
cipher.tar.gz	Driver for cipher 9000 ATC-16 card w/ M995 9-track tape
config/	Various configuration utilities
images/	Floppy disk images for booting and installing Linux
kdebug-1.1.tgz	Package to allow simple kernel debugging
kernel.txt.gz	Some unofficial docs on kernel compiling
kguide-0.2.tgz	Help on compiling a new kernel
linux-1.0.patch.alpha.gz	Patch from ALPHA 1.0 to 1.0
linux-1.0.tar.gz	Source tree for Linux 1.0
menu2.01.linux.tar.gz	Menu based shell tool w/ user customizations
modules-1.1.87.tar.gz@	Utilities for making/using kernel modules
old/	Old versions of the kernel - history mostly
patches/	Various kernel enhancements and fixes
pcmcia/	Support for PCMCIA card & card services
scend-0.5.tar.gz	Full-screen editor for structured configuration data
sound/	Support for SoundBlaster, PRO-16, GUS, etc.
tapes/	Various tape backup drivers
v1.0/	Version 1.0 patches (obsolete)

(continues)

V

Upgrading and Adding

Table 16.1 Continued	
Item	**Description**
v1.1/	Version 1.1 developers track (obsolete)
v1.2/	Version 1.2 and patches (stable)
v1.3/	Latest development kernels (ALPHA)

Getting the Full Kernel Source

If you want to start from scratch and grab a full version of kernel source, first you need to move your old source directory to another location. Your kernel source, if you have it on your system, is in the directory /usr/src/linux. As **root**, simply move this to another directory (e.g., /usr/src/linux-old).

You could also have no real /usr/src/linux directory, and instead put kernel source into directories related to the version (e.g., /usr/src/linux-1.2.13) and then make a soft link from the current version's directory to /usr/src/linux.

Now, set up your source for compilation. Log in as **root** and FTP to Sunsite or your favorite mirror site.

Change to the directory /pub/linux/kernel.

Then, change to the directory v1.2 unless Linux has reached version 1.4 at the time that you are following these instructions; then, change to v1.4.

Tip

If an experimental kernel has options you want to use, it's often safe to try it out. Ask around on the Linux newsgroups and see if the problems it has will affect you, and be sure to test it out for a while before trusting it completely. If you choose to use one, you'll be going to 1.3 or 1.5.

Currently, the latest kernel version is 1.2.13, so I'll download the file linux-1.2.13.tar.gz. This is about a 2.3M file, so depending on the speed of your connection, it might take a while. Then, move the file to /usr/src, gunzip and untar it.

Tip

If you're short on hard drive space, then go ahead and delete the old kernel when you're sure the new one is working fine.

Getting Patches To Apply to Kernel Source

If you want to add a patch or a few patches to the source you already have instead of downloading a whole new source version, follow these instructions. Log in as **root**, and FTP to Sunsite or your favorite mirror site.

Change to the directory /pub/linux/kernel, and then to the directory v1.2 (same version notation as in previous section). All of the files that start with *patch* are the patch files. You must apply all patches below the one you want in the end, as they make changes to your source code. For example, if you want to apply patch 1.2.5, you need to get patches 1.2.1 through 1.2.5. Then, just move the patch files to /usr/src.

Applying Patches to Source

If you downloaded patches, you need to apply them to the source code before you can compile it. To apply your patches, log in as **root** and change to /usr/src. You *must* apply the patches in order. To actually apply a patch, type **zcat patchname.gz | patch -p0** (e.g., **zcat patch-2.1.1.gz | patch -p0**).

Caution

You must apply the patches in numerical order. Each one makes changes to the source code, and so the source must be in the full state it's expecting.

Apply the next patch in line. Continue applying patches until you've reached the last one you need. If the patch fails, double-check and make sure you have the patch for exactly the next kernel after the source you're using. You can even look through the patch file and see the changes that are being made, and make them by hand.

If you can't seem to solve the patch problem, you can always download the full version of the source for the kernel you want to compile.

Configuring the Source To Fit Your Needs

Now, it's time to configure the kernel so it's compiled for your site's specific needs. Because the instructions here are for when this book was written, I recommend you read the README file in your new /usr/src/linux directory. In the "INSTALLING the kernel" section, you will find detailed instructions on how to proceed.

I'll walk you through the compiling of this kernel: version 1.2.13. First, I'll make sure that everything is properly in place, as follows:

1. Change to the directory /usr/include.

2. Type **rm –rf linux** to remove any old C header files.

3. Type **ln –s /usr/src/linux/include/linux linux** to make a soft link that points your system to the new C header files included with the new kernel source.

4. Type **rm –rf asm** to remove any old assembler header files.

5. Type **ln –s /usr/src/linux/include/asm–i386 asm** to make a soft link that points your system to the new assembler header files included with the new kernel source.

6. Change to /usr/src/linux.

7. Type **make mrproper** to clean up any additional extra source that could cause problems with your compilation.

Now, to configure the kernel to suit your needs, do the following as **root**:

1. Change to /usr/src/linux if you're not already there.

2. Type **make config** to start the script that walks you through specific configuration options. From here, I will walk you through the questions I got and the answers I gave in this particular version.

> **Tip**
>
> When in doubt over whether you need a feature, it's generally safe to choose *y* for *yes*. Then at least, you won't have to recompile to add a needed feature. If you choose no for something, it's not included in the compiled kernel, and you'll have to go back and compile it all over again! The main difference is the more things you say yes to, the larger the kernel.

3. Kernel math emulation: Answer **n** for *no* unless you are running a 386 without a coprocessor on this machine.

4. Normal floppy disk support: Answer **y** for *yes* so your kernel will support standard PC floppy disks.

5. Normal (MFM/RLL disk and IDE disk/cdrom support: Answer **y** if you need support for any of this hardware. Otherwise, answer **n.**

6. Now you're given a few options, and you only want to choose one of them, as follows:

- Use old disk-only driver for primary: This driver would only allow one interface with up to two drives. If this is all you require for the computer you're working on, press **y** for *yes*. Otherwise, press **n** for *no.*

- Use old IDE driver for primary/secondary: This driver allows a secondary interface (through which would add items like IDE/ATAPI CD-ROM drives). If you intend to use this equipment on your computer, press **y** for *yes*. Otherwise, press **n** for *no.*

- Include support for IDE/ATAPI CD-ROMs: If you intend to use this equipment, press **y.** If not, press **n.**

> **Tip**
>
> The hardware discussed here is explained in more detail in chapter 2.

7. XT hard disk support: If you intend to use this equipment, press **y.** If not, press **n.**

8. Networking support: Because you're running an Internet site, choose **y.**

9. Limit memory to low 16M: This item is directly related to some 386 machines. If you have a 386 machine and it has a DMA controller that doesn't properly handle over 16M of RAM, then choose **y.** Otherwise, choose **n.**

10. PCI bios support: If the computer you're working on uses PCI BIOS, choose **y.** Otherwise, choose **n.** If you choose yes, you'll be asked for more information on your PCI bridge organization.

11. System V IPC: Perl uses this option to allow processes to talk to one another. Choose **y.**

12. Kernel support for ELF binaries: You installed an all-ELF Slackware version, so choose **y.**

13. Use –m486 flag for 486-specific optimizations: If the computer you're working on is a 486 or Pentium machine, choose **y.** It will optimize things to run on its processor.

14. Set version information on all symbols for modules: This tells modules to check your kernel version and, if the module's version doesn't match, it won't run. Often, a module will work okay even if it's older than the kernel you're using, so this can be a pain as it requires you to compile modules every time you update your kernel. However, if you don't want to take the chance of running into problems, go ahead and choose **y.** Otherwise, choose **n.**

> ### Note
>
> A module, or loadable module, is a piece of kernel code that isn't always needed. Instead, it's saved out into a piece of code that can be loaded into memory when it's necessary (e.g., FTAPE). This helps to keep down on how much RAM your system kernel eats up on a regular basis.

15. TCP/IP networking: Your computers need this option to speak to the Internet (which uses the TCP/IP protocol), so choose **y.**

16. IP forwarding/gatewaying: You need this on your main server, but not on other machines. Choose the appropriate answer.

17. IP multicasting: This is the capability of a machine to have multiple IP addresses. If you don't need this option, choose **n.**

18. IP firewalling: You won't need this option because if you want to use a firewall, you'll install Socks, which doesn't require it. Choose **n.**

19. IP accounting: Choose **n.**

20. You should leave the following options at their defaults:

> PC/TCP compatibility mode
>
> Reverse ARP
>
> Assume subnets are local
>
> Disable NAGLE algorithm
>
> The IPX protocol

21. SCSI support: If you have any SCSI hardware, choose **y.** It will ask you further configuration questions. If you don't have SCSI hardware, choose **n.**

22. Network device support: Choose **y.** You need this to connect to your provider.

23. Dummy net driver: This allows you to set up "dummy addresses," such as aliases for a machine named "ftp" that physically doesn't exist. Choose **y** to be able to use this.

24. SLIP (serial line) support: If you want to be able to use SLIP or allow your users to use SLIP, choose **y.**

25. CSLIP compressed headers: Choose **y.** This will make your SLIP connections more secure.

26. 16 channels instead of 4:   By default, you can have only four simultaneous SLIP connections. If you want to be able to offer more than four, choose **y.** Otherwise, choose **n.**

27. PPP support: If you're using PPP, choose **y.**

28. PLIP support: This allows you to connect computers using parallel ports. You can only connect two machines in this way because computers generally only have one parallel port. Choose **n** unless you intend to use this.

29. Do you want to be offered ALPHA test drivers: Because you're running a site, you probably don't want to risk running experimental drivers unless it's a driver that isn't available otherwise. It doesn't automatically add them, so if you're not sure, choose **y.** Otherwise, choose **n.**

30. Now you'll be asked which networking card you're using. Choose **n** for all of those you're not using and **y** for the one you are:

> Western Digital/SMC
>
> AMD LANCE and Pcnet
>
> 3COM (default)
>
> Other ISA cards
>
> EISA, VLB, PCI, and other on board controllers
>
> Pocket and portable adapters

31. Now you'll be asked if you need a number of CD-ROM drivers, none of which are for SCSI or IDE/ATAPI drives. Answer **n** for anything you don't have and **y** for anything you do:

Sony CDU31A/CDU33A

Mitsumi (not IDE/ATAPI)

Matsushita/Panasonic

Matsushita/Panasonic second controller

Aztech/Orchid/Okano/Wearnes non IDE

Sony CDU535

32. Now you are asked which file systems you want to support:

- Standard (minix) fs support: Choose **y** for this one. It's nice and small and good for making rescue disks.

- Extended fs support: This is a slightly older file system than the one you used during your Linux installation. Choose **n**.

- Second extended fs support: Choose **y**. You installed Linux with this file system initially.

- xiafs file system support: If you used xiafs instead of ext2fs, choose **y**. Otherwise, choose **n**.

- msdos fs support: Choose **y** if you want to be able to read from MS-DOS formatted disks, floppies, or hard drives.

- umsdos: Choose **n**. UMSDOS (UNIX in MS-DOS) is a Linux filesystem that operates much like an MS-DOS FAT file system, but allows the user to have long file names, permissions, group ownerships, and other UNIX-like file settings.

- /proc file system support: Choose **y**. This item makes up for some deficiencies in the Linux kernel compared to other UNIX systems when it comes to process handling. You definitely want this for your site.

- NFS file system support: If you want to mount any file systems via NFS, choose **y**.

- ISO9660 cdrom file system support: If you use a CD-ROM at all, choose **y**.

- OS/2 HPFS file system support: If you want to access an OS/2 file system, choose **y.**

- System V and Coherent file system support: If you have access to a machine that runs one of these flavors of UNIX and therefore will have access to disks formatted for them, choose **y.** Otherwise, choose **n.**

33. You'll now be asked which character devices (mouse, printer, etc.) you want to use:

- Cyclades asynch mux: This is a multiport serial card. If you have one, choose **y.**

- Parallel printer: If you want to hook a parallel printer up to this machine, choose **y.**

- Logitech busmouse: If the mouse on this machine is a Logitech busmouse, choose **y.**

- PS/2 mouse: If you have a PS/2 mouse on this machine, choose **y.**

- Microsoft busmouse: If you have a Microsoft busmouse on this machine, choose **y.**

- ATIXL busmouse: If you have this type of mouse, choose **y.**

- QIC-02 tape: If you have this kind of tape drive on your machine, choose **y.**

- QIC-117:   If you have this kind of tape drive on your machine, choose **y.**

34. Sound card support: If you have a sound card on the machine you're configuring the kernel for, choose **y.** If you do, you will be asked for specific configuration information involving your sound card.

35. The Kernel hacking section: Answer **n** to Kernel profiling support to avoid any problems with your site.

36. Don't be startled if your system briefly compiles something! If it does, that's because there are some special configuration options it can continue with to make your life easier down the road. For example, if you said you have a sound card, it compiles a small program to configure sound support.

37. The configuration program exits. Look through the Makefile and make sure that it's what you want.

Creating Your Kernel

Now, you can create your kernel! This requires the following steps:

1. Log in as **root**.

2. Change to `/usr/src/linux`.

3. Type **make dep** to make sure key files are in the right place.

4. Type **make clean** to be assured that everything is up-to-date.

5. Now, to compile the kernel itself, type **make zImage.**

> **Note**
>
> The speed it takes to compile a kernel depends on how fast your machine is and how much RAM it has. On a 386 machine, it can take over an hour, while on a Pentium or high end 486, it may take less than 30 minutes. You'll probably want to recompile your kernel when you have something else you can do while you wait.

6. Move `/vmlinuz` to `/vmlinuz2` so you don't overwrite your previous kernel.

7. Edit the file `/etc/lilo`.

> **Note**
>
> Instead of completely replacing the old kernel at the moment, I'm going to add a reference for the new one. This way, I can reboot with the new kernel and test it to make sure it works. Then, if it works satisfactorily, I can come back and remove the old one.

8. Locate the section

```
image = /vmlinuz

label = Linux

root = /dev/hda1
```

> **Note**
>
> The value assigned to root may be different if you didn't use /dev/hda1
> initially. Just make sure the original root reference and the following one
> match.

9. Copy this section and create a new one below it.

10. Change it to read

```
image = /zImage2

label = linux-new

root = /dev/hda1
```

11. Save and exit the file.

12. Type **lilo** to install the new settings.

Now, when you boot with LILO, you can type **linux-new** instead of **linux**
and boot with the new kernel. When you're confident it's stable, erase the
old kernel (the old zImage file) and move zImage2 to zImage.

Upgrading Your Servers

When new versions of servers come out, it often means that they have—or
are meant to have—fewer bugs than previous versions. This in itself is a good
reason to upgrade. There might also be new features added that are useful to
you, as in more functions being automated, or even more functions available.
Also, if new standards have come out, a new server will be released to support
those standards.

To actually upgrade a server, first download the new source code for the
server. You should be able to find its home location in its own documentation files. If you can't, try looking on Sunsite first. Then, move it to /usr/src.

Next, take a look through the information files (e.g., README) that came
with the source to see what you need to do before compilation. The differences between the previous version and the new version could be minor or
massive, depending on how many bug fixes there are, how many new features were added, how standards have changed, and how the interface has
changed.

> **Tip**
>
> Back up your old server in case you find you would rather return to it, or the new server simply doesn't work.

Follow the precompilation instructions carefully. After all, if there are any options that need to be configured *before* you compile the program, you don't want to forget about them until you're almost finished setting up! Then you'd have to turn around and start all over. Then, once you've set it up for compilation, compile the program according to the instructions in the README files.

As you've seen throughout this book, once you get the program compiled there is often more configuration to do. Follow the instructions in the information files on any post-compilation configuration necessary.

Test the new server and make sure it does what you expected and wanted it to do. If you don't like the new server, erase it. If you do like it, erase the old server. Though, you may want to keep the old one around for a week or so in case it takes a while for problems with the new server to show themselves.

Adding New Applications

Every once in awhile, you'll see a new application that you decide you want for your site, a particular machine, or even a particular user (could be an IRC client or server, a game, a WAIS server, graphics viewer for a graphics-capable machine where you don't have to use X-Windows, fax programs, or any other number of applications available on the Internet).

> **Tip**
>
> To find most of the applications, go to Sunsite in /pub/Linux and look through the directories there. You can also find the Linux Software Map on the Linux Documentation Project pages, which is a catalog of applications available for Linux and where to find them.

The difficulty or ease of installing this application depends on the application itself and how diligently you read the instructions before going at it.

The basic instructions for installing a new application are similar to the instructions listed in the previous section.

Download the application, and take a look through the information files (e.g., README) that came with it. It may have come as source, or as a binary. If it came as source, see what configuration you need to do before compilation, follow the instructions, and compile the program according to the instructions in the README files.

Follow the instructions in the information files on any further setup, whether you got the file as source or as a binary. Then, test the program to make sure it does what you want and does it the way you want it done.

Part VI

Appendixes

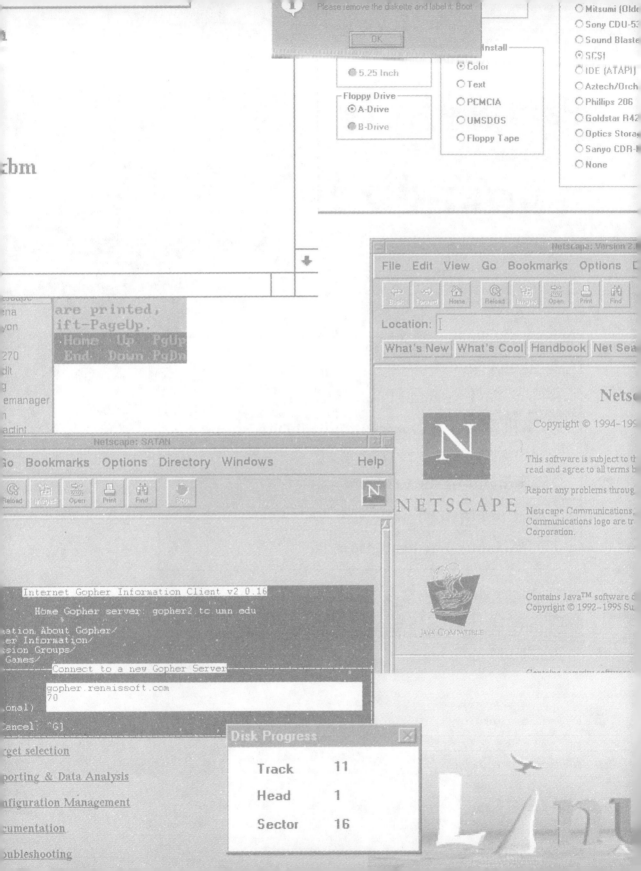

Linux Archive Sites

Two definitive archive sites contain the latest and greatest Linux system software. They are huge, busy sites that are primary archive systems on the Internet—which makes connecting to them difficult and transfer rates painfully slow. Therefore, I am providing you with references to both of the primary sites as well as their *mirrors*—sites whose contents duplicate the primary locations in order to take the load off the primary system.

> **Note**
>
> Data on the Internet changes quickly. The list of mirror sites in this appendix are accurate as of when this book was written, but they may no longer be correct. If you prefer to use mirror sites and have problems with the sites in this list, FTP to Sunsite and/or TSX-11. If the FTP access fails, the server will give you an up-to-date list of mirror sites before it disconnects.

Sunsite

To get to Sunsite's Linux archives, FTP to **sunsite.unc.edu** and go to the directory /pub/Linux. Sunsite fortunately has a large list of mirror sites, which are listed by region of the world.

Africa

Site: **ftp.sun.ac.za**
Directory: **/pub/linux/sunsite/**

Site: **ftp.is.co.za**
Directory: **/linux/sunsite/**

Asia

Site: **ftp.cs.cuhk.hk**
Directory: **/pub/Linux/**

Site: **ftp.spin.ad.jp**
Directory: **/pub/linux/sunsite.unc.edu/**

Site: **ftp.nuri.net**
Directory: **/pub/Linux/**

Site: **ftp.nus.sg**
Directory: **/pub/unix/Linux/**

Site: **ftp.nectec.or.th**
Directory: **/pub/mirrors/linux/**

Australia

Site: **ftp.dstc.edu.au**
Directory: **/pub/linux/**

Site: **bond.edu.au**
Directory: **/pub/OS/Linux/**

Europe

Site: **ftp.tu-graz.ac.at**
Directory: **/pub/Linux/**

Site: **ftp.univie.ac.at**
Directory: **/systems/linux/sunsite/**

Site: **ftp.fi.muni.cz**
Directory: **/pub/UNIX/linux/**

Site: **pub.vse.cz**
Directory: **/pub/386-unix/linux/**

Site: **ftp.univ-angers.fr**
Directory: **/pub/Linux/**

Site: **ftp.ibp.fr**
Directory: **/pub/linux/sunsite/**

Site: **ftp.loria.fr**
Directory: **/pub/linux/sunsite/**

Site:	**ftp.dfv.rwth-aachen.de**
Directory:	**/pub/linux/sunsite/**
Site:	**ftp.germany.eu.net**
Directory:	**/pub/os/Linux/Mirror.SunSITE/**
Site:	**ftp.tu-dresden.de**
Directory:	**/pub/Linux/sunsite/**
Site:	**ftp.uni-erlangen.de**
Directory:	**/pub/Linux/MIRROR.sunsite/**
Site:	**ftp.gwdg.de**
Directory:	**/pub/linux/mirrors/sunsite/**
Site:	**ftp.ba-mannheim.de**
Directory:	**/pub/linux/mirror.sunsite/**
Site:	**ftp.uni-paderborn.de**
Directory:	**/pub/Mirrors/sunsite.unc.edu/**
Site:	**ftp.uni-rostock.de**
Directory:	**/Linux/sunsite/**
Site:	**ftp.rus.uni-stuttgart.de**
Directory:	**/pub/unix/systems/linux/MIRROR.sunsite/**
Site:	**ftp.uni-tuebingen.de**
Directory:	**/pub/linux/Mirror.sunsite/**
Site:	**ftp.rz.uni-ulm.de**
Directory:	**/pub/mirrors/linux/sunsite/**
Site:	**ftp.kfki.hu**
Directory:	**/pub/linux/**
Site:	**ftp.italnet.it**
Directory:	**/pub/Linux/**
Site:	**cnuce-arch.cnr.it**
Directory:	**/pub/Linux/**
Site:	**ftp.nvg.unit.no**
Directory:	**/pub/linux/sunsite/**
Site:	**sunsite.icm.edu.pl**
Directory:	**/pub/Linux/**

VI

Appendixes

Site: **ftp.cs.us.es**
Directory: **/pub/Linux/sunsite-mirror/**

Site: **ftp.etsimo.uniovi.es**
Directory: **/pub/linux/**

Site: **ftp.switch.ch**
Directory: **/mirror/linux/**

Site: **ftp.metu.edu.tr**
Directory: **/pub/linux/sunsite/**

Site: **unix.hensa.ac.uk**
Directory: **/mirrors/sunsite/pub/Linux/**

Site: **ftp.maths.warwick.ac.uk**
Directory: **/mirrors/linux/sunsite.unc-mirror/**

Site: **ftp.idiscover.co.uk**
Directory: **/pub/Linux/sunsite.unc-mirror/**

Site: **src.doc.ic.ac.uk**
Directory: **/packages/linux/sunsite.unc-mirror/**

Site: **ftp.dungeon.com**
Directory: **/pub/linux/sunsite-mirror/**

North America

Site: **ftp.io.org**
Directory: **/pub/systems/linux/**

Site: **ftp.cc.gatech.edu**
Directory: **/pub/linux/**

Site: **sunsite.unc.edu**
Directory: **/pub/Linux/**

Site: **ftp.cdrom.com**
Directory: **/pub/linux/sunsite/**

Site: **ftp.siriuscc.com**
Directory: **/pub/Linux/Sunsite/**

Site: **lss.afit.af.mil**
Directory: **/pub/Linux/**

Site: **ftp.engr.uark.edu**
Directory: **/pub/linux/sunsite/**

Site: **ftp.infomagic.com**
Directory: **/pub/mirrors/linux/sunsite/**

Site: **ftp.iquest.com**
Directory: **/pub/linux/sunsite/**

Site: **ftp.linux.org**
Directory: **/pub/mirrors/sunsite/**

Site: **ftp.cps.cmich.edu**
Directory: **/pub/linux/sunsite/**

Site: **ftp.uoknor.edu**
Directory: **/linux/sunsite/**

Site: **ftp.rge.com**
Directory: **/pub/systems/linux/sunsite/**

Site: **ftp.pht.com**
Directory: **/mirrors/linux/sunsite/**

Site: **ftp.yggdrasil.com**
Directory: **/mirrors/sunsite/**

Site: **ftp.wit.com**
Directory: **/systems/unix/linux/**

Site: **uiarchive.cso.uiuc.edu**
Directory: **/pub/systems/linux/sunsite/**

South America
Site: **ftp.inf.utfsm.cl**
Directory: **/pub/Linux/**

TSX-11

While Sunsite (and its mirrors) is considered to be the main Linux archive site, TSX-11 is another primary site. TSX-11 gets the files soon after Sunsite does, so their content is virtually identical. A key use for TSX-11 is that the Linux X-Windows developers place their code on this site first, so you can find the most up-to-date experimental X-Windows code on TSX-11 in /pub/ linux/Alpha.

VI

Appendixes

To get to TSX-11's Linux archives, FTP to **tsx-11.mit.edu** and go to the directory /pub/linux. TSX-11 fortunately has a large list of mirror sites, which are listed by region of the world here.

Africa
Site: **ftp.sun.ac.za**
Directory: **/pub/linux**

Asia
Site: **ftp.menut.edu.tr**
Directory: **/pub/linux/tsx**

Site: **ftp.metu.edu.tr**
Directory: **/pub/linux**

Australia
Site: **kirk.bond.edu.au**
Directory: **/pub/OS/Linux**

Europe
Site: **ftp.fgb.mw.tu-muenchen.de**
Directory: **/pub/linux**

Site: **ftp.ibp.fr**
Directory: **/pub/linux**

Site: **ftp.win.tue.nl**
Directory: **/pub/linux/SLS**

Site: **src.doc.ic.ac.uk**
Directory: **/packages/Linux**

North America
Site: **ftp.pht.com**
Directory: **/pub/linux**

Site: **ftp.rge.com**
Directory: **/pub/systems/linux/tsx-11/**

Site: **ftp.uu.net**
Directory: **/systems/unix/linux/**

Site: **sunsite.unc.edu**
Directory: **/pub/Linux**

Site: **uiarchive.cso.uiuc.edu**
Directory: **/pub/systems/linux/tsx-11**

Site: **wuarchive.wustl.edu**
Directory: **/systems/linux**

Appendix B

The GNU General Public License

As stated in chapter 1, "Why Create Your Own Site with Linux?", Linux is covered under the GNU (Gnu's Not Unix) General Public License. The following is the complete text of the GPL.

GNU GENERAL PUBLIC LICENSE

Version 2, June 1991

Copyright © 1989, 1991 Free Software Foundation, Inc., 675 Mass Ave, Cambridge, MA 02139, USA

Everyone is permitted to copy and distribute verbatim copies of this license document, but changing it is not allowed.

Preamble

The licenses for most software are designed to take away your freedom to share and change it. By contrast, the GNU General Public License is intended to guarantee your freedom to share and change free software—to make sure the software is free for all its users. This General Public License applies to most of the Free Software Foundation's software and to any other program whose authors commit to using it. (Some other Free Software Foundation software is covered by the GNU Library General Public License instead.) You can apply it to your programs, too.

When we speak of free software, we are referring to freedom, not price. Our General Public Licenses are designed to make sure that you have the freedom to distribute copies of free software (and charge for this service if you wish), that you receive source code or can get it if you want it, that you can change the software or use pieces of it in new free programs; and that you know you can do these things.

To protect your rights, we need to make restrictions that forbid anyone to deny you these rights or to ask you to surrender the rights.

These restrictions translate to certain responsibilities for you if you distribute copies of the software, or if you modify it.

For example, if you distribute copies of such a program, whether gratis or for a fee, you must give the recipients all the rights that you have. You must make sure that they, too, receive or can get the source code. And you must show them these terms so they know their rights.

We protect your rights with two steps: (1) copyright the software, and (2) offer you this license which gives you legal permission to copy, distribute and/or modify the software.

Also, for each author's protection and ours, we want to make certain that everyone understands that there is no warranty for this free software. If the software is modified by someone else and passed on, we want its recipients to know that what they have is not the original, so that any problems introduced by others will not reflect on the original authors' reputations.

Finally, any free program is threatened constantly by software patents. We wish to avoid the danger that redistributors of a free program will individually obtain patent licenses, in effect making the program proprietary. To prevent this, we have made it clear that any patent must be licensed for everyone's free use or not licensed at all.

The precise terms and conditions for copying, distribution and modification follow.

GNU GENERAL PUBLIC LICENSE

TERMS AND CONDITIONS FOR COPYING, DISTRIBUTION AND MODIFICATION

0. This License applies to any program or other work which contains a notice placed by the copyright holder saying it may be distributed under the terms of this General Public License. The "Program," below, refers to any such program or work, and a "work based on the Program" means either the Program or any derivative work under copyright law: that is to say, a work containing the Program or a portion of it, either verbatim or with modifications and/or translated into another language. (Hereinafter, translation is included without limitation in the term "modification.") Each licensee is addressed as "you."

Activities other than copying, distribution and modification are not covered by this License; they are outside its scope. The act of running the Program is not restricted, and the output from the Program is covered only if its contents constitute a work based on the Program (independent of having been made by running the Program).

Whether that is true depends on what the Program does.

1. You may copy and distribute verbatim copies of the Program's source code as you receive it, in any medium, provided that you conspicuously and appropriately publish on each copy an appropriate copyright notice and disclaimer of warranty; keep intact all the notices that refer to this License and to the absence of any warranty; and give any other recipients of the Program a copy of this License along with the Program.

   You may charge a fee for the physical act of transferring a copy, and you may at your option offer warranty protection in exchange for a fee.

2. You may modify your copy or copies of the Program or any portion of it, thus forming a work based on the Program, and copy and distribute such modifications or work under the terms of Section 1 above, provided that you also meet all of these conditions:

   a) You must cause the modified files to carry prominent notices stating that you changed the files and the date of any change.

   b) You must cause any work that you distribute or publish, that in whole or in part contains or is derived from the Program or any part thereof, to be licensed as a whole at no charge to all third parties under the terms of this License.

   c) If the modified program normally reads commands interactively when run, you must cause it, when started running for such interactive use in the most ordinary way, to print or display an announcement including an appropriate copyright notice and a notice that there is no warranty (or else, saying that you provide a warranty) and that users may redistribute the program under these conditions, and telling the user how to view a copy of this License. (Exception: if the Program itself is interactive but does not normally print such an announcement, your work based on the Program is not required to print an announcement.)

VI

Appendixes

These requirements apply to the modified work as a whole. If identifiable sections of that work are not derived from the Program, and can be reasonably considered independent and separate works in themselves, then this License, and its terms, do not apply to those sections when you distribute them as separate works. But when you distribute the same sections as part of a whole which is a work based on the Program, the distribution of the whole must be on the terms of this License, whose permissions for other licensees extend to the entire whole, and thus to each and every part regardless of who wrote it.

Thus, it is not the intent of this section to claim rights or contest your rights to work written entirely by you; rather, the intent is to exercise the right to control the distribution of derivative or collective works based on the Program.

In addition, mere aggregation of another work not based on the Program with the Program (or with a work based on the Program) on a volume of a storage or distribution medium does not bring the other work under the scope of this License.

3. You may copy and distribute the Program (or a work based on it, under Section 2) in object code or executable form under the terms of Sections 1 and 2 above provided that you also do one of the following:

   a) Accompany it with the complete corresponding machine-readable source code, which must be distributed under the terms of Sections 1 and 2 above on a medium customarily used for software interchange; or,

   b) Accompany it with a written offer, valid for at least three years, to give any third party, for a charge no more than your cost of physically performing source distribution, a complete machine-readable copy of the corresponding source code, to be distributed under the terms of Sections 1 and 2 above on a medium customarily used for software interchange; or,

   c) Accompany it with the information you received as to the offer to distribute corresponding source code. (This alternative is allowed only for noncommercial distribution and only if you received the program in object code or executable form with such an offer, in accord with Subsection b above.)

The source code for a work means the preferred form of the work for making modifications to it. For an executable work, complete source code means all the source code for all modules it contains, plus any associated interface definition files, plus the scripts used to control compilation and installation of the executable. However, as a special exception, the source code distributed need not include anything that is normally distributed (in either source or binary form) with the major components (compiler, kernel, and so on) of the operating system on which the executable runs, unless that component itself accompanies the executable.

If distribution of executable or object code is made by offering access to copy from a designated place, then offering equivalent access to copy the source code from the same place counts as distribution of the source code, even though third parties are not compelled to copy the source along with the object code.

4. You may not copy, modify, sublicense, or distribute the Program except as expressly provided under this License. Any attempt otherwise to copy, modify, sublicense or distribute the Program is void, and will automatically terminate your rights under this License.

   However, parties who have received copies, or rights, from you under this License will not have their licenses terminated so long as such parties remain in full compliance.

5. You are not required to accept this License, since you have not signed it. However, nothing else grants you permission to modify or distribute the Program or its derivative works. These actions are prohibited by law if you do not accept this License. Therefore, by modifying or distributing the Program (or any work based on the Program), you indicate your acceptance of this License to do so, and all its terms and conditions for copying, distributing or modifying the Program or works based on it.

6. Each time you redistribute the Program (or any work based on the Program), the recipient automatically receives a license from the original licensor to copy, distribute or modify the Program subject to these terms and conditions. You may not impose any further restrictions on the recipients' exercise of the rights granted herein.

   You are not responsible for enforcing compliance by third parties to this License.

VI

Appendixes

7. If, as a consequence of a court judgment or allegation of patent infringement or for any other reason (not limited to patent issues), conditions are imposed on you (whether by court order, agreement or otherwise) that contradict the conditions of this License, they do not excuse you from the conditions of this License. If you cannot distribute so as to satisfy simultaneously your obligations under this License and any other pertinent obligations, then as a consequence you may not distribute the Program at all. For example, if a patent license would not permit royalty-free redistribution of the Program by all those who receive copies directly or indirectly through you, then the only way you could satisfy both it and this License would be to refrain entirely from distribution of the Program.

    If any portion of this section is held invalid or unenforceable under any particular circumstance, the balance of the section is intended to apply and the section as a whole is intended to apply in other circumstances.

    It is not the purpose of this section to induce you to infringe any patents or other property right claims or to contest validity of any such claims; this section has the sole purpose of protecting the integrity of the free software distribution system, which is implemented by public license practices. Many people have made generous contributions to the wide range of software distributed through that system in reliance on consistent application of that system; it is up to the author/donor to decide if he or she is willing to distribute software through any other system and a licensee cannot impose that choice.

    This section is intended to make thoroughly clear what is believed to be a consequence of the rest of this License.

8. If the distribution and/or use of the Program is restricted in certain countries either by patents or by copyrighted interfaces, the original copyright holder who places the Program under this License may add an explicit geographical distribution limitation excluding those countries, so that distribution is permitted only in or among countries not thus excluded. In such case, this License incorporates the limitation as if written in the body of this License.

9. The Free Software Foundation may publish revised and/or new versions of the General Public License from time to time. Such new versions will be similar in spirit to the present version, but may differ in detail to address new problems or concerns.

Each version is given a distinguishing version number. If the Program specifies a version number of this License which applies to it and "any later version," you have the option of following the terms and conditions either of that version or of any later version published by the Free Software Foundation. If the Program does not specify a version number of this License, you may choose any version ever published by the Free Software Foundation.

10. If you wish to incorporate parts of the Program into other free programs whose distribution conditions are different, write to the author to ask for permission. For software which is copyrighted by the Free Software Foundation, write to the Free Software Foundation; we sometimes make exceptions for this. Our decision will be guided by the two goals of preserving the free status of all derivatives of our free software and of promoting the sharing and reuse of software generally.

NO WARRANTY

11. BECAUSE THE PROGRAM IS LICENSED FREE OF CHARGE, THERE IS NO WARRANTY FOR THE PROGRAM, TO THE EXTENT PERMITTED BY APPLICABLE LAW. EXCEPT WHEN OTHERWISE STATED IN WRITING THE COPYRIGHT HOLDERS AND/OR OTHER PARTIES PROVIDE THE PROGRAM "AS IS" WITHOUT WARRANTY OF ANY KIND, EITHER EXPRESSED OR IMPLIED, INCLUDING, BUT NOT LIMITED TO, THE IMPLIED WARRANTIES OF MERCHANTABILITY AND FITNESS FOR A PARTICULAR PURPOSE. THE ENTIRE RISK AS TO THE QUALITY AND PERFORMANCE OF THE PROGRAM IS WITH YOU. SHOULD THE PRO-GRAM PROVE DEFECTIVE, YOU ASSUME THE COST OF ALL NECES-SARY SERVICING, REPAIR OR CORRECTION.

12. IN NO EVENT UNLESS REQUIRED BY APPLICABLE LAW OR AGREED TO IN WRITING WILL ANY COPYRIGHT HOLDER, OR ANY OTHER PARTY WHO MAY MODIFY AND/OR REDISTRIBUTE THE PROGRAM AS PERMITTED ABOVE, BE LIABLE TO YOU FOR DAMAGES, INCLUD-ING ANY GENERAL, SPECIAL, INCIDENTAL OR CONSEQUENTIAL DAMAGES ARISING OUT OF THE USE OR INABILITY TO USE THE PROGRAM (INCLUDING BUT NOT LIMITED TO LOSS OF DATA OR DATA BEING RENDERED INACCURATE OR LOSSES SUSTAINED BY YOU OR THIRD PARTIES OR A FAILURE OF THE PROGRAM TO OPER-ATE WITH ANY OTHER PROGRAMS), EVEN IF SUCH HOLDER OR OTHER PARTY HAS BEEN ADVISED OF THE POSSIBILITY OF SUCH DAMAGES.

END OF TERMS AND CONDITIONS

Appendix: How to Apply These Terms to Your New Programs

If you develop a new program, and you want it to be of the greatest possible use to the public, the best way to achieve this is to make it free software which everyone can redistribute and change under these terms.

To do so, attach the following notices to the program. It is safest to attach them to the start of each source file to most effectively convey the exclusion of warranty; and each file should have at least the "copyright" line and a pointer to where the full notice is found.

> <one line to give the program's name and a brief idea of what it does.>
>
> Copyright© 19yy <name of author>
>
> This program is free software; you can redistribute it and/or modify it under the terms of the GNU General Public License as published by the Free Software Foundation; either version 2 of the License, or (at your option) any later version.
>
> This program is distributed in the hope that it will be useful, but WITHOUT ANY WARRANTY; without even the implied warranty of MERCHANTABILITY or FITNESS FOR A PARTICULAR PURPOSE. See the GNU General Public License for more details.
>
> You should have received a copy of the GNU General Public License along with this program; if not, write to the Free Software Foundation, Inc., 675 Mass Ave, Cambridge, MA 02139, USA.

Also add information on how to contact you by electronic and paper mail.

If the program is interactive, make it output a short notice like this when it starts in an interactive mode:

> Gnomovision version 69, Copyright © 19yy name of author
>
> Gnomovision comes with ABSOLUTELY NO WARRANTY; for details type 'show w'.
>
> This is free software, and you are welcome to redistribute it under certain conditions; type 'show c' for details.

The hypothetical commands 'show w' and 'show c' should show the appropriate parts of the General Public License. Of course, the commands you use may be called something other than 'show w' and 'show c'; they could even be mouse-clicks or menu items—whatever suits your program.

You should also get your employer (if you work as a programmer) or your school, if any, to sign a "copyright disclaimer" for the program, if necessary. Here is a sample; alter the names:

> Yoyodyne, Inc., hereby disclaims all copyright interest in the program 'Gnomovision' (which makes passes at compilers) written by James Hacker.

> <signature of Ty Coon>, 1 April 1989

> Ty Coon, President of Vice

> This General Public License does not permit incorporating your program into proprietary programs. If your program is a subroutine library, you may consider it more useful to permit linking proprietary applications with the library. If this is what you want to do, use the GNU Library General Public License instead of this License.

Appendix C

Where To Find Linux Help and Discussions on the Net

Because Linux is developed, maintained, and distributed over the Internet, Linux users have a strong support network online. This appendix is broken down into what you can find within newsgroups and on the Web.

Newsgroups

A number of newsgroups offer discussions on a wide range of Linux topics. Newsgroups are presented in this appendix according to their top-level hierarchy (indicated by the first part of each newsgroup's full name, e.g., **comp**).

> **Tip**
>
> If a particular top-level hierarchy contains a UNIX group but not a Linux group, and you want to discuss Linux within that hierarchy, the UNIX group is often the appropriate location.

The comp.os.linux Hierarchy

The hierarchy **comp.os.linux** is the primary collection of Linux newsgroups on the net. These groups are where the majority of Linux discussions, support, and development take place in Internet news forums.

Linux Newsgroup	Topic
comp.os.linux.advocacy	Reasons that Linux is better than other operating systems
comp.os.linux.announce	Linux-related announcements
comp.os.linux.answers	Helpful documents that are posted monthly to the comp.os.linux.* groups: FAQs, How-Tos, READMEs, and so on
comp.os.linux.development.apps	Writing applications for Linux and porting applications from other operating systems to Linux
comp.os.linux.development.system	The development of Linux kernels, device drivers, and modules
comp.os.linux.hardware	Linux and hardware compatibility
comp.os.linux.misc	General Linux topics that don't fit into one of the other groups in the comp.os.linux.* hierarchy
comp.os.linux.networking	Networking and communications under Linux
comp.os.linux.setup	Setting up Linux, and Linux system administration
comp.os.linux.x	X-Windows with Linux

Other Linux Newsgroups

A number of other Linux newsgroups are on the Internet. Many of these are local groups, used by Linux user groups in various cities around the world. A sample of the groups available are listed below, sorted according to the top-level hierarchy they're found in.

alt

The **alt** hierarchy stands for *alternative*. This set of newsgroups contains anything and everything, and is the most loosely governed of the newsgroup top-level hierarchies.

alt.os.linux

This old newsgroup is left over from the days before Linux found a home in the **comp.os.*** hierarchy. I recommend that you go to the **comp.os.linux.*** groups instead of **alt.os.linux**.

alt.os.linux.caldera

This Linux group discusses the Caldera Network Desktop.

Note

Discussions in the country or region-specific hierarchies listed below are generally conducted in the country's home language rather than in English. They are also generally comprised of people in or near that country, though others can certainly participate.

---

at

The **at** hierarchy stands for *Austria*.

at.linux

This is an Austrian Linux discussion group.

at.fido.linux

Austrian Fidonet users discuss Linux in this group. (*Fidonet* is a method of linking BBS systems.)

aus

The **aus** hierarchy stands for *Australia*.

aus.computers.linux

This is an Australian Linux discussion group.

dc

The **dc** hierarchy stands for *Washington, DC*.

dc.org.linux-users

Because this is an **org** subhierarchy, this group is somewhat of a club for Washington, DC Linux users.

de

The **de** hierarchy stands for *Germany*.

de.alt.sources.linux.patches

Here, Germans post patches for Linux source code.

de.comp.os.linux

This German group discusses the Linux operating system.

fido

The **fido** hierarchy stands for *Fidonet,* a way of linking BBS systems.

fido.ger.linux

Here, German-speaking Fidonet users discuss Linux.

fj

The **fj** hierarchy stands for *Fiji.*

fj.os.linux

People at or near Fiji discuss Linux here.

fr

The *fr* hierarchy stands for France.

fr.comp.os.linux

This is a French Linux discussion group.

han

The **han** hierarchy contains discussions in Korea and among Koreans.

han.comp.linux

This is a Korean Linux discussion group.

han.sys.linux

This Korean group discusses Linux kernels, device drivers, and modules.

it

The **it** hierarchy stands for *Italy.*

it.comp.linux

This is an Italian Linux discussion group.

linux

The **linux** hierarchy is a top-level hierarchy for Linux itself. It's not as busy as it could be because a lot of sites don't carry the top-levels that don't fall within UseNet's main ones. It contains a lot of Linux development newsgroups.

This hierarchy is large for a non-UseNet top-level one: It has over 55 groups of its own. If you have access to it, you may find it worthwhile. Subscribe to the groups that you find interesting or useful. Note, however, that the primary Linux discussion groups are in the hierarchy **comp.os.linux**.

no

The **no** hierarchy stands for *Norway*.

no.linux

People in or near Norway discuss Linux here.

Web Pages

A number of Internet Web pages are related to Linux, but the definitive one is the page for the Linux Documentation Project (LDP). Bookmark this page in your Web browser because it points to a number of other helpful pages. The URL for the main LDP is:

http://sunsite.unc.edu/mdw/

There are also a number of mirrors for the LDP pages around the world, so you aren't locked into having to web to Austria to read them.

http://bau2.uibk.ac.at/linux/mdw/linux.html

http://wildsau.idv.uni-linz.ac.at/mdw

http://star06.atklab.yorku.ca/linux/linux.html

http://neon.ingenia.com/LDP/linux.html (Canada)

http://www.cs.mun.ca/~slug/mdw/welcome.html

http://engsoc.carleton.ca/ldp/linux.html

http://neon.ingenia.com/LDP/linux.html (Canada)

http://www.amscons.com/mdw/linux.html

http://www.halcyon.com/linuxdoc/linux.html

http://www.infomagic.com/linux/ldp

http://www.entertain.com/jgreene/ldpwww/welcome.html (Denver)

http://www.caldera.com/LDP/

http://www.fi.muni.cz/linuxdoc/linux.html

http://www.jura.uni-sb.de/LDP/linux.html

http://www.uni-paderborn.de/Linux/mdw

http://www.cs.TU-Berlin.DE/ftp/pub/linux/mdw/

http://amelia.db.erau.edu/ldp/

http://petee.stu.rpi.edu/LDP/llinux.html

http://www.cs.unc.edu/linux-docs/linux.html

http://www.oir.ucf.edu/linux_doc/linux.html

http://lennon.engr.wisc.edu/~gerdts/ldp

http://www.cc.gatech.edu/linux/ldp/

http://helios.ee.ucla.edu/mirrors/ldpwww/

http://inorganic5.chem.ufl.edu/ldp

http://confused.ume.maine.edu/mdw/

http://www.gui.uva.es/linux

http://www.cs.us.es/archive/

http://weikko.tky.hut.fi/LDP/linux.html

http://garbo.uwasa.fi/ldp/

http://hatutu.imag.fr/mdw

http://www.loria.fr/linux/linuxdoc/

http://www.resus.univ-mrs.fr/Fr/CS/Linux/Mdw/linux.html

http://www.eee.hku.hk/LDP/

http://www.vma.bme.hu/linuxdoc/linux.html

http://skynet.ul.ie/ldp

http://www.cs.huji.ac.il/papers/mdw/linux.html

http://www.dsi.unimi.it/ftp/pub/os/Linux/Docs/
ldp-mirror/linux.html

http://www.gee.kyoto-u.ac.jp/LDP/

http://www.gbnet.net/net/Linux/docs/

http://www.nijenrode.nl/~steven/ldp/linux.html

http://www.nvg.unit.no/linux/ldp/linux.html

http://www1.oslohd.no/linux/

http://www.dtek.chalmers.se/Datorsys/Project/linux/LDP/
linux.html

ftp://ftp.ox.ac.uk/pub/linux/LDP_WWW/linux.html

http://www.idiscover.co.uk/linux/linux.html

http://www.mcc.ac.uk/LinuxDoc/linux.html

http://www.ivc.cc.ca.us/ldp

Contents of the CD-ROM

The CD-ROM included with this book is full of software and documentation. Since most of the software and applications are labeled sufficiently to tell you what they're used for, this appendix addresses what exactly the things on the CD-ROM are. This appendix is broken down into the directories you'll find on the CD-ROM, so it will be easy for you to find information on the package you're looking for.

All the text files on this CD are in "Linux/Unix" format—each line ends only with a CR, not CR-LF. This means that if the files are viewed with Notepad in Windows, they'll be unreadable. Use Word, Write, or Wordpad instead of Notepad, and, of course, once in Linux, any text editor will work.

The text files each have two names, one is the long name for Linux, the other is the short name for MS-DOS, MS-Windows, and Windows 95. The file trans.tbl in each directory stores the names for the files in DOS on the left, and Linux on the right.

The / (root) Directory

The root directory on the CD-ROM contains everything that comes with the Slackware 3.0 distribution, plus a directory called /extras that contains most of the servers we install in this book.

Files Contained in the root Directory

There are a few informative files included in this directory:

MS-DOS	Linux	Description
booting.txt	BOOTING.TXT	Advice on what to do if, once your system is installed, you have trouble booting it.

continues

MS-DOS	Linux	Description
catalog.txt	catalog.txt	An ad from Infomagic, the producer of the CD-ROM included with this book. There is also an insert in the book with a coupon for a discount on a Slackware CD-ROM package from this manufacturer.
copying	COPYING	The GNU General Public License. This same document is Appendix B in the book.
changelo	ChangeLog	Log of changes made in this directory structure since it was updated to the 3.0 distribution.
copyrigh	Copyright	The copyright Linux falls under.
faq.txt	FAQ.TXT	The Slackware FAQ. A helpful document if you run into problems that aren't covered in this book.
install.txt	INSTALL.TXT	This is the Linux Installation How-To file. An excellent resource for installing the operating system.
lowmem.txt	LOMEM.TXT	A document on how to install Linux on a machine with 4 megabytes or less of RAM.
ls_lr	ls_lr	A complete listing of the files included in the Slackware 3.0 distribution.readme30.txt Introduction to Slackware 3.0, its disk sets, and other general helpful information.
trans.tbl	TRANS.TBL	Table containing both MS-DOS/MS-WINDOWS names for program items in this directory, and the Linux equivalents (since Linux uses long file names).
upgrade.txt	UPGRADE.TXT	Advice on upgrading your Linux system using the Slackware distributions.

The /bootdsks.12 Directory

The disk images necessary to create the 5 1/4" boot disk specific to your needs if you choose to use this size. These files are broken down into a few categories.

The /bootdsks.12 Informative Files

There are a few files in this directory meant to help you choose what particular 5 1/4" boot disk you need.

MS-DOS	Linux	Description
00_index.txt	00_index.txt	An index explaining what each file in this directory contains.
README.TXT	README.TXT	A listing of what each boot disk is for, and hints on what to do if you have problems booting your Linux system with the disks.
Trans.tbl	TRANS.TBL	The MS-DOS and Linux names of each item in this directory.
WHICH.ONE	WHICH.ONE	Recommendations on how to choose the appropriate disk.

The /bootdsks.12 Disk Images

The remaining files in this directory are all 5 1/4" boot disk images. Instructions on how to select one are listed in the files discussed in the previous section, and also in chapter 3, "Getting Ready To Install Linux from the CD-ROM."

The items in this directory that are not informative files, nor listed in chapter 3, are boot disks for the experimental 1.3 Linux kernel version.

The /bootdsks.144 Directory

The disk images necessary to create the 3 1/2" boot disk specific to your needs if you choose to use this size. These files are broken down into a few categories.

The /bootdsks.144 Informative Files

There are a few files in this directory meant to help you choose what particular 3 1/2" boot disk you need.

MS-DOX	Linux	Description
00_index.txt	00-index.txt	An index explaining what each file in this directory contains.
README.TXT	README.TXT	A listing of what each boot disk is for, and hints on what to do if you have problems booting your Linux system with the disks.
Trans.tbl	TRANS.TBL	List of MS-DOS and Linux filename for each item in this directory.
WHICH.ONE	WHICH.ONE	Recommendations on how to choose the appropriate disk.

There are a few files in this directory advertising CD-ROM Slackware distributions as well.

File	Linux	Description
00_cdrom.txt	00-CDROM.TXT	An ad for the CDs distributed by ftp.cdrom.com.
00_cdrom.htm	00-CDROM.html	An HTML version of the previous text file, to allow you to view it with your Web browser and follow its links.
header	HEADER	Another small advertisement.

The /bootdsks.144 Disk Images

The remaining files in this directory are all 3 1/2" boot disk images. Instructions on how to select one are listed in the files discussed in the previous section, and also in chapter 3, "Getting Ready To Install Linux from the CD-ROM."

The items in this directory that are not informative files, nor listed in chapter 3, are boot disks for the experimental 1.3 Linux kernel version.

The /contents Directory

This directory lists all the programs contained in this particular Slackware distribution of Linux. This is just a list; none of the files here are the actual programs or source referenced.

The /contents/scripts Directory

This directory lists all the scripts contained in this particular Slackware distribution. As before, this is just a list; none of these files are the actual scripts referenced.

The /contrib Directory

This directory contains information about the packages contributed to Slackware by users around the world, and some of the packages themselves. These files are in the following formats:

txt   Text

lsm   Andrew word processor, which is available for Linux.

tgz   A tar and gzipped package.

unknown   Anything with an unclear extension tends to be a standard text file.

The `00_index.txt` file lists what the documents included are. The file `package_descriptions` contains information on the packages included in this directory.

The /contrib/smail-3.1.29 Directory

This directory contains a number of patches, documents, and the source for the smail mail server. The Sendmail server is the one I'm covering in this book. See the READ.ME file for more information on the contents of this directory.

The /docs Directory

This directory tree contains a large amount of documentation useful in setting up various things in Linux. This directory itself contains a number of the Linux Documentation Project How-To files. The names of the files speak for themselves, but if you are unsure, refer to the `00_index.txt` file for a description.

The subdirectories contain the following information:

Subdirectory	Linux	Description
catalog	catalog	The catalog subdirectory contains Walnut Creek CD-ROM catalogs in a variety of languages.
kernel12	kernel.12	This subdirectory contains documentation for various items for the production series kernel tree we're using.
kernel13	kernel.13	Contains documentation for various items for the experimental series kernel tree paralleling the production tree we're using.
linux.faq	linux.faq	Contains the Linux FAQ.
mini	mini	Contains the Linux Documentation Project Mini How-To files for a variety of things.
slack-docs	slack-docs	Contains the slackware documentation.

The /extras Directory

This directory contains most of the servers and packages we use in this book. These particular items don't come with Slackware as a default.

VI

Appendixes

The /install Directory

This directory contains programs used in Linux Slackware installations, such as:

GZIP.EXE	The MS-DOS version of the gzip UNIX program.
RAWRITE.EXE	One program used to create boot and root disks.
FIPS	Directory containing one program used to reallocate hard drive space.

The /kernels Directory

This directory contains all of the default Linux kernels (in subdirectories), and various programs used to install them by hand. In this book, we use the install program provided with Slackware.

The /lininst Directory

This directory contains the program, Lininst, used to create your boot and root disks during the Linux installation process. Installing Linux is covered in chapter 3, "Getting Ready To Install Linux from the CD-ROM."

The /rootdsks Directory

This directory contains the root disk images you'll use to create your root disk for your Linux installation. Choosing a disk is covered in chapter 3, "Getting Ready To Install Linux from the CD-ROM."

The /slaktest Directory

These items are used if you tell the install program that you only want to do a minimal test installation. Only a few files are actually installed to your hard drive, and you run Linux instead mostly from the CD-ROM.

The /slakware Directory

This is the directory that contains the disk sets you'll use to install Linux on your computer. These disk sets are discussed in further detail in chapter 3, "Getting Ready To Install Linux from the CD-ROM."

The /source Directory

This directory contains all of the source code for the Slackware files, as required by the GNU Public License.

Appendix E

Setting Up a Firewall

Sometimes the standard security precautions aren't considered stringent enough to protect a site's data. If this is the case for your site, you may need to set up a firewall to protect your systems from intrusive data. (See chapter 12, "Security," for help on deciding whether or not your site needs a firewall.)

The firewall software you'll install with this book is Socks version 5. It allows the hosts behind your firewall to access the Internet without permitting hosts outside the firewall access them.

> **Note**
>
> Be sure to have a separate machine for your firewall for good security. Then, the machine that contains your servers (e.g., ftpd, httpd) should be outside the firewall, so people from the outside world can access it. Your users should be inside the firewall.

> **Note**
>
> There are also commercial firewall packages available for Linux, but they are often too expensive for anyone except those who are running large sites. The best way to find the commercial system (generally software and hardware) is by searching the Web. For example, try **http://www.zebu.com**.

Compiling and Installing the Binaries

First, you need to get the binaries compiled before you can set up your server. So, let's go through that process now.

Preparing To Compile Socks

Before you can compile Socks, you need to set up a Makefile containing the specific settings you need for your site. This will ensure that the firewall software is compiled for your needs.

To configure your source for compilation, complete the following steps on the machine you intend to use as your firewall server (as root):

1. FTP to **ftp.nec.com**.

2. Go to the directory /pub/security/socks.cstc/socks5.

3. Get the source file socks 5-beta-0.10.tar.gz.

4. Copy the source to /user/src.

5. Gunzip the source.

6. Untar the source.

7. Change to the socks5 directory.

8. Type **configure** to run the script that will look over your system and configure things for you. This is an automated script that locates all of the items it needs to be able to compile Socks, and sets up the Makefile and a list of other necessary files accordingly. A few screens worth of information slide by as it looks for what it needs and then creates the files.

Compiling and Installing the Binaries

Compiling and installing the general Socks binary is fairly simple. Just do the following (as root):

1. Go to your Socks directory.

2. Type **make** to compile Socks. Use what you've learned throughout this book about fixing source (e.g. in chapter 10, "Installing FTP Server Software") that won't compile to get it working if you run into any problems.

3. Type **make check** to run any self-test programs included with the distribution.

4. Type **make install** to install the binaries and documentation for Socks.

5. Type **make clean** to get rid of the mess of interim files created during the compilation.

6. Type **make distclean** to get rid of the interim files the configuration script created.

Setting Up Your Socks Server

Now, it's time to set up your firewall itself. Take your time and put a lot of thought into this section. Whatever you leave out now, you'll have to add later.

Setting Up socks5.conf

The socks5.conf file is where you will define most of your firewall's permissions and how it handles access. To set this file up, do the following (as root):

1. Edit the file /etc/services.

2. Add the line:

```
socks 1080/tcp
```

3. Edit the file /etc/socks5.conf.

4. First, you're going to determine your site's most basic IP address and your netmask. For example, my site's IP addresses all start with 199.60.103. with one more number specifying the machine. If I use 199.60.103.0, the 0 in the last digit tells Socks that any machine with the same inital three parts of the IP address is one of mine. For the netmask, because I have a class C address, I'd use 255.255.255.0. This item is used in a few of the definitions you'll encounter in this file.

5. Now, assign what kind of authentication is required for each location. Your choices are as follows:

n	no authentication required
u	username, plus password if you require one
k	kerberos 5 required
-	any form of authentication required

For each item you want to assign a type of authentication to, you need to have a line containing the following items:

■ Use the word auth to tell the server this is an authentication assignment line.

- Supply the address for the service the authentication type is being assigned to. This address can be the one determined in step 4: a full host + domain name or a domain name.

- Specify the port for the above mentioned service.

- Specify the type of authentication required.

If, for example, I had a Web server on port 80 with the address **www.renaissoft.com** and I didn't want to require authentication so outside users could access it, I would use the following for its authentication line:

```
auth www.renaissoft.com 80 n
```

6. If you have any machines with multiple IP addresses, you need to tell your firewall how to handle them. The items you need to have on a line assigning routing are the following:

- Use the word `route` to tell the server this is a routing definition.

- Supply the address for the service or host you are defining. This address can be expressed in the form of step 4: a full host + domain name or a domain name.

- Specify the port number of the service you are defining or the name of the service.

- Specify the IP address of the interface card or the name assigned to the interface.

> **Caution**
>
> If you don't have machines with multiple IP addresses, a routing definition is not necessary.

For example, if the Web server I referred to in the previous example is on a machine with two IP addresses, I need to assign its routing here. If the name of the interface card is `le1`, the definition would be as follows:

```
route www.renaissoft.com 80 le1
```

7. Now, you can set how you want your server to log some items, and what kinds of messages it should display. A line with this type of definition consists of the following items:

- Include the word `set` to tell it you're setting a logging or display definition.

- Specify the variable you want to set. The items you can set are as follows:

SOCKS5_DEBUG	Turns on all debugging information
SOCKS5_LOG_STDERR	Logs all messages to `stderr`
SOCKS5_LOG_SYSLOG	Logs all messages to `syslog`

For example, I can send all messages to initially go to the `syslog`. Then, I can set the `syslog` to separate these items according to type and save them to specific files. To do this, I would:

```
set SOCKS5_LOG_SYSLOG
```

8. If your Socks server has services it needs to access through other Socks servers, you need to assign some proxies. A proxy definition line contains the following items:

   - Indicate the type of proxy, which can be `s5` (socks5), `s4` (socks4), or `np` (no proxy necessary).

   - Indicate the address for the service or host you are defining. This address can be expressed in the form of step 4: a full host + domain name or a domain name.

   - Specify either the port number or the name of the service you're defining.

   - Specify either the IP address or the name of the proxy server to use for the service.

   - Indicate the port on the proxy server to contact for the service.

   For example, if the Web service I discussed earlier has to go through another Socks server, and if this proxy server is also a Socks5 setup at **proxy.renaissoft.com** and is set to wait for Web items at port 85, I would enter the following:

   ```
   s5 www.renaissoft.com 80 proxy.renaissoft.com 85
   ```

9. Now set access controls to determine which requests for services will be honored and which will be denied. There are two types of access definitions: *permit* and *deny*. Both options require the same list of parameters, as follows:

- Determine the type of authentication methods necessary to trust the service connecting. Your choices are one or more of the following:

  n no authentication necessary

  u username authentication required with optional password

  k Kerberos 5 authentication required

- Establish the types of commands your server will accept from the process making the connection. You can choose one or more of the following:

  c Accept connections

  b Accept bind

  u Accept udp

  a Accept any and all commands

- Decide the address for the service or host the command is approved to come from. This address can be expressed in the form of step 4: a full host + domain name or a domain name.

- Decide the address for the service or host the command is approved to go to. This address can be expressed in the form of item 4: a full host + domain name or a domain name.

- Specify the port for the service or host the command is authorized to come from.

- Specify the port for the service or host the command is authorized to go to.

- Create an optional list of user names you are specifically authorizing, excluding all others.

For example, if I wanted to authorize all commands from the site **neighbor.com** from port 40, to be sent to the machine **catherine.renaissoft.com** on port 45 with no authentication required, then my line would read as follows:

```
permit a neighbor.com catherine.renaissoft.com 40 45
```

If I wanted to ensure that three particular users (Ralph, Jane, and Spot) from the site **enemy.com** on port 40 could not get into the same area, I would use the following:

```
deny a enemy.com catherine.renaissoft.com 40 45 ralph jane spot
```

10. Save and exit the file.

Preparing Your Clients

All of your client applications need to be recompiled to know how to talk to your firewall. Fortunately, even if your client of choice doesn't have an option in its source to work with a firewall, it's simple to add the necessary code (if you have access to the source).

> **Tip**
>
> Some preconfigured clients come with the firewall software in the `clients` directory. Compile them and give them a try if you like.

To determine whether a client's source can be changed to allow it to work with your firewall, do the following:

1. Go to the source directory for the client you want to convert.

2. Search it for the following item:

```
SOCK_DGRAM
```

To do this search, use **grep SOCK_DGRAM *** to search all of the files in the directory for the term SOCK_DGRAM.

3. If this shows up, you cannot use this client with Socks. `SOCK_DGRAM` is a UDP item and does not get along with this firewall software.

4. Find another acceptable client that does not contain this item.

To change a client's source to allow it to work with your firewall, do the following:

1. Edit the file.

2. Locate the beginning of the main procedure.

3. Enter the following near the beginning of this procedure:

```
SOCKSinit(argv[0]);
```

VI

Appendixes

4. Locate all lines that begin with cc. Add the following to the end of each of those lines:

```
-Dconnect=Rconnect -Dgetsockname=Rgetsockname -Dbind=Rbind \
-Daccept=Raccept -Dlisten=Rlisten -Dselect=Rselect
```

> **Tip**
>
> If the client is compiled with a Makefile, add the above to the CFLAGS macro.

5. Locate the final target in the Makefile, which starts with cc or ld.

6. Add the following library:

```
-DSHORTENED_RBIND
```

7. Compile the client.

8. Test the client.

Locating Assistance

If you need assistance in setting up your firewall, there are a number of excellent sources you can look to for help. These sources are supported by the people who program the server itself.

The NEC Socks Home Page

NEC has an excellent home page with everything you want to know about Socks. Check it out at

http://www.socks.nec.com/

The Socks Mailing List

You can subscribe to a mailing list for discussions of Socks problems, postings of new FAQs, announcements, etc. To subscribe, send e-mail to

majordomo@syl.dl.nec.com

This mail should have no subject and have in the body only

subscribe socks your_e-mail_address

Appendix F

The Linux Hardware How-To

In order for an operating system to work properly with a computer system, the appropriate software drivers for all of the hardware components must be available. Fortunately, the "Linux Hardware Compatibility HOWTO" tells you exactly what hardware is and is not supported by Linux, so you don't have to guess! It is important that you consult this document to avoid any incompatibility problems.

Linux Hardware Compatibility HOWTO

FRiC (Boy of Destiny), frac@pobox.com
v6969, 16 July 1995

This document lists most of the hardware supported by Linux and helps you locate any necessary drivers.

1. Introduction

1.1. Welcome

Welcome to the Linux Hardware Compatibility HOWTO. This document lists most of the hardware supported by Linux, now if only people would read this first before posting their questions on Usenet.

Subsections titled Others list hardware with alpha or beta drivers in varying degrees of usability or other drivers that aren't included in standard kernels. Note that some drivers only exist in alpha kernels, so if you see something listed as supported but isn't in your version of the Linux kernel, upgrade.

The latest version of this document can be found on the net at the usual sites where the Linux HOWTO's are kept.

If you know of any Linux hardware (in)compatibilities not listed here please let me know. Send mail (note my new e-mail address) or find me on IRC. Thanks.

1.2. System architectures

This document only deals with Linux for Intel platforms, for other platforms check the following:

- Linux/68k

    <http://www-users.informatik.rwth-aachen.de/~hn/linux68k.html>

- Linux/MIPS

    <http://www.waldorf-gmbh.de/linux-mips-faq.html>

- Linux/PowerPC

    <ftp://sunsite.unc.edu/pub/Linux/docs/ports/Linux-PowerPC-FAQ.gz>

- Linux for Acorn

    <http://www.ph.kcl.ac.uk/~amb/linux.html>

- MacLinux

    <http://www.ibg.uu.se/maclinux/>

2. Computers/Motherboards/BIOS

ISA, VLB, EISA, and PCI buses are all supported.

PS/2 and Microchannel (MCA) is not supported in the standard kernel. Alpha test PS/2 MCA kernels are available but not yet recommended for beginners or serious use.

2.1. Specific systems

- Compaq Deskpro XL

    <http://www-c724.uibk.ac.at/XL/>

- IBM PS/2 MCA systems

    <ftp://invaders.dcrl.nd.edu/pub/misc/>

3. Laptops

Some laptops have unusual video adapters or power management, it is not uncommon to be unable to use the power management features.

PCMCIA drivers currently support all common PCMCIA controllers, including Databook TCIC/2, Intel i82365SL, Cirrus PD67xx, and Vadem VG-468 chipsets. Motorola 6AHC05GA controller used in some Hyundai laptops is not supported. (Read the PCMCIA HOWTO.)

- APM

    <ftp://tsx-11.mit.edu/pub/linux/packages/laptops/apm/>

- PCMCIA

    <ftp://cb-iris.stanford.edu/pub/pcmcia/>

- non-blinking cursor

    <ftp://sunsite.unc.edu/pub/Linux/kernel/patches/console/noblink-1.5.tar.gz>

- power savings (WD7600 chipset)

    <ftp://sunsite.unc.edu/pub/Linux/system/Misc/low-level/pwrm-1.0.tar.Z>

- other general info

    <ftp://tsx-11.mit.edu/pub/linux/packages/laptops/>

3.1. Specific laptops

- Compaq Contura Aero

    <http://domen.uninett.no/~hta/linux/aero-faq.html>

- IBM ThinkPad

    <http://peipa.essex.ac.uk/tp-linux/tp-linux.html>

- NEC Versa M and P

    <http://www.santafe.edu:80/Ânelson/versa-linux/>

- Tadpole P1000

    <http://peipa.essex.ac.uk/tadpole-linux/tadpole-linux.html>

VI

Appendixes

■ Linux, X, and the WD90C24A2 video chipset

   <http://www.castle.net/~darin/>

4. CPU/FPU

Intel/AMD/Cyrix 386SX/DX/SL/DXL/SLC, 486SX/DX/SL/SX2/DX2/DX4, Pentium. Basically all 386 or better processors will work. Linux has built-in FPU emulation if you don't have a math coprocessor.

Linux does not support SMP yet. Multi-processor systems will run Linux but only the first processor will be used. There's some work being done right now, check the Linux Project Map for details.

A few very early AMD 486DX's may hang in some special situations. All current chips should be okay and getting a chip swap for old CPU's should not be a problem.

ULSI Math*Co series has a bug in the FSAVE and FRSTOR instructions that causes problems with all protected mode operating systems. Some older IIT and Cyrix chips may also have this problem.

There are problems with TLB flushing in UMC U5S chips. Fixed in newer kernels.

■ enable cache on Cyrix processors

   <ftp://sunsite.unc.edu/pub/Linux/kernel/patches/CxPatch030.tar.z>

■ Cyrix software cache control

   <ftp://sunsite.unc.edu/pub/Linux/kernel/patches/linux.cxpatch>

5. Video cards

Linux will work with all video cards in text mode, VGA cards not listed below probably will still work with mono VGA and/or standard VGA drivers.

If you're looking into buying a cheap video card to run X, keep in mind that accelerated cards (ATI Mach, ET4000/W32p, S3) are MUCH faster than unaccelerated or partially accelerated (Cirrus, WD) cards. S3 801 (ISA), S3 805 (VLB), ET4000/W32p, and ATI Graphics Wonder (Mach32) are good low-end accelerated cards.

"32 bpp" is actually 24 bit color aligned on 32 bit boundaries. It does NOT mean the cards are capable of 32 bit color, it's still 24 bit color (16,777,216

colors). 24 bit packed pixels modes are not supported in XFree86, so cards
that can do 24 bit color modes in other OS's may not able to do this in X.
These cards include Mach32, Cirrus 542x, S3 801/805, ET4000, and others.

5.1. Diamond video cards

Most recent Diamond cards ARE supported by the current release of XFree86.
Early Diamond cards are not supported by XFree86, but there are ways of
getting them to work.

- Diamond support for XFree86

  <http://www.diamondmm.com/linux.html>

- Diamond FAQ (for older cards)

  <ftp://sunsite.unc.edu/pub/Linux/X11/Diamond.FAQ>

- Diamond Disgruntled Users Page (for older cards)

  <http://gladstone.uoregon.edu/~trenton/diamond/>

5.2. SVGALIB

- VGA

- EGA

- ATI Mach32

- Cirrus 542x

- OAK OTI-037/67/77/87

- Trident TVGA8900/9000

- Tseng ET3000/ET4000/W32

5.3. XFree86 3.1.1, Accelerated

- ATI Mach8

- ATI Mach32 (16 bpp—does not work with all Mach32 cards)

- ATI Mach64 (16/32 bpp)

- Cirrus Logic 5420, 542x/5430 (16 bpp), 5434 (16/32 bpp), 62×5

- IBM 8514/A

- IBM XGA, XGA-II

- IIT AGX-010/014/015/016

- Oak OTI-087

- S3 911, 924, 801, 805, 928, 864, 964, Trio32, Trio64, 868, 968

- see Appendix A for long list of supported cards

- Tseng ET4000/W32/W32i/W32p

- Weitek P9000 (16/32 bpp)

- Diamond Viper VLB/PCI

- Orchid P9000

- Western Digital WD90C31/33

5.4. XFree86 3.1.1, Unaccelerated

- ATI VGA Wonder series

- Avance Logic AL2101/2228/2301/2302/2308/2401

- Chips & Technologies 65520/65530/65540/65545

- Cirrus Logic 6420/6440

- Compaq AVGA

- Genoa GVGA

- MCGA (320×200)

- MX MX68000/MX68010

- NCR 77C22, 77C22E, 77C22E+

- Oak OTI-067, OTI-077

- Trident TVGA8800, TVGA8900, TVGA9xxx (not very fast)

- Tseng ET3000, ET4000AX

- VGA (standard VGA, 4 bit, slow)

- Video 7 / Headland Technologies HT216-32

- Western Digital/Paradise PVGA1, WD90C00/10/11/24/30/31/33

5.5. Monochrome

- Hercules mono

- Hyundai HGC-1280

- Sigma LaserView PLUS

- VGA mono

5.6. Others

- EGA (ancient, from c. 1992)

  <ftp://ftp.funet.fi/pub/OS/Linux/BETA/Xega/>

5.7. Works in progress

- Compaq QVision

- Number Nine Imagine 128

No, I do not know when support for these cards will be finished, please don't ask me. If you want support for these cards now get Accelerated-X.

5.8. Commercial X servers

Commercial X servers provide support for cards not supported by XFree86, and might give better performances for cards that are supported by XFree86. In general, they support many more cards than XFree86, so I'll only list cards that aren't supported by XFree86 here. Contact the vendors directly or check the Commercial HOWTO for more info.

5.8.1. Accelerated-X 1.2

- ARK Logic

- Chips & Technologies 82C45x, 82C48x, F655xx

- Compaq QVision 2000

- Matrox MGA-I, MGA-II

- Number Nine I-128

- S3 Trio32 (732), Trio64 (764), 866, 868, 968

- Weitek P9100

VI

Appendixes

$199, X Inside, Inc. <info@xinside.com>.

Accel-X supports most cards in 16 and 32 bpp modes and it also supports 24 bit packed pixel modes for cards that have these modes, including ATI Mach32, Mach64 (1280hr ×1024@24bpp), ET4000/W32p, S3-866/868/968, and more.

Accel-X also supports XVideo (Xv) extensions (on Matrox Comet, Marvel-II, and SPEA ShowTime Plus), PEX, and XIE.

5.8.2. Metro-X 2.3.2

$199, Metro Link <sales@metrolink.com>.

Metro-X supports more boards than XFree but less than Accel-X, however

I don't have much more information as I can't seem to view the PostScript files they sent me. Mail them directly for more info.

6. Controllers (hard drive)

Linux will work with standard IDE, MFM and RLL controllers. When using MFM/RLL controllers it is important to use ext2fs and the bad block checking options when formatting the disk.

Enhanced IDE (EIDE) interfaces are supported. With up to two IDE interfaces and up to four hard drives and/or CD-ROM drives.

ESDI controllers that emulate the ST-506 (that is MFM/RLL/IDE) interface will also work. The bad block checking comment also applies to these controllers.

Generic 8 bit XT controllers also work.

7. Controllers (SCSI)

It is important to pick a SCSI controller carefully. Many cheap ISA SCSI controllers are designed to drive CD-ROM's rather than anything else. Such low end SCSI controllers are no better than IDE. See the SCSI HOWTO and look at performance figures before buying a SCSI card.

7.1. Supported

- AMI Fast Disk VLB/EISA (BusLogic compatible)

- Adaptec AVA-1505/1515 (ISA) (Adaptec 152x compatible)

- Adaptec AHA-1510/152x (ISA) (AIC-6260/6360)

- Adaptec AHA-154x (ISA) (all models)

- Adaptec AHA-174x (EISA) (in enhanced mode)

- Adaptec AHA-274x (EISA) / 284x (VLB) (AIC-7770)

- Adaptec AHA-294x (PCI) (AIC-7870)

- Always IN2000

- BusLogic (ISA/EISA/VLB/PCI) (all models)

- DPT PM2001, PM2012A (EATA-PIO)

- DPT Smartcache (EATA-DMA) (ISA/EISA/PCI) (all models)

- DTC 329x (EISA) (Adaptec 154x compatible)

- Future Domain TMC-16×0, TMC-3260 (PCI)

- Future Domain TMC-8xx, TMC-950

- NCR 53c7x0, 53c8x0 (PCI)

- Pro Audio Spectrum 16 SCSI (ISA)

- Qlogic / Control Concepts SCSI/IDE (FAS408) (ISA/VLB/PCMCIA)
  PCMCIA cards must boot DOS to init card

- Seagate ST-01/ST-02 (ISA)

- SoundBlaster 16 SCSI-2 (Adaptec 152x compatible) (ISA)

- Trantor T128/T128F/T228 (ISA)

- UltraStor 14F (ISA), 24F (EISA), 34F (VLB)

- Western Digital WD7000 SCSI

7.2. Others

- AMD AM53C974, AM79C974 (PCI) (Compaq, Zeos onboard SCSI)

  <ftp://sunsite.unc.edu/pub/Linux/kernel/patches/scsi/
  AM53C974-0.3.tgz>

- Adaptec ACB-40xx SCSI-MFM/RLL bridgeboard

  <ftp://sunsite.unc.edu/pub/Linux/kernel/patches/scsi/
  adaptec-40XX.tar.gz>

VI

Appendixes

- Adaptec APA-1460 SlimSCSI (PCMCIA)

  <ftp://cb-iris.stanford.edu/pub/pcmcia/>

- Acculogic ISApport / MV Premium 3D SCSI (NCR 53c406a)

  <ftp://sunsite.unc.edu/pub/Linux/kernel/patches/scsi/
  ncr53c406-0.10.patch.gz>

- Always AL-500

  <ftp://sunsite.unc.edu/pub/Linux/kernel/patches/scsi/
  al500_0.1.tar.gz>

- BusLogic (ISA/EISA/VLB/PCI) (new beta driver)

  <ftp://ftp.dandelion.com/BusLogic-1.0-beta.tar.gz>

- Iomega PC2/2B

  <ftp://sunsite.unc.edu/pub/Linux/kernel/patches/scsi/
  iomega_pc2-1.1.x.tar.gz>

- New Media Bus Toaster PCMCIA

  <ftp://lamont.ldeo.columbia.edu/pub/linux/
  bus_toaster-1.5.tgz>

- Qlogic (ISP1020) (PCI)

  <ftp://sunsite.unc.edu/pub/Linux/Incoming/>

- Ricoh GSI-8

  <ftp://tsx-11.mit.edu/pub/linux/ALPHA/scsi/gsi8.tar.gz>

- Trantor T130B (NCR 53c400)

  <ftp://sunsite.unc.edu/pub/Linux/kernel/patches/scsi/
  53c400.tar.gz>

7.3. Unsupported

- Parallel port SCSI adapters

- Non Adaptec compatible DTC boards (327x, 328x)

8. Controllers (I/O)

Any standard serial/parallel/joystick/IDE combo cards. Linux supports 8250, 16450, 16550, and 16550A UART's.

See National Semiconductor's "Application Note AN-493" by Martin S. Michael. Section 5.0 describes in detail the differences between the NS16550 and NS16550A. Briefly, the NS16550 had bugs in the FIFO circuits, but the NS16550A (and later) chips fixed those. However, there were very few NS16550's produced by National, long ago, so these should be very rare. And many of the "16550" parts in actual modern boards are from the many manufacturers of compatible parts, which may not use the National "A" suffix. Also, some multiport boards will use 16552 or 16554 or various other multiport or multifunction chips from National or other suppliers (generally in a dense package soldered to the board, not a 40 pin DIP). Mostly, don't worry about it unless you encounter a very old 40 pin DIP National "NS16550" (no A) chip loose or in an old board, in which case treat it as a 16450 (no FIFO) rather than a 16550A.—Zhahai Stewart <zstewart@hisys.com>

9. Controllers (multiport)

9.1. Supported

- AST FourPort and clones
- Accent Async-4
- Bell Technologies HUB6
- Boca BB-1004, 1008 (4, 8 port)—no DTR, DSR, and CD
- Boca BB-2016 (16 port)
- Boca IO/AT66 (6 port)
- Boca IO 2by4 (4S/2P)—works with modems, but uses 5 IRQ's
- Cyclades Cyclom-8Y/16Y (8, 16 port)
- PC-COMM 4-port
- STB 4-COM
- Twincom ACI/550
- Usenet Serial Board II

VI

Appendixes

9.2. Others

- Comtrol RocketPort (8/16/32 port)

  <ftp://tsx-11.mit.edu/pub/linux/packages/comtrol/>

- DigiBoard COM/Xi

  contact Simon Park <si@wimpol.demon.co.uk>

- DigiBoard PC/Xe (ISA) and PC/Xi (EISA)

  <ftp://ftp.digibd.com/drivers/linux/>

- Specialix SIO/XIO (modular, 4 to 32 ports)

  <ftp://sunsite.unc.edu/pub/Linux/kernel/patches/serial/sidrv0_5.taz>

- Stallion EasyIO (ISA) / EasyConnection 8/32 (ISA/MCA)

  <ftp://sunsite.unc.edu/pub/Linux/kernel/patches/serial/
  stallion-0.1.9.tar.gz>

- Stallion EasyConnection 8/64 / ONboard (ISA/EISA/MCA) / Brumby /
  Stallion (ISA)

  <ftp://sunsite.unc.edu/pub/Linux/kernel/patches/serial/
  stallion-0.1.9.tar.gz>

10. Network adapters

Ethernet adapters vary greatly in performance. In general, the newer the design the better. Some very old cards like the 3C501 are only useful because they can be found in junk heaps for $5 a time. Be careful with clones, not all are good clones and bad clones often cause erratic lockups under Linux. Read the Ethernet HOWTO for full detailed descriptions of various cards.

10.1. Supported

10.1.1. Ethernet

- 3Com 3C501—"avoid like the plague"

- 3Com 3C503, 3C505, 3C507, 3C509/3C509B (ISA) / 3C579 (EISA)

- AMD LANCE (79C960) / PCnet-ISA/PCI (AT1500, HP J2405A,
  NE1500/NE2100)

- AT&T GIS WaveLAN

- Allied Telesis AT1700

- Ansel Communications AC3200 EISA

- Apricot Xen-II

- Cabletron E21xx

- DEC DE425 (EISA) / DE434/DE435 (PCI)

- DEC DEPCA and EtherWORKS

- HP PCLAN (27245 and 27xxx series)

- HP PCLAN PLUS (27247B and 27252A)

- Intel EtherExpress

- Intel EtherExpress Pro

- NE2000/NE1000 (be careful with clones)

- New Media Ethernet

- Racal-Interlan NI5210 (i82586 Ethernet chip)

- Racal-Interlan NI6510 (am7990 lance chip)—doesn't work with more than 16 megs RAM

- PureData PDUC8028, PDI8023

- SEEQ 8005

- SMC Ultra

- Schneider & Koch G16

- Western Digital WD80x3

- Zenith Z-Note / IBM ThinkPad 300 built-in adapter

10.1.2. Pocket and portable adapters

- AT-Lan-Tec/RealTek parallel port adapter

- D-Link DE600/DE620 parallel port adapter

VI

Appendices

10.1.3. Slotless

■ SLIP/CSLIP/PPP (serial port)

■ EQL (serial line load balancing)

■ PLIP (parallel port)—using "LapLink cable" or bi-directional cable

10.1.4. ARCnet

■ works with all ARCnet cards

10.1.5. Token Ring

■ IBM Tropic chipset cards

10.2. Others

10.2.1. Ethernet

■ 3Com Vortex Ethercards (3C590, 3C595 (100 mbps)) (PCI)

    <http://cesdis.gsfc.nasa.gov/pub/linux/drivers/vortex.html>

■ DEC 21040/21140 "Tulip" / SMC PCI EtherPower 10/100

    <http://cesdis.gsfc.nasa.gov/linux/drivers/tulip.html>

10.2.2. ISDN

■ Diehl SCOM card

    <ftp://sunsite.unc.edu/pub/Linux/kernel/patches/network/isdndrv-0.1.1.tar.gz>

■ ICN ISDN card

    <ftp://ftp.franken.de/pub/isdn4linux/>

■ Teles ISDN card

    <ftp://ftp.franken.de/pub/isdn4linux/>

10.2.3. Amateur radio cards

■ AX.25 networking

    <ftp://sunacm.swan.ac.uk/pub/misc/Linux/Radio/>

- Ottawa PI/PI2

- Most generic 8530 based HDLC boards

- No support for the PMP/Baycom board

10.2.4. PCMCIA cards

- 3Com 3C589

- Accton EN2212 EtherCard

- D-Link DE650

- IBM Credit Card Adapter

- IC-Card

- Kingston KNE-PCM/M

- LANEED Ethernet

- Linksys EthernetCard

- Network General "Sniffer"

- Novell NE4100

- Thomas-Conrad Ethernet

- possibly more

10.2.5. ATM

- Efficient Networks ENI155P-MF 155 Mbps ATM adapter

  <http://lrcwww.epfl.ch/linux-atm/>

10.3. Unsupported

- Xircom adapters are not supported.

11. Sound cards

11.1. Supported

- 6850 UART MIDI

- Adlib (OPL2)

- Audio Excell DSP16

- Aztech Sound Galaxy NX Pro

- ECHO-PSS cards (Orchid SoundWave32, Cardinal DSP16)

- Ensoniq SoundScape

- Gravis Ultrasound

- Gravis Ultrasound 16-bit sampling daughterboard

- Gravis Ultrasound MAX

- Logitech SoundMan Games (SBPro, 44kHz stereo support)

- Logitech SoundMan Wave (Jazz16/OPL4)

- Logitech SoundMan 16 (PAS-16 compatible)

- MPU-401 MIDI

- MediaTriX AudioTriX Pro

- Media Vision Premium 3D (Jazz16)

- Media Vision Pro Sonic 16 (Jazz)

- Media Vision Pro Audio Spectrum 16

- Microsoft Sound System (AD1848)

- OAK OTI-601D cards (Mozart)

- OPTi 82C928/82C929 cards (MAD16/MAD16 Pro)

- Sound Blaster

- Sound Blaster Pro

- Sound Blaster 16 family

- Wave Blaster (and other SB16 daughterboards)

11.2. Others

- MPU-401 MIDI (intelligent mode)

  <ftp://sunsite.unc.edu/pub/Linux/kernel/sound/
  mpu401.0.11a.tar.gz>

- PC speaker / Parallel port DAC

  <ftp://ftp.informatik.hu-berlin.de/pub/os/linux/hu-sound/>

■ Turtle Beach MultiSound/Tahiti/Monterey

<ftp://ftp.cs.colorado.edu/users/mccreary/archive/tbeach/multisound/>

11.3. Unsupported

The ASP chip on Sound Blaster 16 series and AWE32 is not supported. AWE32's onboard MIDI synthesizer is not supported. They will probably never be supported.

Sound Blaster 16's with DSP 4.11 and 4.12 have a hardware bug that causes hung/stuck notes when playing MIDI and digital audio at the same time. The problem happens with either Wave Blaster daughterboards or MIDI devices attached to the MIDI port. There is no known fix.

12. Hard drives

All hard drives should work if the controller is supported.

(From the SCSI HOWTO) All direct access SCSI devices with a block size of 256, 512, or 1024 bytes should work. Other block sizes will not work. (Note that this can often be fixed by changing the block and/or sector sizes using the MODE SELECT SCSI command.)

Large IDE (EIDE) drives work fine with newer kernels. The boot partition must lie in the first 1024 cylinders due to PC BIOS limitations.

Some Conner CFP1060S drives may have problems with Linux and ext2fs. The symptoms are inode errors during e2fsck and corrupt file systems. Conner has released a firmware upgrade to fix this problem, contact Conner at 1-800-4CONNER (US) or +44-1294-315333 (Europe). Have the microcode version (found on the drive label, 9WA1.6x) handy when you call.

Certain Micropolis drives have problems with Adaptec and BusLogic cards, contact the drive manufacturers for firmware upgrades if you suspect problems.

■ Multiple device driver (RAID-0, RAID-1)

<ftp://sweet-smoke.ufr-info-p7.ibp.fr/public/Linux/>

VI

Appendixes

13. Tape drives

13.1. Supported

- SCSI tape drives

  (From the SCSI HOWTO) Drives using both fixed and variable length blocks smaller than the driver buffer length (set to 32k in the distribution sources) are supported. Virtually all drives should work. (Send mail if you know of any incompatible drives.)

- QIC-02

- QIC-117, QIC-40/80 drives (Ftape)

  <ftp://sunsite.unc.edu/pub/Linux/kernel/tapes>—Most tape drives using the floppy controller should work. Check the Ftape HOWTO for details. Various dedicated QIC-80 controllers (Colorado FC-10, Iomega Tape Controller II) are also supported.

13.2. Unsupported

- Emerald and Tecmar QIC-02 tape controller cards—Chris Ulrich

  <insom@math.ucr.edu>

- Drives that connect to the parallel port (eg: Colorado Trakker)

- Some high speed tape controllers (Colorado TC-15 / FC-20)

- Irwin AX250L/Accutrak 250 (not QIC-80)

- IBM Internal Tape Backup Unit (not QIC-80)

- COREtape Light

14. CD-ROM drives

14.1. Supported

- SCSI CD-ROM drives

  (From the CD-ROM HOWTO) Any SCSI CD-ROM drive with a block size of 512 or 2048 bytes should work under Linux; this includes the vast majority of CD-ROM drives on the market.

- EIDE (ATAPI) CD-ROM drives

- Aztech CDA268, Orchid CDS-3110, Okano/Wearnes CDD-110

- GoldStar R420

- LMS Philips CM 206

- Matsushita/Panasonic, Kotobuki (SBPCD)

- Mitsumi

- Optics Storage Dolphin 8000AT

- Sanyo H94A

- Sony CDU31A/CDU33A

- Sony CDU-535/CDU-531

- Teac CD-55A SuperQuad

14.2. Others

- LMS/Philips CM 205/225/202

    <ftp://sunsite.unc.edu/pub/Linux/kernel/patches/cdrom/lmscd0.3d.tar.gz>

- NEC CDR-35D (old)

    <ftp://sunsite.unc.edu/pub/Linux/kernel/patches/cdrom/linux-neccdr35d.patch>

- Sony SCSI multisession CD-XA

    <ftp://tsx-11.mit.edu/pub/linux/patches/sony-multi-0.00.tar.gz>

14.3. Notes

PhotoCD (XA) is supported.

All CD-ROM drives should work similarly for reading data. There are various compatibility problems with audio CD playing utilities. (Especially with some NEC drives.) Some alpha drivers may not have audio support yet.

Early (single speed) NEC CD-ROM drives may have trouble with currently available SCSI controllers.

15. Removable drives

All SCSI drives should work if the controller is supported, including optical drives, WORM, CD-R, floptical, and others. Iomega Bernoulli and Zip drives, and SyQuest drives all work fine.

Linux supports both 512 and 1024 bytes/sector disks.

VI

Appendixes

16. Mice

16.1. Supported

- Microsoft serial mouse

- Mouse Systems serial mouse

- Logitech Mouseman serial mouse

- Logitech serial mouse

- ATI XL Inport busmouse

- C&T 82C710 (QuickPort) (Toshiba, TI Travelmate)

- Microsoft busmouse

- Logitech busmouse

- PS/2 (auxiliary device) mouse

16.2. Others

- Sejin J-mouse

  <ftp://sunsite.unc.edu/pub/Linux/kernel/patches/console/
  jmouse.1.1.70-jmouse.tar.gz>

- MultiMouse—use multiple mouse devices as single mouse

  <ftp://sunsite.unc.edu/pub/Linux/system/Misc/MultiMouse-1.0.tgz>

16.3. Notes

Those pad devices like Glidepoint also work, so long they're compatible with another mouse protocol.

Newer Logitech mice (except the Mouseman) use the Microsoft protocol and all three buttons do work. Even though Microsoft's mice have only two buttons, the protocol allows three buttons.

The mouse port on the ATI Graphics Ultra and Ultra Pro use the Logitech busmouse protocol. (See the Busmouse HOWTO for details.)

17. Modems

All internal modems or external modems connected to the serial port.

A small number of modems come with DOS software that downloads the control program at runtime. These can normally be used by loading the program under DOS and doing a warm boot. Such modems are probably best avoided as you won't be able to use them with non PC hardware in the future.

PCMCIA modems should work with the PCMCIA drivers.

Fax modems need appropriated fax software to operate.

- Digicom Connection 96+/14.4+—DSP code downloading program

  <ftp://sunsite.unc.edu/pub/Linux/system/Serial/
  smdl-linux.1.02.tar.gz>

- ZyXEL U-1496 series—ZyXEL 1.4, modem/fax/voice control program

  <ftp://sunsite.unc.edu/pub/Linux/system/Serial/ZyXEL-1.4.tar.gz>

18. Printers/Plotters

All printers and plotters connected to the parallel or serial port should work.

- HP LaserJet 4 series—free-lj4, printing modes control program

  <ftp://sunsite.unc.edu/pub/Linux/system/Printing/
  free-lj4-1.1p1.tar.gz>

- BiTronics parallel port interface

  <ftp://sunsite.unc.edu/pub/Linux/kernel/misc/
  bt-ALPHA-0.0.1.tar.gz>

18.1. Ghostscript

Many Linux programs output PostScript files. Non-PostScript printers can emulate PostScript Level 2 using Ghostscript.

- Ghostscript

  <ftp://ftp.cs.wisc.edu/pub/ghost/aladdin/>

18.1.1. Ghostscript supported printers

- Apple Imagewriter
- C. Itoh M8510
- Canon BubbleJet BJ10e, BJ200
- Canon LBP-8II, LIPS III
- DEC LA50/70/75/75plus
- DEC LN03, LJ250

- Epson 9 pin, 24 pin, LQ series, Stylus, AP3250

- HP 2563B

- HP DesignJet 650C

- HP DeskJet/Plus/500

- HP DeskJet 500C/520C/550C/1200C color

- HP LaserJet/Plus/II/III/4

- HP PaintJet/XL/XL300 color

- IBM Jetprinter color

- IBM Proprinter

- Imagen ImPress

- Mitsubishi CP50 color

- NEC P6/P6+/P60

- Okidata MicroLine 182

- Ricoh 4081

- SPARCprinter

- StarJet 48 inkjet printer

- Tektronix 4693d color 2/4/8 bit

- Tektronix 4695/4696 inkjet plotter

- Xerox XES printers (2700, 3700, 4045, etc.)

18.1.2. Others

- Canon BJC600 and Epson ESC/P color printers

  <ftp://petole.imag.fr/pub/postscript/>

19. Scanners

- A4 Tech AC 4096

  <ftp://ftp.informatik.hu-berlin.de/pub/local/linux/ac4096.tgz>

- Fujitsu SCSI-2 scanners

  contact Dr. G.W. Wettstein <greg%wind.UUCP@plains.nodak.edu>

- Genius GS-B105G

  <ftp://tsx-11.mit.edu/pub/linux/ALPHA/scanner/gs105-0.0.1.tar.gz>

- Genius GeniScan GS4500 handheld scanner

  <ftp://tsx-11.mit.edu/pub/linux/ALPHA/scanner/gs4500-1.3.tar.gz>

- HP ScanJet, ScanJet Plus

  <ftp://ftp.ctrl-c.liu.se/unix/linux/wingel/>

- HP ScanJet II series SCSI

  <ftp://sunsite.unc.edu/pub/Linux/apps/graphics/scanners/
  hpscanpbm-0.3a.tar.gz>

- Logitech Scanman 32 / 256

  <ftp://tsx-11.mit.edu/pub/linux/ALPHA/scanner/
  logiscan-0.0.2.tar.gz>

- Mustek M105 handheld scanner with GI1904 interface

  <ftp://tsx-11.mit.edu/pub/linux/ALPHA/scanner/
  scan-driver-0.1.8.tar.gz>

- UMAX SCSI scanners

  contact Craig Johnston <mkshenk@u.washington.edu>

20. Other hardware

20.1. VESA Power Savings Protocol (DPMS) monitors

20.2. Joysticks

- Joystick driver

  <ftp://sunsite.unc.edu/pub/Linux/kernel/patches/console/
  joystick-0.7.3.tgz>

- Joystick driver (module)

  <ftp://sunsite.unc.edu/pub/Linux/kernel/patches/console/
  joyfixed.tgz>

20.3. Video capture boards

- FAST Screen Machine II

  <ftp://sunsite.unc.edu/pub/Linux/apps/video/
  ScreenMachineII_1.1.tgz>

VI

Appendixes

- ProMovie Studio

  <ftp://sunsite.unc.edu/pub/Linux/apps/video/PMS-grabber.tgz>

- VideoBlaster, Rombo Media Pro+

  <ftp://sunsite.unc.edu/pub/Linux/apps/video/vid_src.gz>

- WinVision video capture card

  <ftp://sunsite.unc.edu/pub/Linux/apps/video/fgrabber-1.0.tgz>

20.4. UPS

- APC SmartUPS

  <ftp://sunsite.unc.edu/pub/Linux/system/UPS/apcd-0.1.tar.gz>

- UPS's with RS-232 monitoring port (unipower package)

  <ftp://sunsite.unc.edu/pub/Linux/system/UPS/unipower-1.0.0.tgz>

- various other UPS's are supported, read the UPS HOWTO

20.5. Miscellaneous

- Analog Devices RTI-800/815 ADC/DAC board

  contact Paul Gortmaker<gpg109@anu.edu.au>

- HP IEEE-488 (HP-IB) interface

  <ftp://beaver.chemie.fu-berlin.de/pub/linux/IEEE488/>

- Maralu chip-card reader/writer

  <ftp://ftp.thp.uni-koeln.de/pub/linux/chip/>

- Mattel Powerglove

  <ftp://sunsite.unc.edu/pub/Linux/apps/linux-powerglove.tgz>

- Reveal FM Radio card

  <ftp://magoo.uwsuper.edu/pub/fm-radio/>

- Videotext cards

  <ftp://sunsite.unc.edu/pub/Linux/apps/video/videoteXt-0.5.tar.gz>

21 Related sources of information

- Cameron Spitzer's hardware FAQ archive

  <ftp://rahul.net/pub/cameron/PC-info/>

- Computer Hardware and Software Vendor Phone Numbers

  <http://mtmis1.mis.semi.harris.com/comp_ph1.html>

- Guide to Computer Vendors

  <http://www.ronin.com/SBA/>

- System Optimization Information

  <http://www.dfw.net/~sdw/>

22. Acknowledgments

Thanks to all the authors and contributors of other HOWTO's, many things here are shamelessly stolen from their works; to Zane Healy and Ed Carp, the original authors of this list; and to everyone else who sent in updates and feedbacks. Special thanks to Eric Boerner and lilo (the person, not the program) for the sanity checks. And thanks to Dan Quinlan for the original SGML conversion.

23. Appendix A. S3 cards supported by XFree86 3.1.1.

CHIPSET	RAMDAC	CLOCKCHIP
801/805	AT&T 20C490	16
801/805	AT&T 20C490	ICD2061A
805	S3 GENDAC	16
805	SS2410	ICD2061A
928	AT&T 20C490	16
928	Sierra SC15025	ICD2061A
928	Bt485	ICD2061A
928	Bt485	SC11412
928	Bt485	ICD2061A
928	Ti3020	ICD2061A
864	AT&T 20C498	ICS2494
864	AT&T 20C498/	ICD2061A/
	STG1700	ICS9161
864	STG1700	ICD2061A
864	AT&T 20C498/	ICS2595
	AT&T 21C498	
864	S3 86C716 SDAC	
864	ICS5342	ICS5342
864	AT&T 20C490	ICD2061A
864	AT&T 20C498-13	ICD2061A
964	AT&T 20C505	ICD2061A
964	Bt485	ICD2061A
964	Bt9485	ICS9161A
964	Ti3020	ICD2061A
964	Ti3025	Ti3025
764	(Trio64)	
	(all Trio64 based cards)	
868		
968	TVP3026	

BPP	CARD
Actix GE 32	Orchid Fahrenheit 1280+
16	STB PowerGraph X.24
Miro 10SD VLB/PCI	SPEA Mirage VLB
8	Diamond Stealth 24 VLB
Actix Ultra	
32	ELSA Winner 1000 ISA/VLB/EISA
32	STB Pegasus VL
16	SPEA Mercury VLB
32	#9 GXE Level 10/11/12
32	#9 GXE Level 14/16
32	Miro 20SD (BIOS 1.x)
32	ELSA Winner 1000 PRO VLB/PCI
	MIRO 20SD (BIOS 2.x)
32	Actix GE 64 VLB
16	SPEA Mirage P64 DRAM (BIOS 3.x)
32	ELSA Winner 1000 PRO
	Miro 20SD (BIOS 3.x)
	SPEA Mirage P64 DRAM (BIOS 4.x)
	Diamond Stealth 64 DRAM
32	Diamond Stealth 64 DRAM (some)
32	#9 GXE64
32	#9 GXE64 PCI
32	Miro Crystal 20SV PCI
32	Diamond Stealth 64
32	SPEA Mercury 64
8	ELSA Winner 2000 PRO PCI
32	#9 GXE64 Pro VLB/PCI
	Miro Crystal 40SV
32	SPEA Mirage P64 (BIOS 5.x)
	Diamond Stealth 64 DRAM
	#9 FX Vision330
	STB PowerGraph 64
32	ELSA Winner 1000AVI
32	ELSA Winner 2000PRO/X
	Diamond Stealth 64 Video VRAM

Index

X

Before using the software on this CD-ROM, consult the list of compatible hardware in appendix F. The contents of the CD-ROM are detailed in appendix D. Chapters 3 and 4 describe the installation of the Linux operating system.

Technical support for the CD-ROM with this book is provided through InfoMagic. Technical support for the CD-ROM by e-mail is free and can be reached at **support@InfoMagic.com**. Technical support by phone for the CD-ROM is available for a charge at 900-786-5555. The rate is currently $2.00 per minute and is subject to change without notice. If you have problems with the book, *Running a Perfect Internet Site with Linux,* please contact Macmillan Technical Support at 317-581-3833 or by e-mail at **support@mcp. com**. Support is provided on CompuServe at **GO QUEBOOKS**. Replacements for defective CD-ROMS will be supplied through Macmillan Technical Support. All other CD-ROM questions must be directed to InfoMagic.

1-800-800-6613
Tel: +1-520-526-9565
Fax: +1-520-526-9573
E-Mail: info@infomagic.com
Web: www.infomagic.com

InfoMagic

11950 N. Highway 89, Flagstaff AZ 86004

ORDER FORM

FIRST NAME:	LAST NAME:

ADDRESS

CITY	STATE
ZIP	COUNTRY

TEL, FAX or E-MAIL:

CD-ROMS & BOOKS available direct from InfoMagic, Inc.:

	PRICE	QTY	AMOUNT
LINUX Developers Resource 5 CD Set - Slackware, RedHat, sources, demos & more! ***QUE SPECIAL OFFER!***	$ 15.00		
LINUX CD-ROM Subscription (includes 6 releases) US/CAN/MEX	$ 150.00		
LINUX CD-ROM Subscription (includes 6 releases) INTERNATIONAL	$ 175.00		
LINUX Installation & Getting Started Guide 250 pg manual by Matt Welsh	$ 12.50		
LINUX Network Administrators Guide 350 pg manual by Olaf Kirch	$ 18.50		
LINUX TOOLBOX - 5 CD Set, 250 pg Install Guide, Internet Guide, more! *see shipping fees below	$ 45.00		
LINUX T-Shirt (circle size) M L XL XXL	$ 15.00		
LINUX Journal Subscription - USA the only monthly magazine for Linux 12 issues!	$ 22.00		
LINUX Journal Subscription - CANADA 12 issues!	$ 27.00		
LINUX Journal Subscription - OVERSEAS 12 issues!	$ 32.00		
MOO-TIFF 2 CD Set for LINUX *100% OSF Motif Compatible* Graphical User Interface for PC's running LINUX	$ 99.00		
BSDISC (NetBSD 1.1 & FreeBSD 2.1) Complete unix-like OS with sources & install scripts	$ 35.00		
MOO-TIFF CD-ROM for FREEBSD *100% OSF Motif Compatible* Graphical User Interface for PC's running FREEBSD	$ 99.00		
CICA Windows 4 CD Set - hundreds of Windows programs & shareware ready to "Plug & Play!"	$ 30.00		
GAMES for DAZE 2 CD Set - over 800 games ready to Plug & Play! X2FTP archive	$ 30.00		
HOBBES OS/2 4 CD Set - hundreds of programs & IBM shareware to "Plug & Play"	$ 35.00		
INTERNET TOOLS CD-ROM - networking tools & utilities for Unix & DOS	$ 30.00		
MOTHER OF PERL 2 CD Set - a powerfull utility language for Unix, Windows NT, OS/2, DOS, more!	$ 35.00		
SOURCE CODE CD-ROM - 4.4 BSD Lite2, MACH, JPEG, GNU, Interviews, GIF Sources and more!	$ 30.00		
STANDARDS 2 CD Set - International & Domestic Telecommunications & Data Standards, RFC's, ITU/CCIT docs	$ 30.00		
TCL/TK CD-ROM - general purpose scripting language & toolkit for rapid X-Windows development	$ 35.00		
TeX 2 CD Set - powerful tools for creating professional-quality typesetting, fonts & more!	$ 35.00		
WORLD WIDE CATALOG CD-ROM - See the best of the WEB without being on-line! Most popular sites included!	$ 35.00		
X-FILES CD-ROM - from the X-Consortium! Includes complete source distribution for X11R6 and XFree86	$ 35.00		

SHIPPING: $5.00 - USA/CAN/MEX $10 - OVERSEAS

(Ship rates are per order up to 5 items)

NOTE: International orders with books or more than 5 items will be charged more for shipping
depending on weight of shipment and country of destination

*Linux Toolbox : $5 per copy US/CAN/MEX $20 per copy OVERSEAS
*Linux CD-ROM Subscriptions & Journal Subscription prices include all shipping

Sub-Total	
5.5% Sales Tax (Arizona Residents ONLY)	
Shipping	
TOTAL	

PAYMENT:

☐ MC/VISA	☐ AMEX	☐ **Check or Money Order Enclosed**

Int'l checks MUST be in U.S. funds and drawn on a U.S. Bank

Acct No. _____   Exp: _____

Name of
Cardholder _____

Signature _____

InfoMagic

11950 N. Highway 89
Flagstaff AZ 86004